STEPHEN KING

THE STAND

No Man's Land

THE STAND: NO MAN'S LAND. Contains material originally published in magazine form as THE STAND: NO MAN'S LAND #1-5. First printing 2011. ISBN# 978-0-7851-3624-8. Published by MARVEL WORLDWIDE, INC., a subsidiary of MARVEL ENTERTAINMENT, LLC. OFFICE OF PUBLICATION: 135 West 50th Street, New York, NY 10020. Copyright © 2011 Stephen King. All rights reserved. $24.99 per copy in the U.S. and $27.99 in Canada (GST #R127032852); Canadian Agreement #40668537. All characters featured in this publication and the distinctive names and likenesses thereof, and all related indicia are trademarks of Stephen King. Published by arrangement with The Doubleday Broadway Publishing Group, a division of Random House, Inc. This publication is produced under license from The Doubleday Broadway Publishing Group and Stephen King. No similarity between any of the names, characters, persons, and/or institutions in this book with those of any living or dead person or institution is intended, and any such similarity which may exist is purely coincidental. Marvel and its logos are TM & © Marvel Characters, Inc. **Printed in the U.S.A.** ALAN FINE, EVP - Office of the President, Marvel Worldwide, Inc. and EVP & CMO Marvel Characters B.V.; DAN BUCKLEY, Publisher & President - Print, Animation & Digital Divisions; JOE QUESADA, Chief Creative Officer; JIM SOKOLOWSKI, Chief Operating Officer; DAVID BOGART, SVP of Business Affairs & Talent Management; TOM BREVOORT, SVP of Publishing; C.B. CEBULSKI, SVP of Creator & Content Development; DAVID GABRIEL, SVP of Publishing Sales & Circulation; MICHAEL PASCIULLO, SVP of Brand Planning & Communications; JIM O'KEEFE, VP of Operations & Logistics; DAN CARR, Executive Director of Publishing Technology; JUSTIN F. GABRIE, Director of Publishing & Editorial Operations; SUSAN CRESPI, Editorial Operations Manager; ALEX MORALES, Publishing Operations Manager; STAN LEE, Chairman Emeritus. For information regarding advertising in Marvel Comics or on Marvel.com, please contact John Dokes, SVP Integrated Sales and Marketing, at jdokes@marvel.com. For Marvel subscription inquiries, please call 800-217-9158. **Manufactured between 6/13/2011 and 7/11/2011 by R.R. DONNELLEY, INC., SALEM, VA, USA.**

10 9 8 7 6 5 4 3 2 1

STEPHEN KING

THE STAND

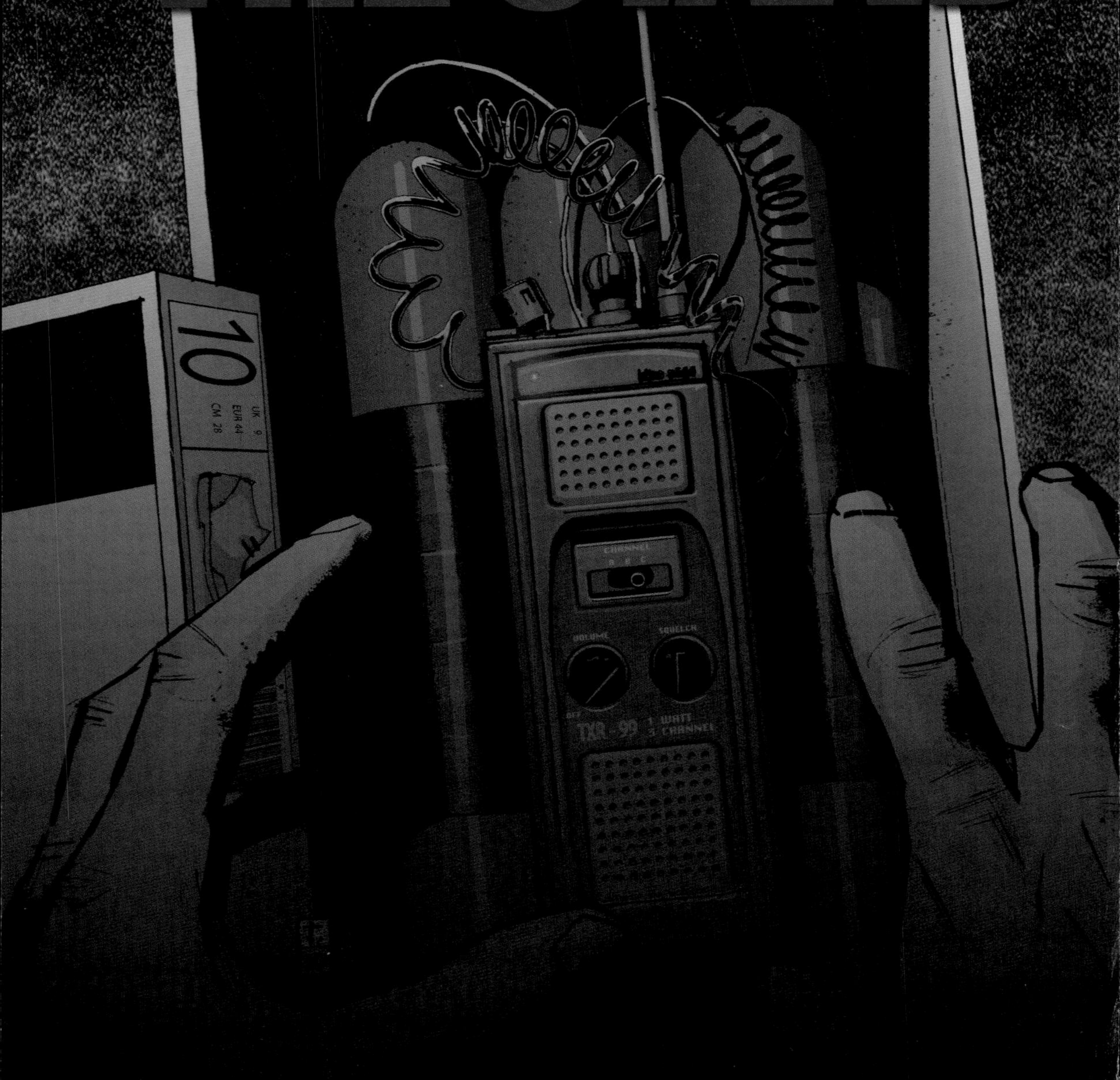
10
10
CHANNEL
VOLUME
SQUELCH
TXR-99

No Man's Land

Creative Director and Executive Director
STEPHEN KING

Script
ROBERTO AGUIRRE-SACASA

Art
MIKE PERKINS

Color Art
LAURA MARTIN

Lettering
VC'S RUS WOOTON

Production
IRENE Y. LEE, RANDALL L. MILLER & MAYELA GUTIERREZ

Assistant Editor
CHARLIE BECKERMAN

Consulting Editor
BILL ROSEMANN

Senior Editor
RALPH MACCHIO

Cover Art
TOMM COKER WITH LAURA MARTIN

Collection Editor
MARK D. BEAZLEY

Editorial Assistants
JOE HOCHSTEIN & JAMES EMMETT

Assistant Editors
NELSON RIBEIRO & ALEX STARBUCK

Editor, Special Projects
JENNIFER GRUNWALD

Senior Editor, Special Projects
JEFF YOUNGQUIST

Senior Vice President of Publishing Sales
DAVID GABRIEL

SVP of Brand Planning & Communications
MICHAEL PASCIULLO

Senior Vice President of Strategic Development
RUWAN JAYATILLEKE

Book Designer
SPRING HOTELING

Editor in Chief
AXEL ALONSO

Chief Creative Officer
JOE QUESADA

Publisher
DAN BUCKLEY

Special Thanks to Chuck Verrill, Marsha DeFilippo, Brian Stark,
Jim Nausedas, Jim McCann, Arune Singh, Lauren Sankovitch & Jeff Suter

For more information on THE STAND comics, visit marvel.com/comics/the_stand

To find Marvel Comics at a local comic shop, call 1-888-COMICBOOK

INTRODUCTION

THE ROAD TAKEN

In *No Man's Land*, the penultimate arc in our adaptation of The Stand, we really get into the nitty gritty of the subject matter: Taking a stand. At one point in the narrative when a crucial decision is reached, Glen Bateman asks a gravely ill Mother Abagail: Do we have a choice? In the specific context of the scene, the choice involves a trek to Las Vegas that some are asked to make to strike a blow for the remnants of humanity who are trying to restructure society against the evil that seeks to destroy them. But in a larger perspective, that is a key question which penetrates to the very heart of the story. If you take a stand on something, you've made a choice. Likewise, if you don't take a stand, you've also made a choice. And both are revelatory of character.

What some members of the cast who are living in Boulder, Colorado must decide is whether they want to continue to reside in the comparative safety of that reawakened city, or take arms against a sea of troubles, and by opposing, end them. In other words, do they want—have they the will—to strike out and make the treacherous voyage to Las Vegas where the Walkin' Dude awaits? To me, this is such a compelling metaphor for our own lives. How often have we been privy to events in our own country, our community, our own homes, that we know in our hearts we should have spoken up against, yet we remained silent? We couldn't find our voice. And so, when good men stand idly by, evil flourishes. We lacked the courage or commitment to plant our feet and take that stand. Wasn't it just easier to turn the other way and pretend nothing bad was happening? Just ignore the screams in the alley, close the window and turn up the volume on the television.

Larry, Stu, Ralph and Glen could remain in the cozy confines of Boulder, pretending the evil festering in Las Vegas courtesy of the Walkin' Dude, Randall Flagg, wasn't really there. They could delude themselves as we all often do, that if we don't act, things will get better on their own. But Mother Abagail has tasked them with going west and confronting the menace that ultimately threatens this small pocket of humanity on this plague-riddled planet.

These four men have taken a stand. Evil shall not prevail on their watch, though it may cost them their very lives.

As with any great novel, this one holds a mirror up to our own lives. Each reader must search his own conscience and wonder whether he would join that intrepid foursome in their foray into the unknown. And if he would not, then know that somewhere in the deserts of Nevada, the Walkin' Dude is wearing his hideous smile just a bit more broadly.

Ralph Macchio
June, 2011

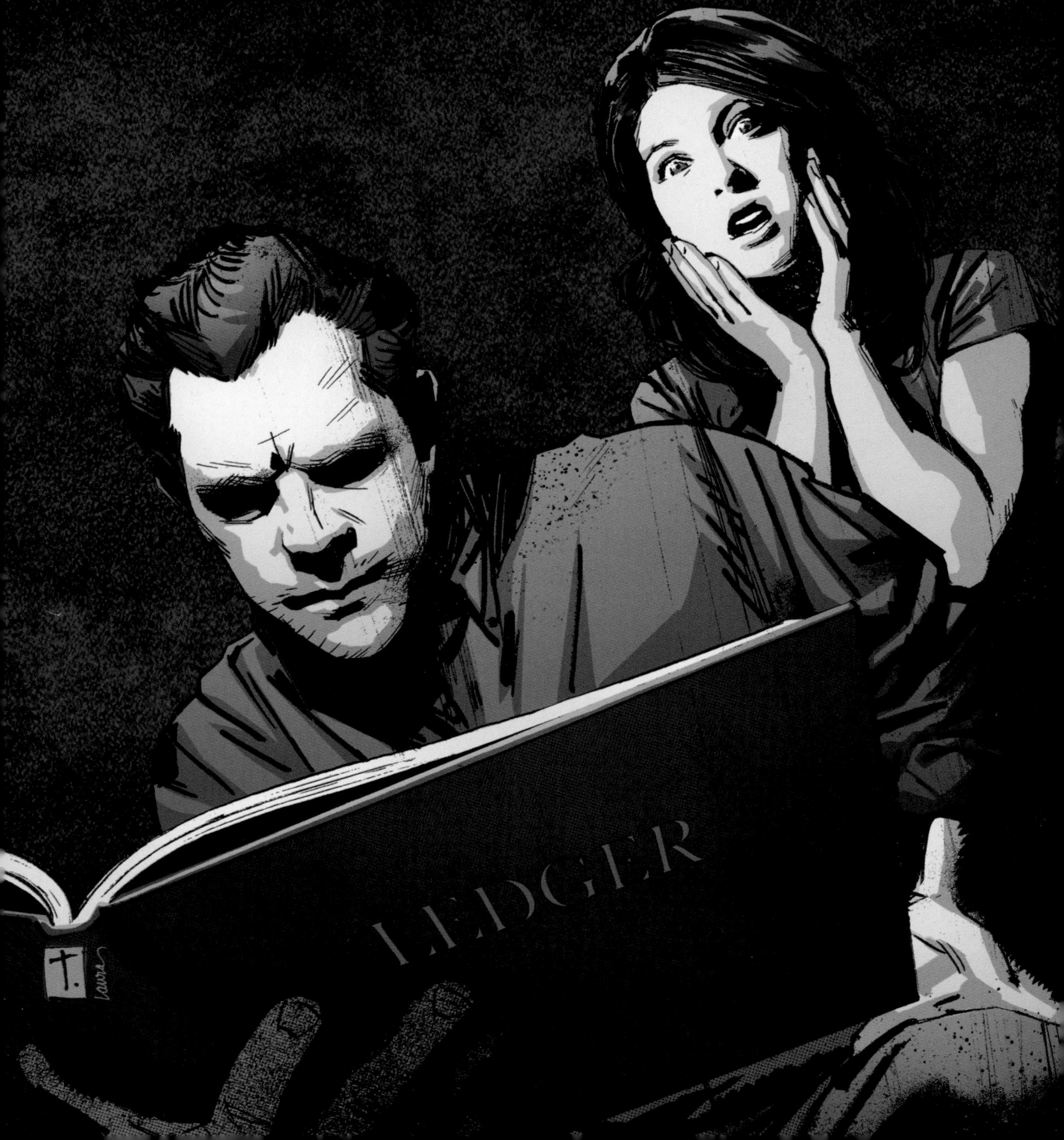
LEDGER

PREVIOUSLY

Two months ago, something happened at Project Blue in California. Within weeks, a flu-like virus—"Captain Trips"—swept through the world, killing off 99% of the population. Now, it's up to the survivors to piece together a new life in a world that has moved on.

The survivors have split into two factions—dark and light. There are those who have heeded the call of Randall Flagg, also known as the Dark Man or the Walkin' Dude, and followed him to Las Vegas. There, he rules with absolute authority, and those who disobey his laws are executed—by crucifixion. Among his disciples are Lloyd Henreid, a former thief who nearly died of starvation when he was imprisoned during the final throes of Captain Trips, and was saved by Flagg. Another is Trashcan Man, or Trashy, a pyromaniac from Illinois who followed Flagg's call across the country, through the desert, and nearly died in the process.

Those who have followed the light flock to the summons of Mother Abagail, who has led her people to Boulder, Colorado. There, a new democracy has been established, and at its head are the seven members of the Free Zone Committee: Stu Redman and his lover, the pregnant Frances Goldsmith, as well as Glen Bateman, Larry Underwood, Sue Stern, the deaf-mute Nick Andros, and Ralph Brentner. The seven of them have re-ratified the Constitution and have begun the process of rebuilding their society.

But they have another task—to counter the oncoming attacks from Las Vegas. Little is known about what the Dark Man is planning, just that he is planning something. The committee decides to send three spies west to investigate: the 70-year-old Judge Farris, the scrappy Dayna Jurgens, and the mentally retarded Tom Cullen.

But the biggest blow comes to the committee just before they have their first public Zone meeting: Mother Abagail disappears in the middle of the night, leaving only a note: "I will be with you again soon if it is God's will." Leaderless and afraid, it is difficult to see how the citizens of the Boulder Free Zone will survive...

chapter ONE

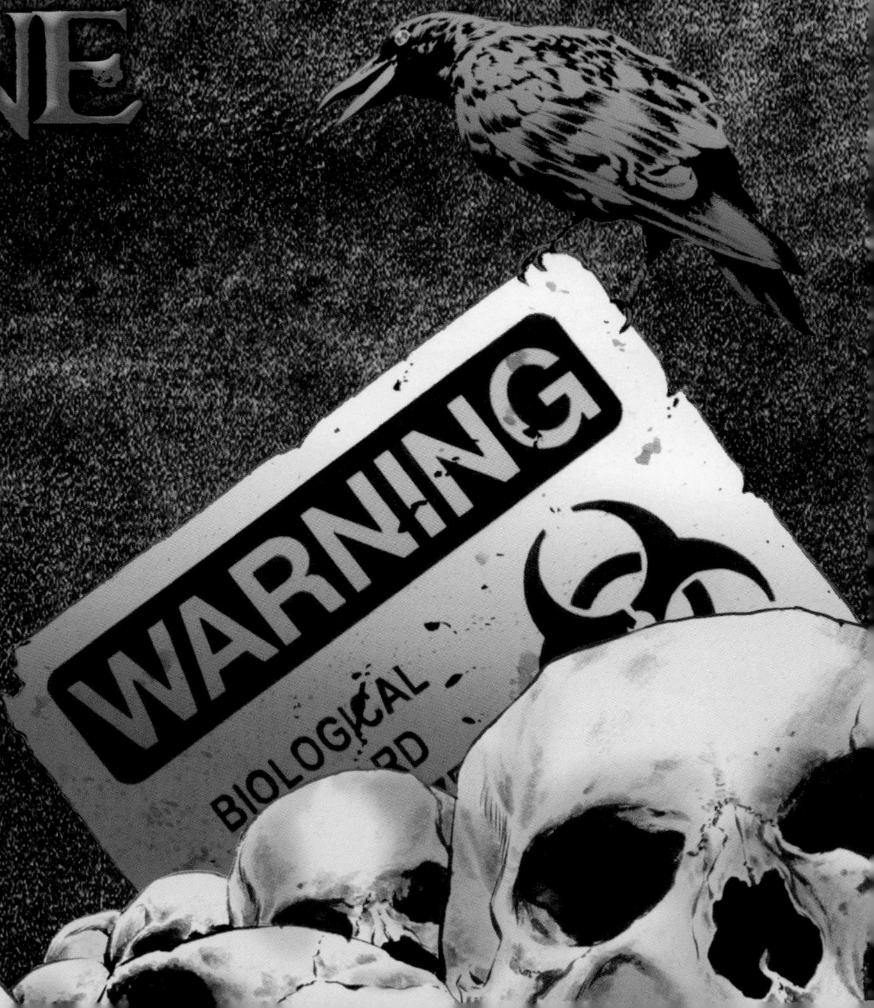
WARNING
BIOLOGICAL

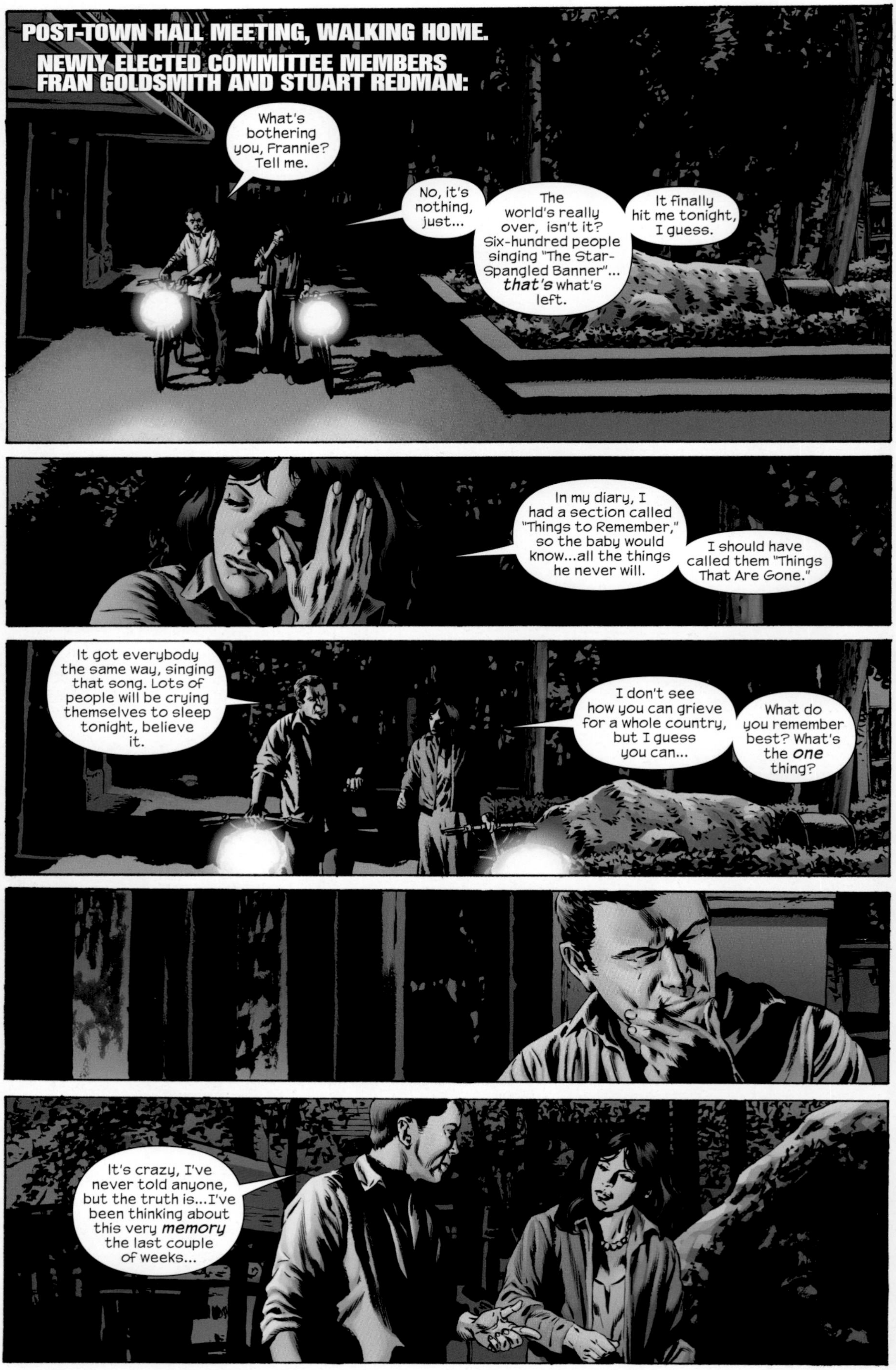
POST-TOWN HALL MEETING, WALKING HOME.
NEWLY ELECTED COMMITTEE MEMBERS FRAN GOLDSMITH AND STUART REDMAN:
What's bothering you, Frannie? Tell me.
No, it's nothing, just...
The world's really over, isn't it? Six-hundred people singing "The Star-Spangled Banner"... *that's* what's left.
It finally hit me tonight, I guess.
In my diary, I had a section called "Things to Remember," so the baby would know...all the things he never will.
I should have called them "Things That Are Gone."
It got everybody the same way, singing that song. Lots of people will be crying themselves to sleep tonight, believe it.
I don't see how you can grieve for a whole country, but I guess you can...
What do you remember best? What's the *one* thing?
It's crazy, I've never told anyone, but the truth is...I've been thinking about this very *memory* the last couple of weeks...

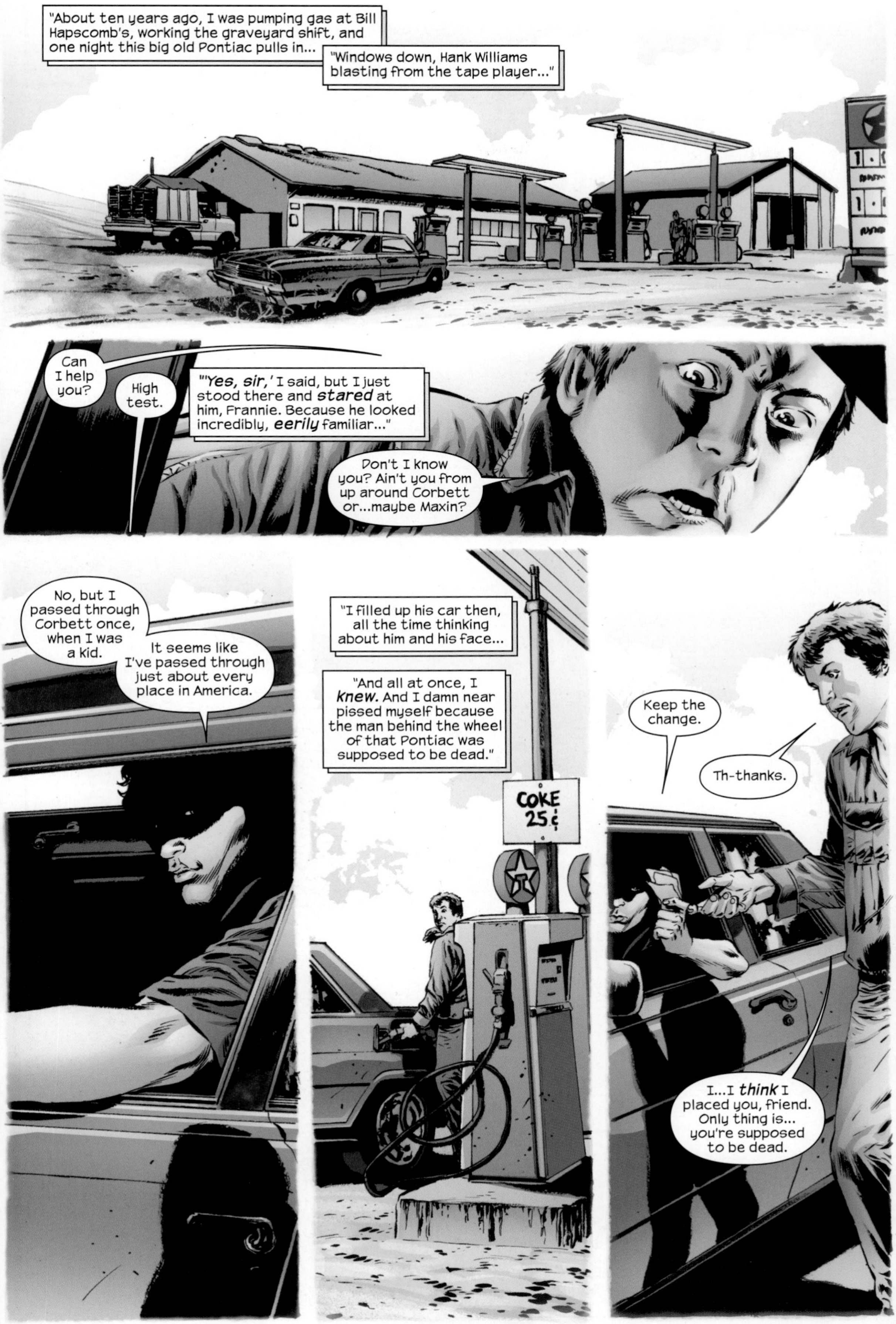
"About ten years ago, I was pumping gas at Bill Hapscomb's, working the graveyard shift, and one night this big old Pontiac pulls in...
"Windows down, Hank Williams blasting from the tape player..."
Can I help you?
High test.
"'Yes, sir,' I said, but I just stood there and stared at him, Frannie. Because he looked incredibly, eerily familiar..."
Don't I know you? Ain't you from up around Corbett or...maybe Maxin?
No, but I passed through Corbett once, when I was a kid.
It seems like I've passed through just about every place in America.
"I filled up his car then, all the time thinking about him and his face...
"And all at once, I knew. And I damn near pissed myself because the man behind the wheel of that Pontiac was supposed to be dead."
COKE 25¢
Keep the change.
Th-thanks.
I...I think I placed you, friend. Only thing is... you're supposed to be dead.

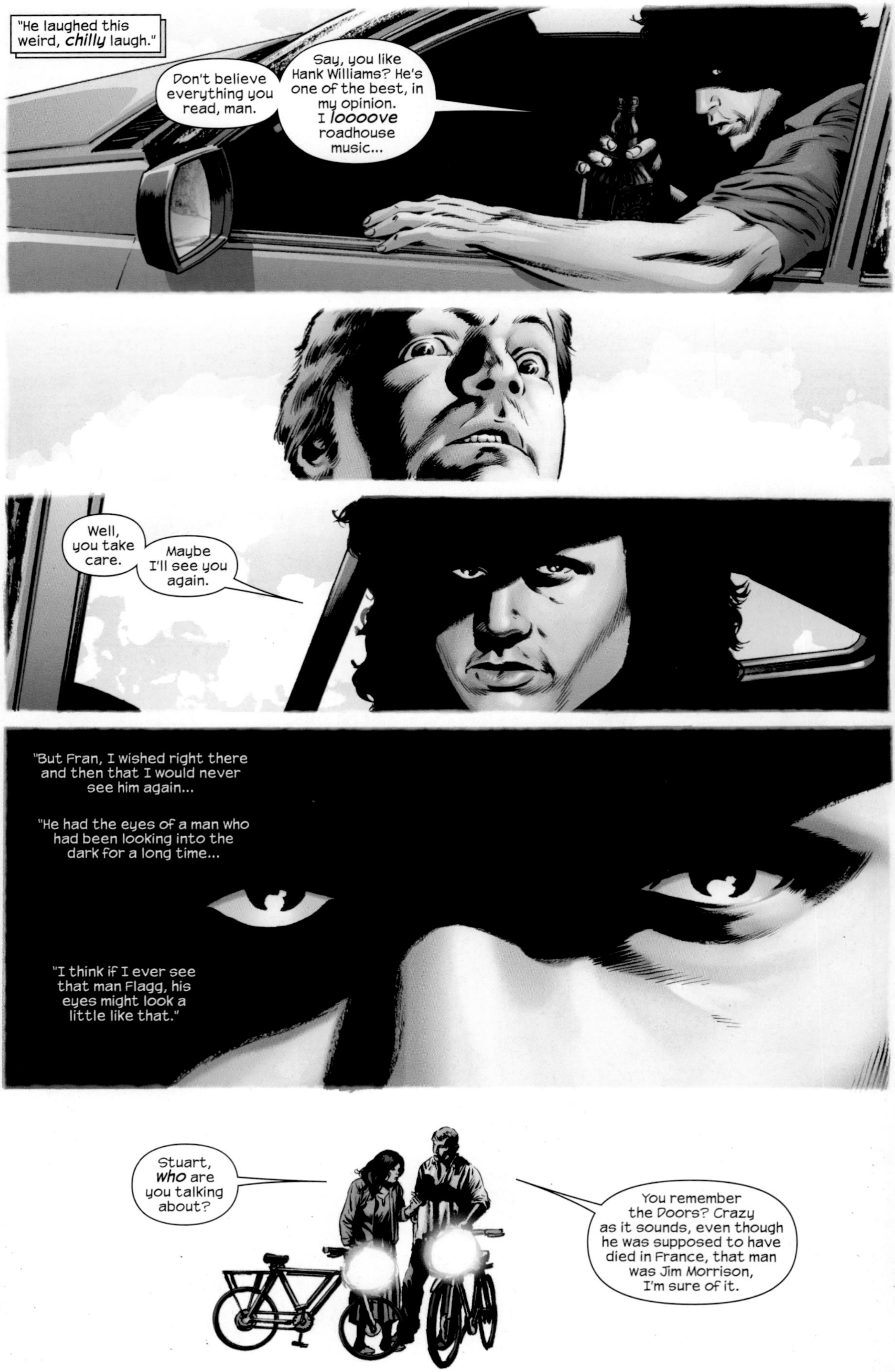
"He laughed this weird, *chilly* laugh."
Don't believe everything you read, man.
Say, you like Hank Williams? He's one of the best, in my opinion. I *loooove* roadhouse music...
Well, you take care.
Maybe I'll see you again.
"But Fran, I wished right there and then that I would never see him again...
"He had the eyes of a man who had been looking into the dark for a long time...
"I think if I ever see that man Flagg, his eyes might look a little like that."
Stuart, *who* are you talking about?
You remember the Doors? Crazy as it sounds, even though he was supposed to have died in France, that man was Jim Morrison, I'm sure of it.

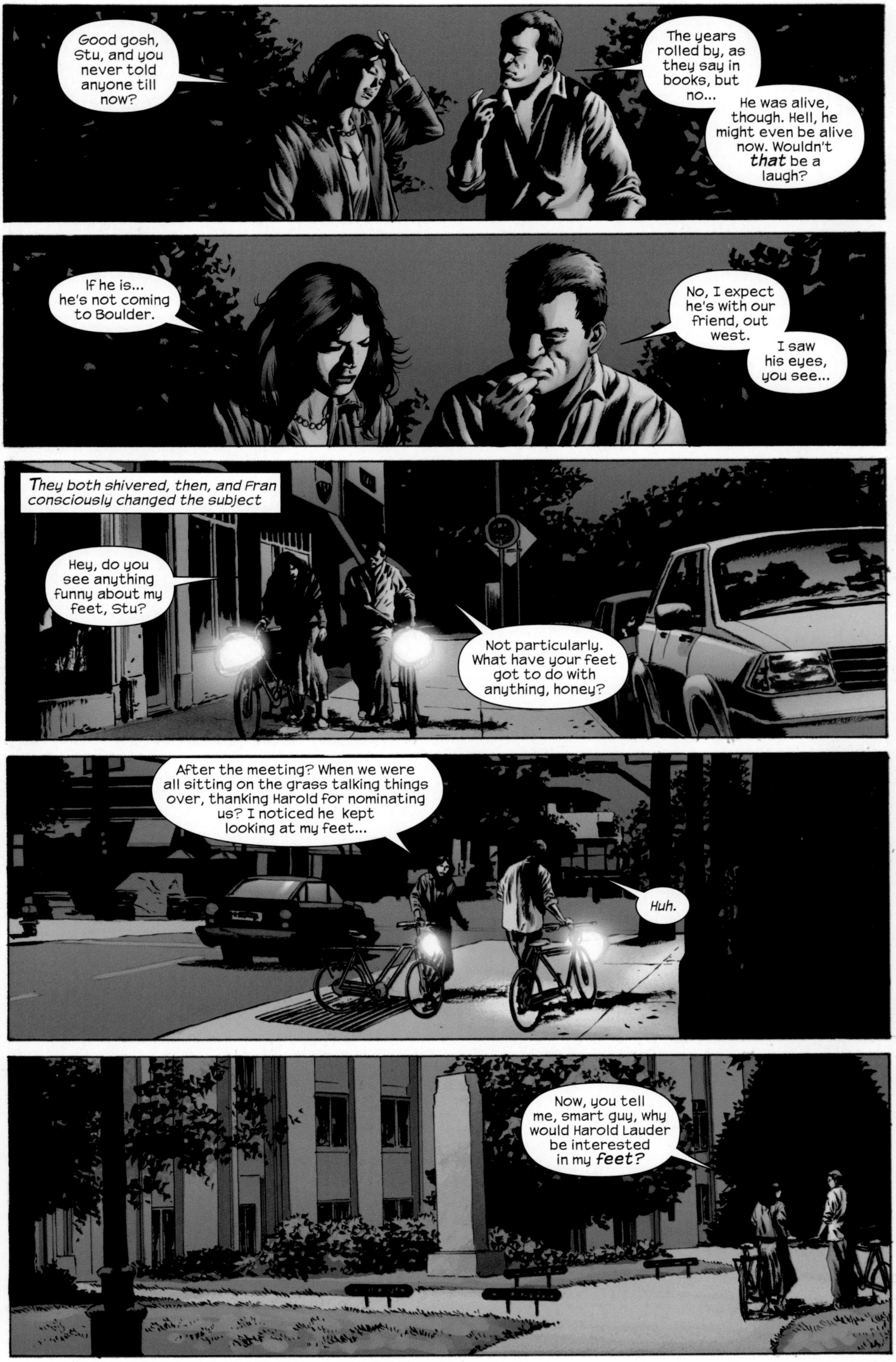
Good gosh, Stu, and you never told anyone till now?
The years rolled by, as they say in books, but no...
He was alive, though. Hell, he might even be alive now. Wouldn't *that* be a laugh?
If he is... he's not coming to Boulder.
No, I expect he's with our friend, out west.
I saw his eyes, you see...
They both shivered, then, and Fran consciously changed the subject
Hey, do you see anything funny about my feet, Stu?
Not particularly. What have your feet got to do with anything, honey?
After the meeting? When we were all sitting on the grass talking things over, thanking Harold for nominating us? I noticed he kept looking at my feet...
Huh.
Now, you tell me, smart guy, why would Harold Lauder be interested in my *feet?*

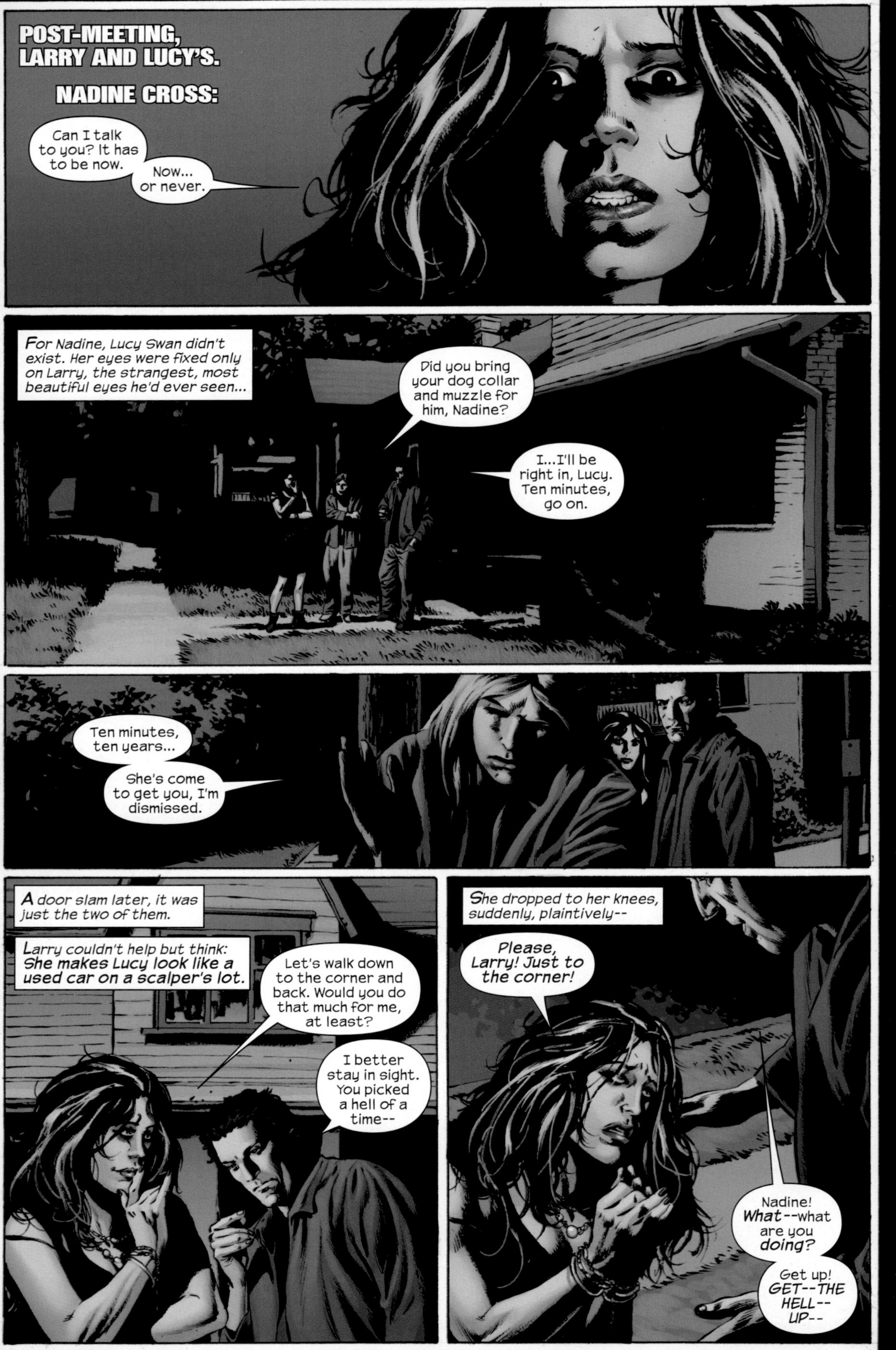
POST-MEETING, LARRY AND LUCY'S.
NADINE CROSS:
Can I talk to you? It has to be now.
Now... or never.
For Nadine, Lucy Swan didn't exist. Her eyes were fixed only on Larry, the strangest, most beautiful eyes he'd ever seen...
Did you bring your dog collar and muzzle for him, Nadine?
I...I'll be right in, Lucy. Ten minutes, go on.
Ten minutes, ten years...
She's come to get you, I'm dismissed.
A door slam later, it was just the two of them.
Larry couldn't help but think: She makes Lucy look like a used car on a scalper's lot.
Let's walk down to the corner and back. Would you do that much for me, at least?
I better stay in sight. You picked a hell of a time--
She dropped to her knees, suddenly, plaintively--
Please, Larry! Just to the corner!
Nadine! What--what are you doing?
Get up! GET--THE HELL--UP--

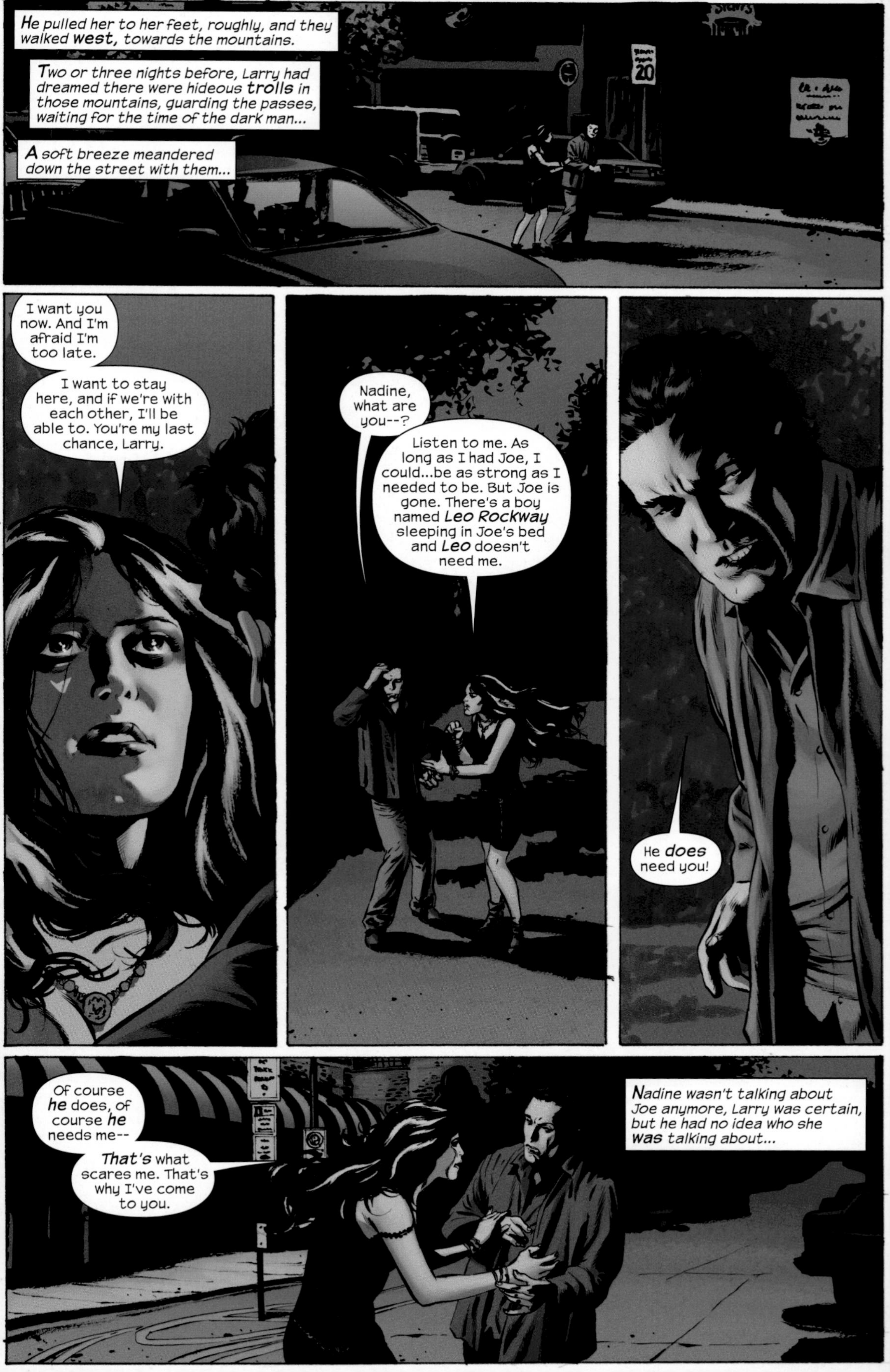
He pulled her to her feet, roughly, and they walked west, towards the mountains.
Two or three nights before, Larry had dreamed there were hideous trolls in those mountains, guarding the passes, waiting for the time of the dark man...
A soft breeze meandered down the street with them...
20
I want you now. And I'm afraid I'm too late.
I want to stay here, and if we're with each other, I'll be able to. You're my last chance, Larry.
Nadine, what are you--?
Listen to me. As long as I had Joe, I could...be as strong as I needed to be. But Joe is gone. There's a boy named Leo Rockway sleeping in Joe's bed and Leo doesn't need me.
He does need you!
Of course he does, of course he needs me--
That's what scares me. That's why I've come to you.
Nadine wasn't talking about Joe anymore, Larry was certain, but he had no idea who she was talking about...

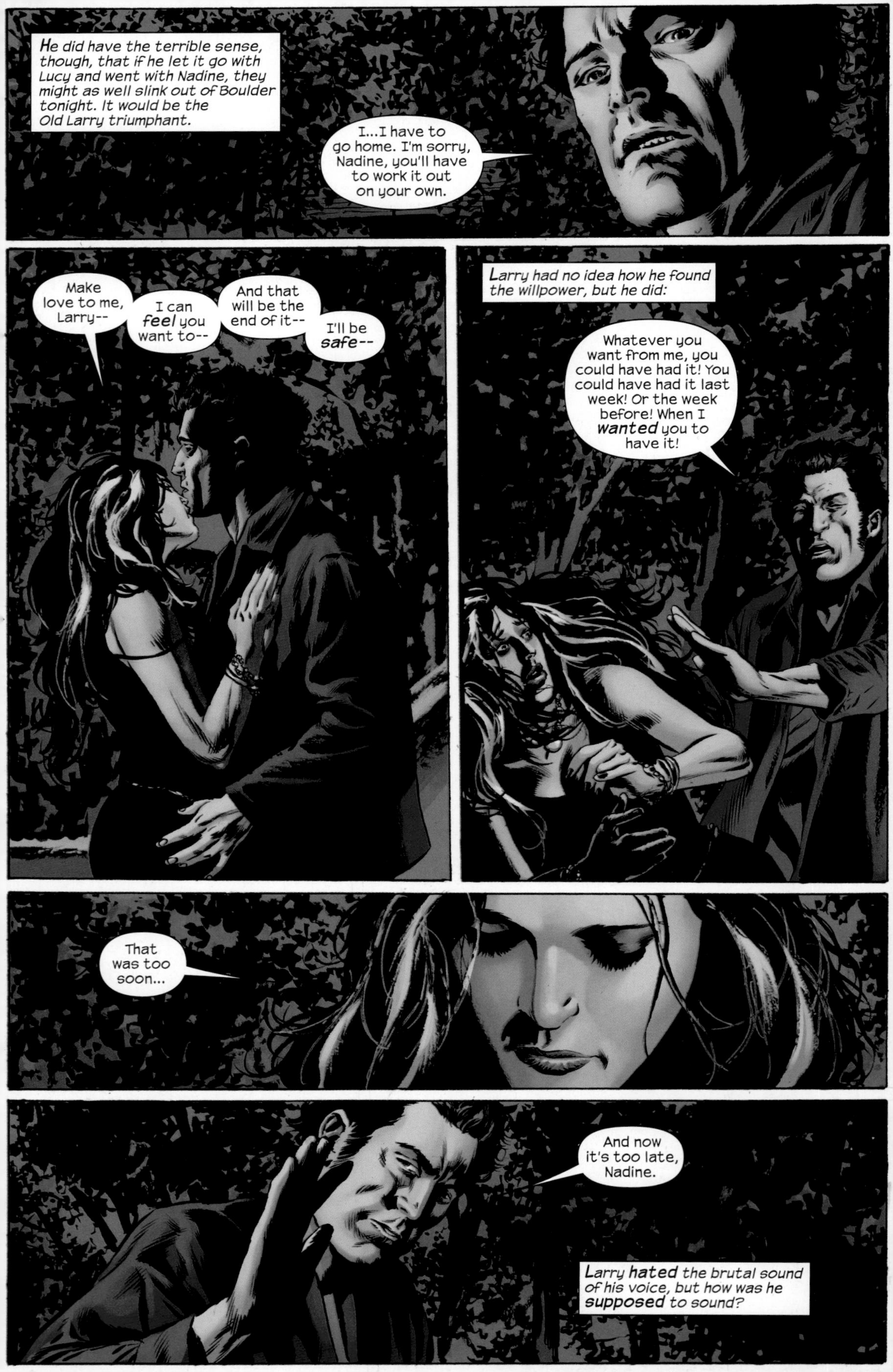

He did have the terrible sense, though, that if he let it go with Lucy and went with Nadine, they might as well slink out of Boulder tonight. It would be the Old Larry triumphant.
I...I have to go home. I'm sorry, Nadine, you'll have to work it out on your own.
Make love to me, Larry--
I can *feel* you want to--
And that will be the end of it--
I'll be *safe*--
Larry had no idea how he found the willpower, but he did:
Whatever you want from me, you could have had it! You could have had it last week! Or the week before! When I **wanted** you to have it!
That was too soon...
And now it's too late, Nadine.
Larry **hated** the brutal sound of his voice, but how was he **supposed** to sound?

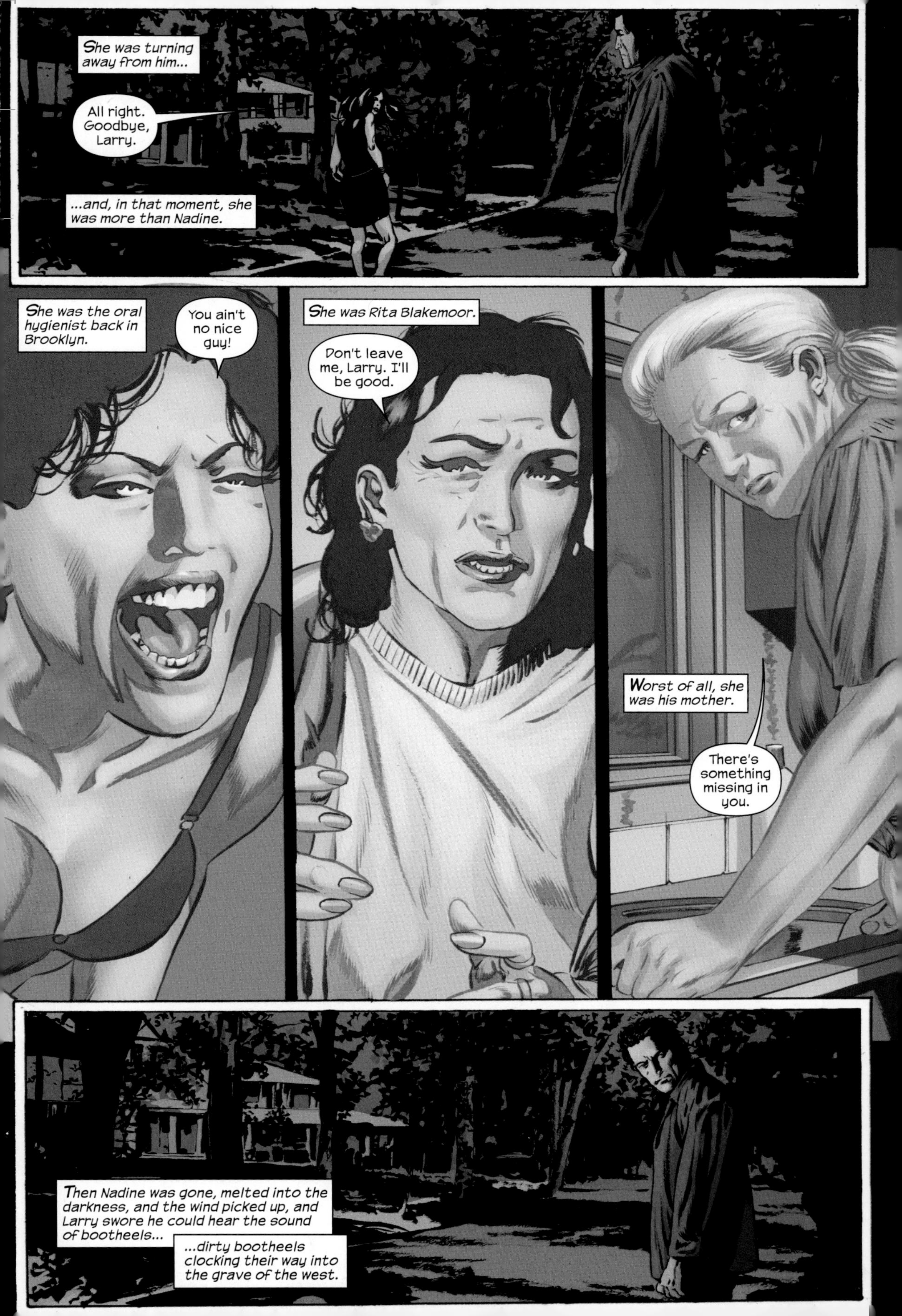
She was turning away from him...
All right. Goodbye, Larry.
...and, in that moment, she was more than Nadine.
She was the oral hygienist back in Brooklyn.
You ain't no nice guy!
She was Rita Blakemoor.
Don't leave me, Larry. I'll be good.
Worst of all, she was his mother.
There's something missing in you.
Then Nadine was gone, melted into the darkness, and the wind picked up, and Larry swore he could hear the sound of bootheels...
...dirty bootheels clocking their way into the grave of the west.

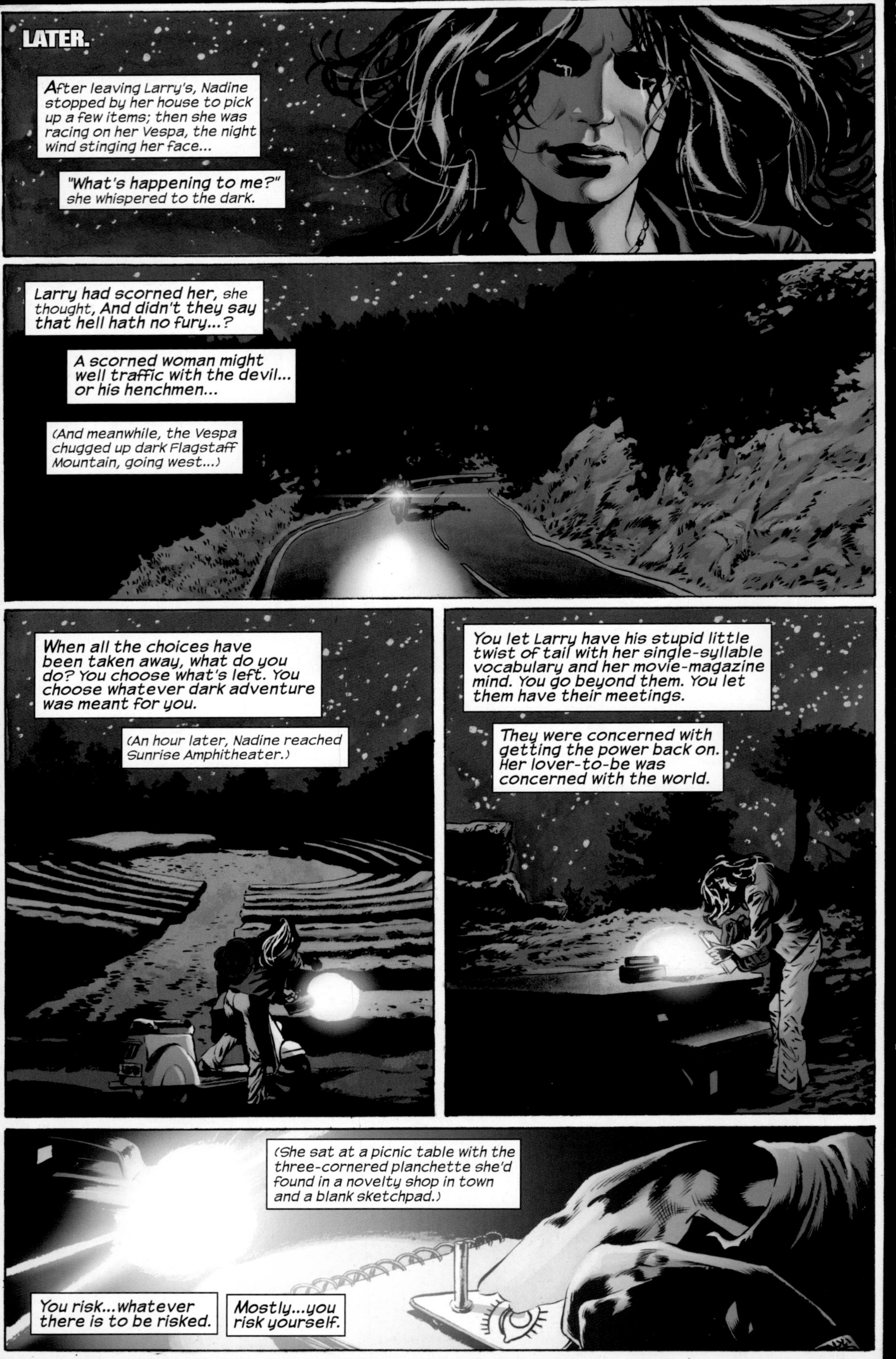
LATER.
After leaving Larry's, Nadine stopped by her house to pick up a few items; then she was racing on her Vespa, the night wind stinging her face...
"What's happening to me?" she whispered to the dark.
Larry had scorned her, she thought, And didn't they say that hell hath no fury...?
A scorned woman might well traffic with the devil... or his henchmen...
(And meanwhile, the Vespa chugged up dark Flagstaff Mountain, going west...)
When all the choices have been taken away, what do you do? You choose what's left. You choose whatever dark adventure was meant for you.
(An hour later, Nadine reached Sunrise Amphitheater.)
You let Larry have his stupid little twist of tail with her single-syllable vocabulary and her movie-magazine mind. You go beyond them. You let them have their meetings.
They were concerned with getting the power back on. Her lover-to-be was concerned with the world.
(She sat at a picnic table with the three-cornered planchette she'd found in a novelty shop in town and a blank sketchpad.)
You risk...whatever there is to be risked.
Mostly...you risk yourself.

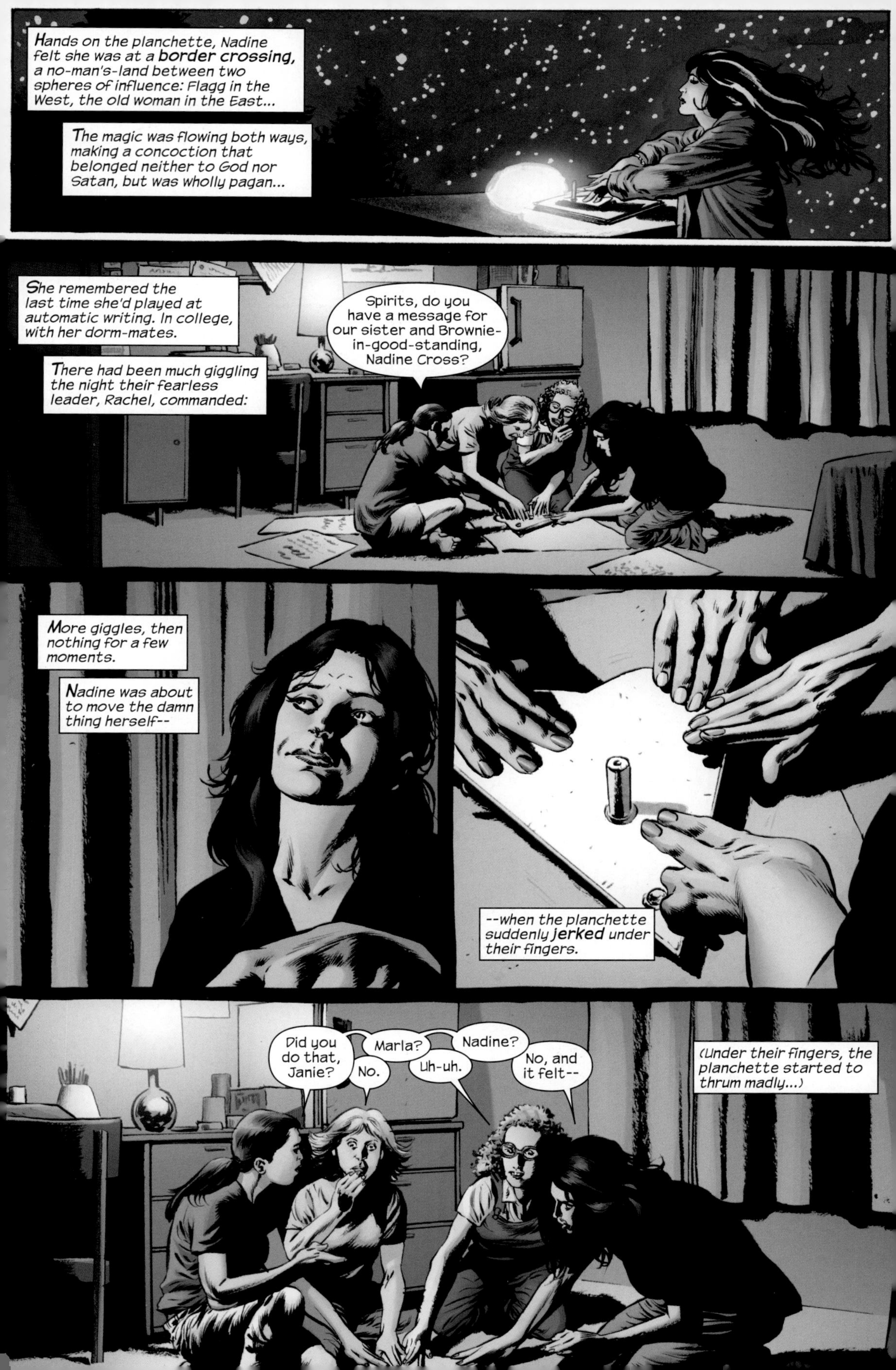
Hands on the planchette, Nadine felt she was at a **border crossing,** a no-man's-land between two spheres of influence: Flagg in the West, the old woman in the East...
The magic was flowing both ways, making a concoction that belonged neither to God nor Satan, but was wholly pagan...
She remembered the last time she'd played at automatic writing. In college, with her dorm-mates.
There had been much giggling the night their fearless leader, Rachel, commanded:
Spirits, do you have a message for our sister and Brownie-in-good-standing, Nadine Cross?
More giggles, then nothing for a few moments.
Nadine was about to move the damn thing herself--
--when the planchette suddenly **jerked** under their fingers.
Did you do that, Janie?
No.
Marla?
Uh-uh.
Nadine?
No, and it felt--
(Under their fingers, the planchette started to thrum madly...)

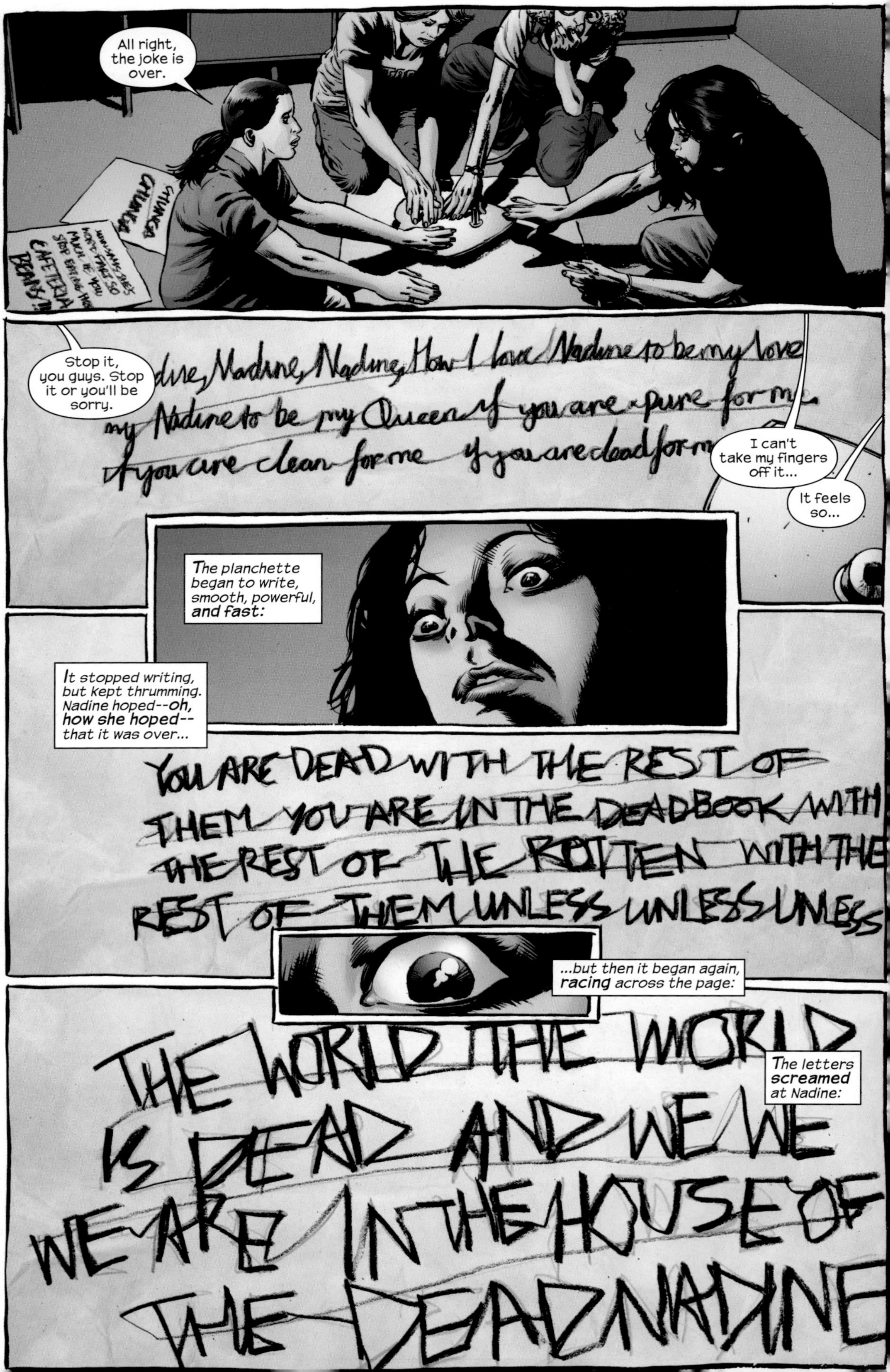

All right, the joke is over.
Stop it, you guys. Stop it or you'll be sorry.
Nadine, Nadine, How I love Nadine to be my love
my Nadine to be my Queen if you are pure for me
if you are clean for me if you are dead for m
I can't take my fingers off it...
It feels so...
The planchette began to write, smooth, powerful, ***and fast:***
It stopped writing, but kept thrumming. Nadine hoped--***oh, how she hoped***--that it was over...
YOU ARE DEAD WITH THE REST OF THEM YOU ARE IN THE DEADBOOK WITH THE REST OF THE ROTTEN WITH THE REST OF THEM UNLESS UNLESS UNLESS
...but then it began again, ***racing*** across the page:
The letters ***screamed*** at Nadine:
THE WORLD THE WORLD IS DEAD AND WE WE WE ARE IN THE HOUSE OF THE DEAD NADINE

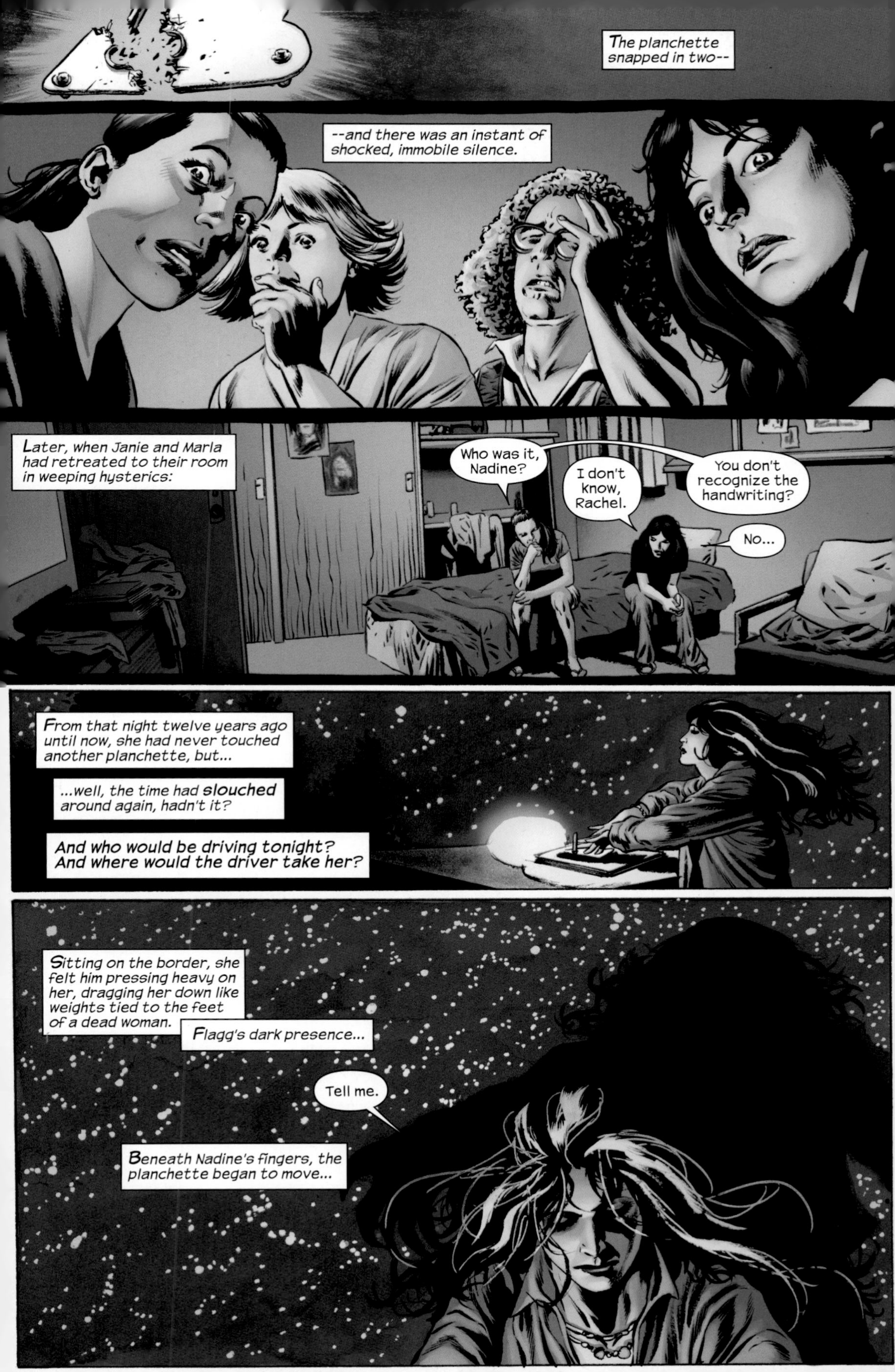
The planchette snapped in two--
--and there was an instant of shocked, immobile silence.
Later, when Janie and Marla had retreated to their room in weeping hysterics:
Who was it, Nadine?
I don't know, Rachel.
You don't recognize the handwriting?
No...
From that night twelve years ago until now, she had never touched another planchette, but...
...well, the time had slouched around again, hadn't it?
And who would be driving tonight? And where would the driver take her?
Sitting on the border, she felt him pressing heavy on her, dragging her down like weights tied to the feet of a dead woman.
Flagg's dark presence...
Tell me.
Beneath Nadine's fingers, the planchette began to move...

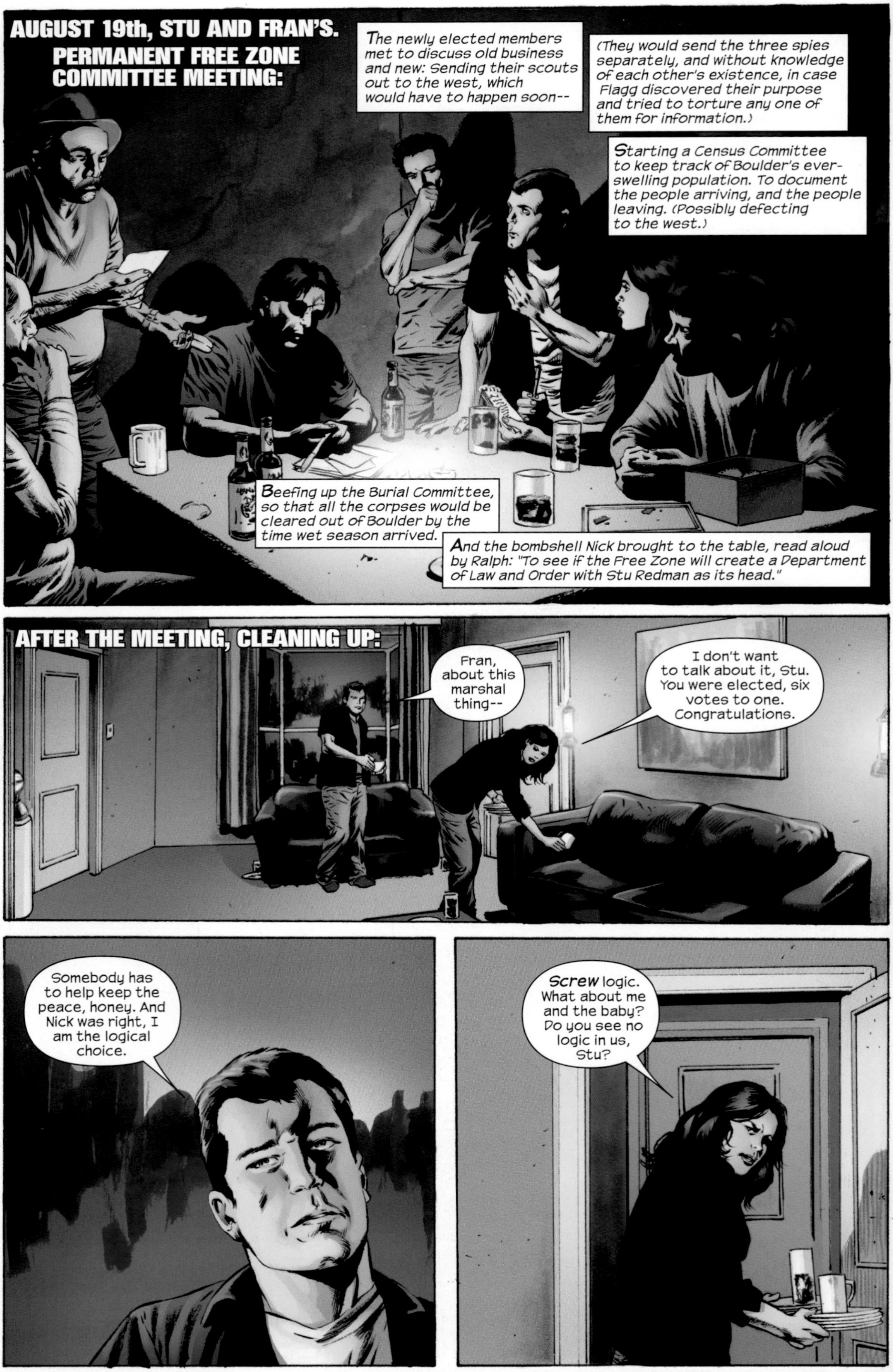
AUGUST 19th, STU AND FRAN'S. PERMANENT FREE ZONE COMMITTEE MEETING:
The newly elected members met to discuss old business and new: Sending their scouts out to the west, which would have to happen soon--
(They would send the three spies separately, and without knowledge of each other's existence, in case Flagg discovered their purpose and tried to torture any one of them for information.)
Starting a Census Committee to keep track of Boulder's ever-swelling population. To document the people arriving, and the people leaving. (Possibly defecting to the west.)
Beefing up the Burial Committee, so that all the corpses would be cleared out of Boulder by the time wet season arrived.
And the bombshell Nick brought to the table, read aloud by Ralph: "To see if the Free Zone will create a Department of Law and Order with Stu Redman as its head."
AFTER THE MEETING, CLEANING UP:
Fran, about this marshal thing--
I don't want to talk about it, Stu. You were elected, six votes to one. Congratulations.
Somebody has to help keep the peace, honey. And Nick was right, I am the logical choice.
Screw logic. What about me and the baby? Do you see no logic in us, Stu?

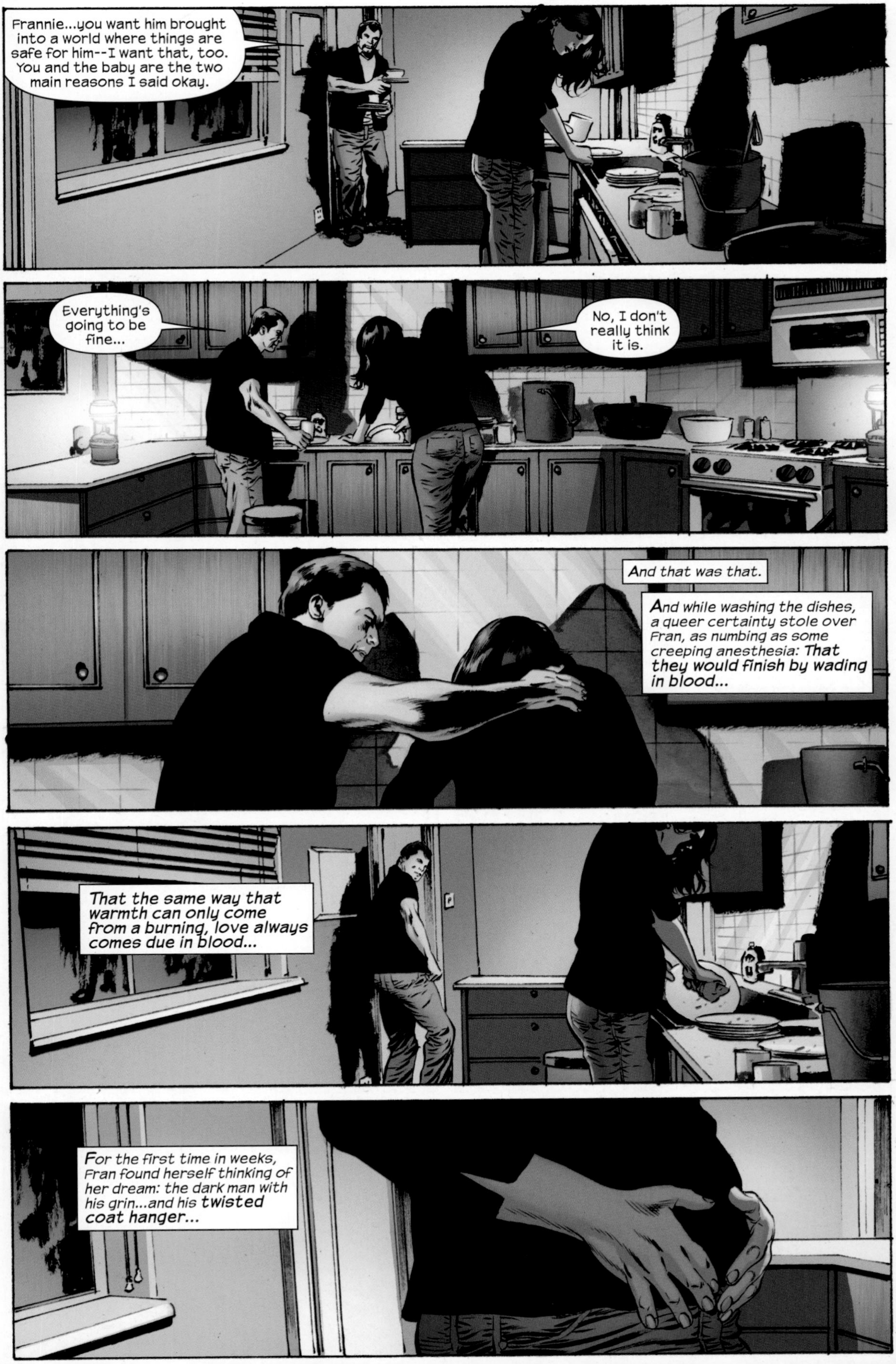
Frannie...you want him brought into a world where things are safe for him--I want that, too. You and the baby are the two main reasons I said okay.
Everything's going to be fine...
No, I don't really think it is.
And that was that.
And while washing the dishes, a queer certainty stole over Fran, as numbing as some creeping anesthesia: That they would finish by wading in blood...
That the same way that warmth can only come from a burning, love always comes due in blood...
For the first time in weeks, Fran found herself thinking of her dream: the dark man with his grin...and his twisted coat hanger...

AUGUST 20th.

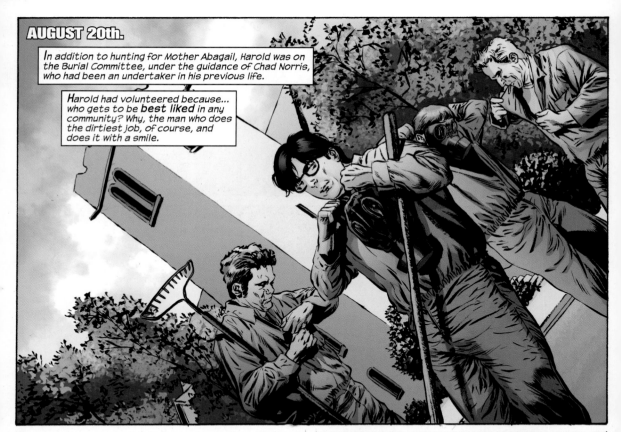

In addition to hunting for Mother Abagail, Harold was on the Burial Committee, under the guidance of Chad Norris, who had been an undertaker in his previous life.

Harold had volunteered because... who gets to be **best liked** in any community? Why, the man who does the dirtiest job, of course, and does it with a smile.

They spent the day emptying the Church of Latter Day Saints on lower Table Mesa Drive. Over seventy dead; the stink was enormous.

"It's going to be like moving and burying cordwood," Chad had promised them, "Nothing but cordwood."

Once the church had been cleared, they drove the bodies to a burial site ten miles southwest of Boulder, in an area that had once been strip-mined for coal.

Watching the bodies tumble out in a grotesque human rain, Harold felt an instant pity, a feeling so deep it was an ache.

Cordwood... That's all that's left. Just cordwood...

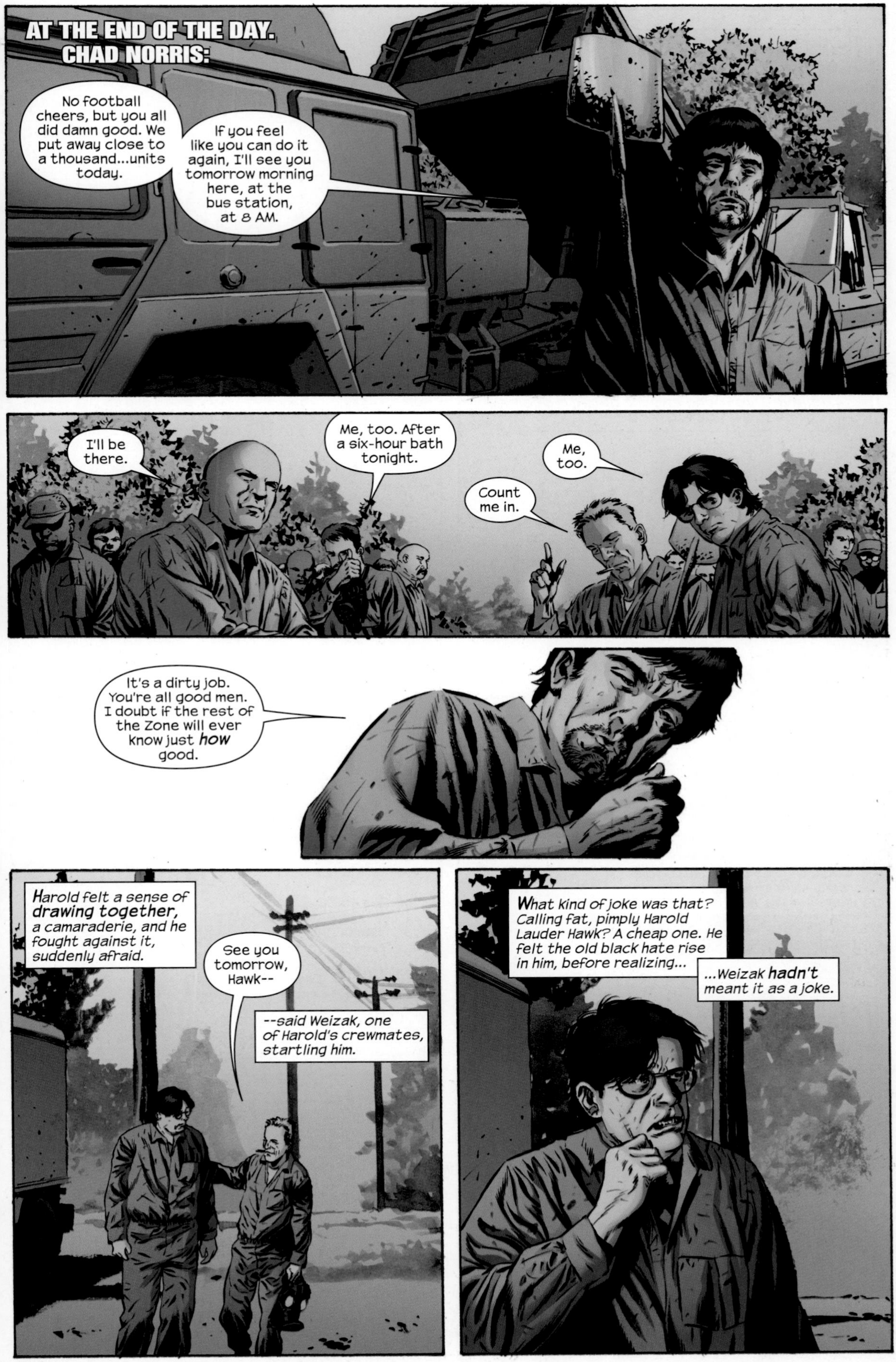
AT THE END OF THE DAY. CHAD NORRIS:
No football cheers, but you all did damn good. We put away close to a thousand...units today.
If you feel like you can do it again, I'll see you tomorrow morning here, at the bus station, at 8 AM.
I'll be there.
Me, too. After a six-hour bath tonight.
Count me in.
Me, too.
It's a dirty job. You're all good men. I doubt if the rest of the Zone will ever know just how good.
Harold felt a sense of drawing together, a camaraderie, and he fought against it, suddenly afraid.
See you tomorrow, Hawk--
--said Weizak, one of Harold's crewmates, startling him.
What kind of joke was that? Calling fat, pimply Harold Lauder Hawk? A cheap one. He felt the old black hate rise in him, before realizing...
...Weizak hadn't meant it as a joke.

The fact was, he **wasn't** fat anymore. And his pimples had cleared up weeks ago. And Weizak didn't know he had once been a school joke. Nor that his father had once asked *Harold* if he was homosexual.

A thought came to him, suddenly: I could be an asset to this community.

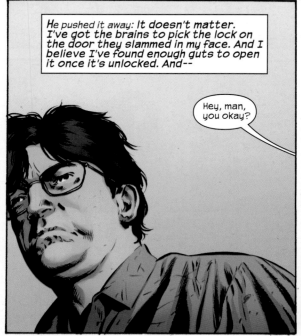

He *pushed* it away: It doesn't matter. I've got the brains to pick the lock on the door they slammed in my face. And I believe I've found enough guts to open it once it's unlocked. And--

Hey, man, you okay?

Me? Oh, I'm fine, Chad. I was just thinking.

Well, you go right along and do that. From what I hear, every time you do that, you coin money for this joint.

Could that be true? Did people really think of him as an idea man? New country, new Harold, except...

...except for Frannie.

See you tomorrow, Hawk!

Eight AM, I'll be there!

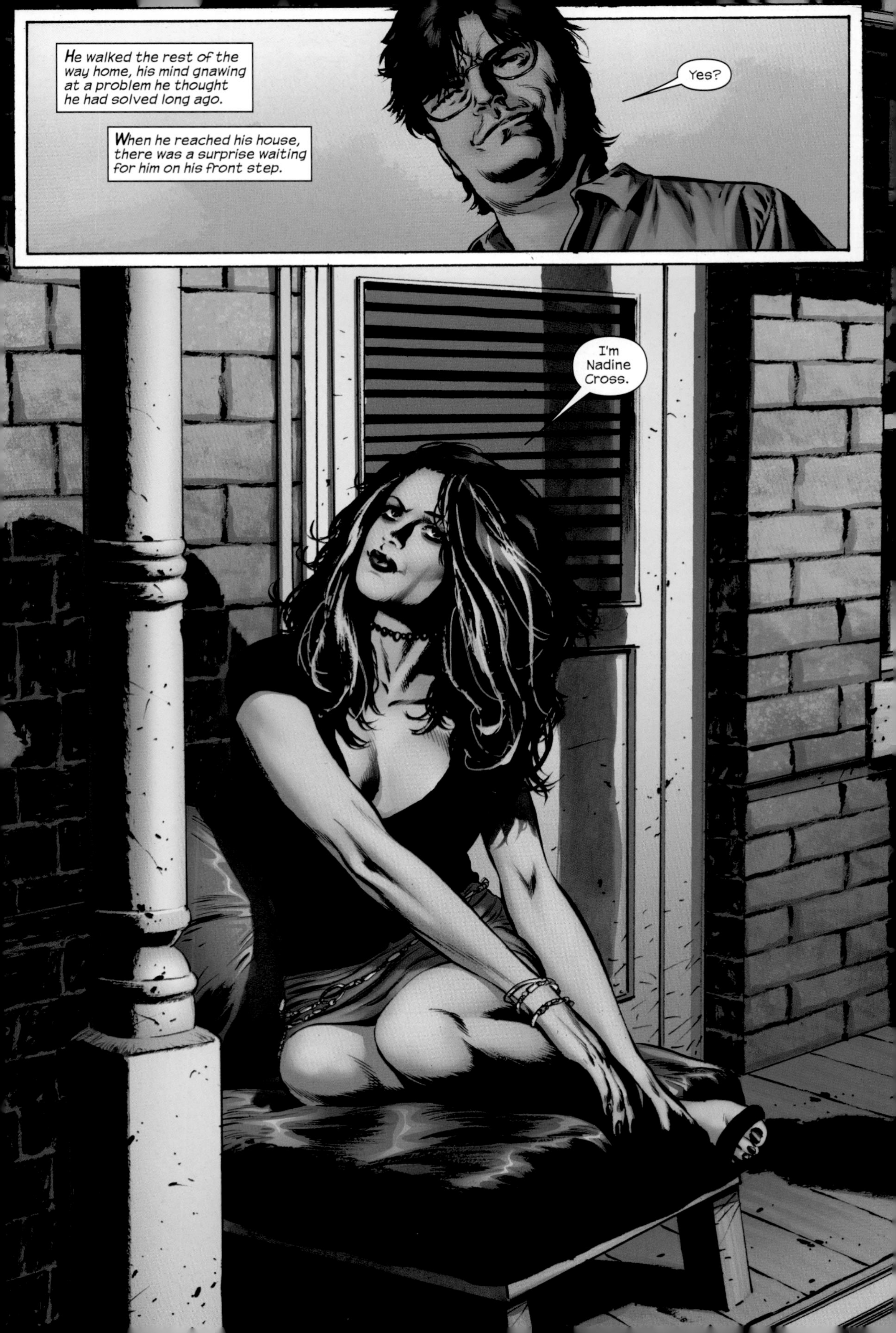
He walked the rest of the way home, his mind gnawing at a problem he thought he had solved long ago.
When he reached his house, there was a surprise waiting for him on his front step.
Yes?
I'm Nadine Cross.

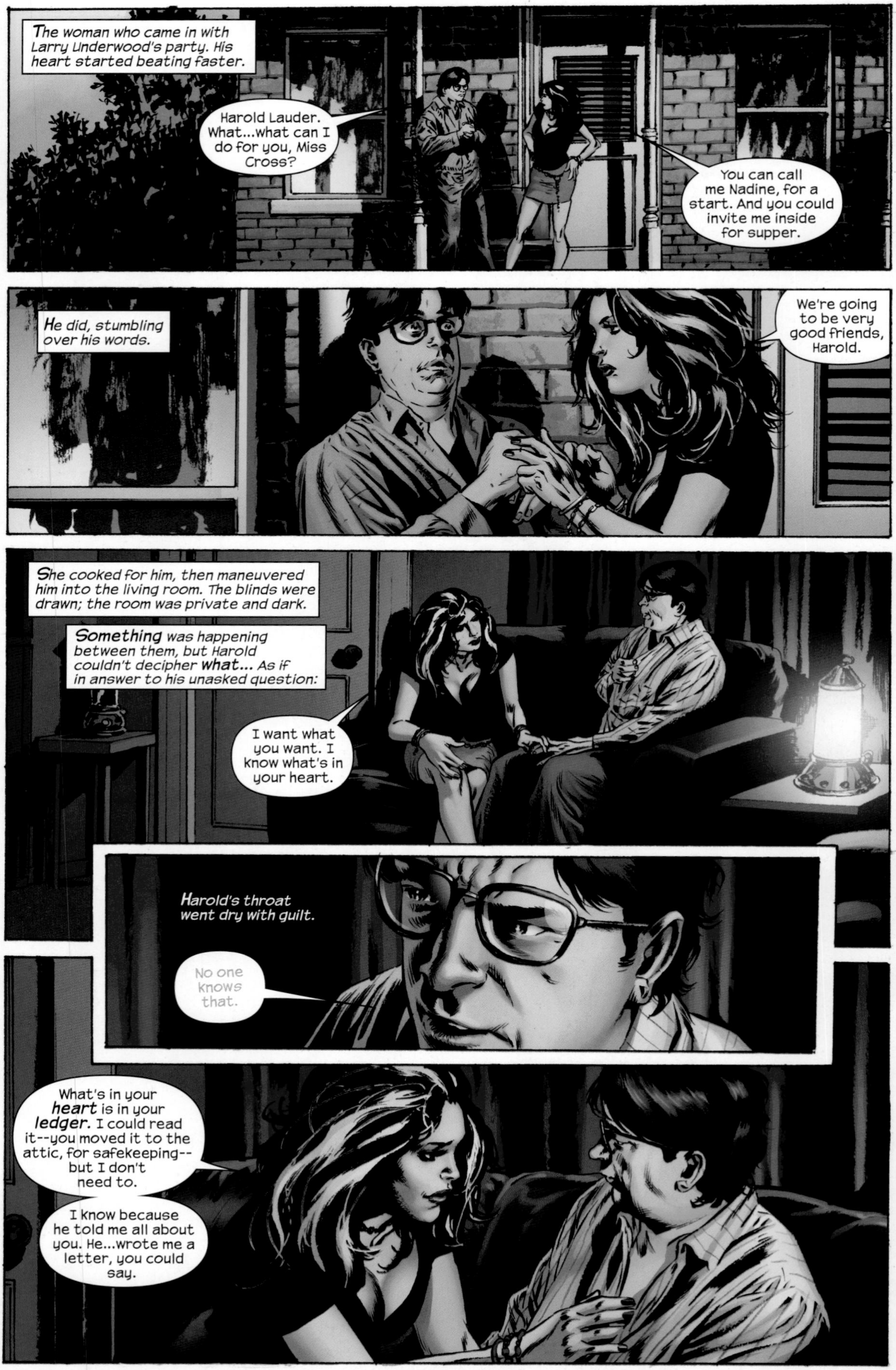
The woman who came in with Larry Underwood's party. His heart started beating faster.
Harold Lauder. What...what can I do for you, Miss Cross?
You can call me Nadine, for a start. And you could invite me inside for supper.
He did, stumbling over his words.
We're going to be very good friends, Harold.
She cooked for him, then maneuvered him into the living room. The blinds were drawn; the room was private and dark.
Something was happening between them, but Harold couldn't decipher what... As if in answer to his unasked question:
I want what you want. I know what's in your heart.
Harold's throat went dry with guilt.
No one knows that.
What's in your heart is in your ledger. I could read it--you moved it to the attic, for safekeeping--but I don't need to.
I know because he told me all about you. He...wrote me a letter, you could say.

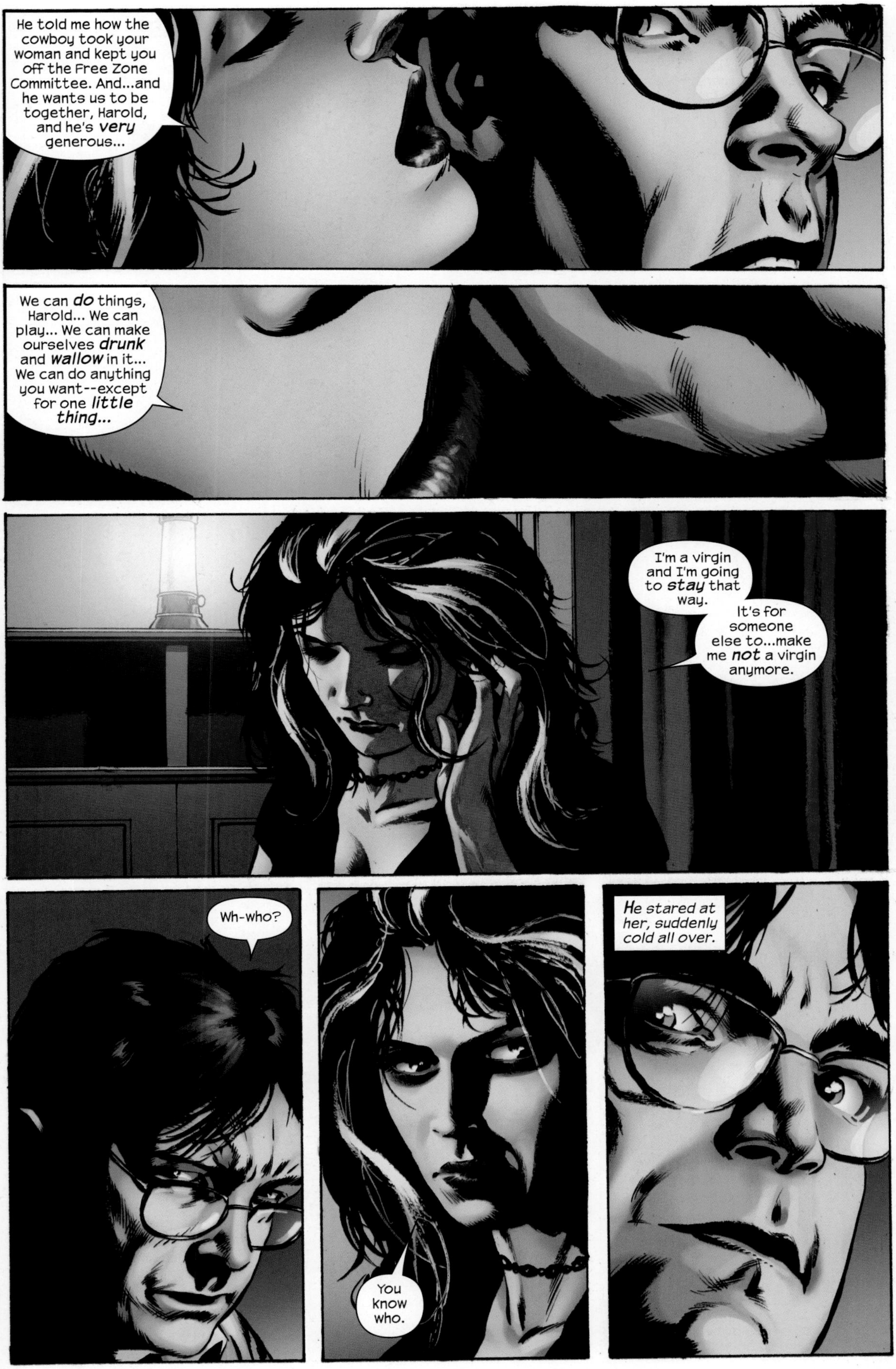
He told me how the cowboy took your woman and kept you off the Free Zone Committee. And...and he wants us to be together, Harold, and he's very generous...
We can do things, Harold... We can play... We can make ourselves drunk and wallow in it... We can do anything you want--except for one little thing...
I'm a virgin and I'm going to stay that way.
It's for someone else to...make me not a virgin anymore.
Wh-who?
You know who.
He stared at her, suddenly cold all over.

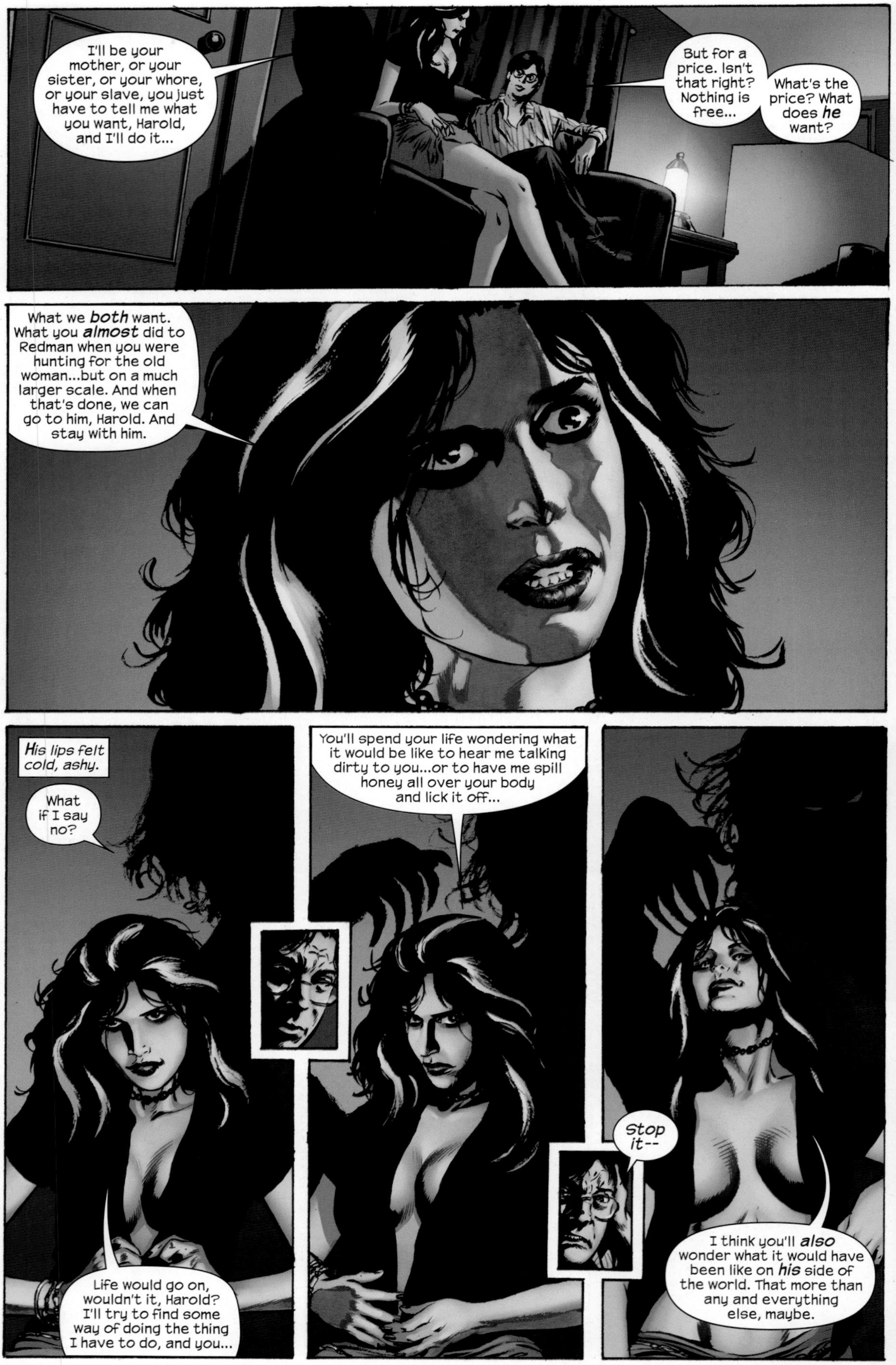

I'll be your mother, or your sister, or your whore, or your slave, you just have to tell me what you want, Harold, and I'll do it...
But for a price. Isn't that right? Nothing is free...
What's the price? What does *he* want?
What we *both* want. What you *almost* did to Redman when you were hunting for the old woman...but on a much larger scale. And when that's done, we can go to him, Harold. And stay with him.
His lips felt cold, ashy.
What if I say no?
Life would go on, wouldn't it, Harold? I'll try to find some way of doing the thing I have to do, and you...
You'll spend your life wondering what it would be like to hear me talking dirty to you...or to have me spill honey all over your body and lick it off...
Stop it--
I think you'll *also* wonder what it would have been like on *his* side of the world. That more than any and everything else, maybe.

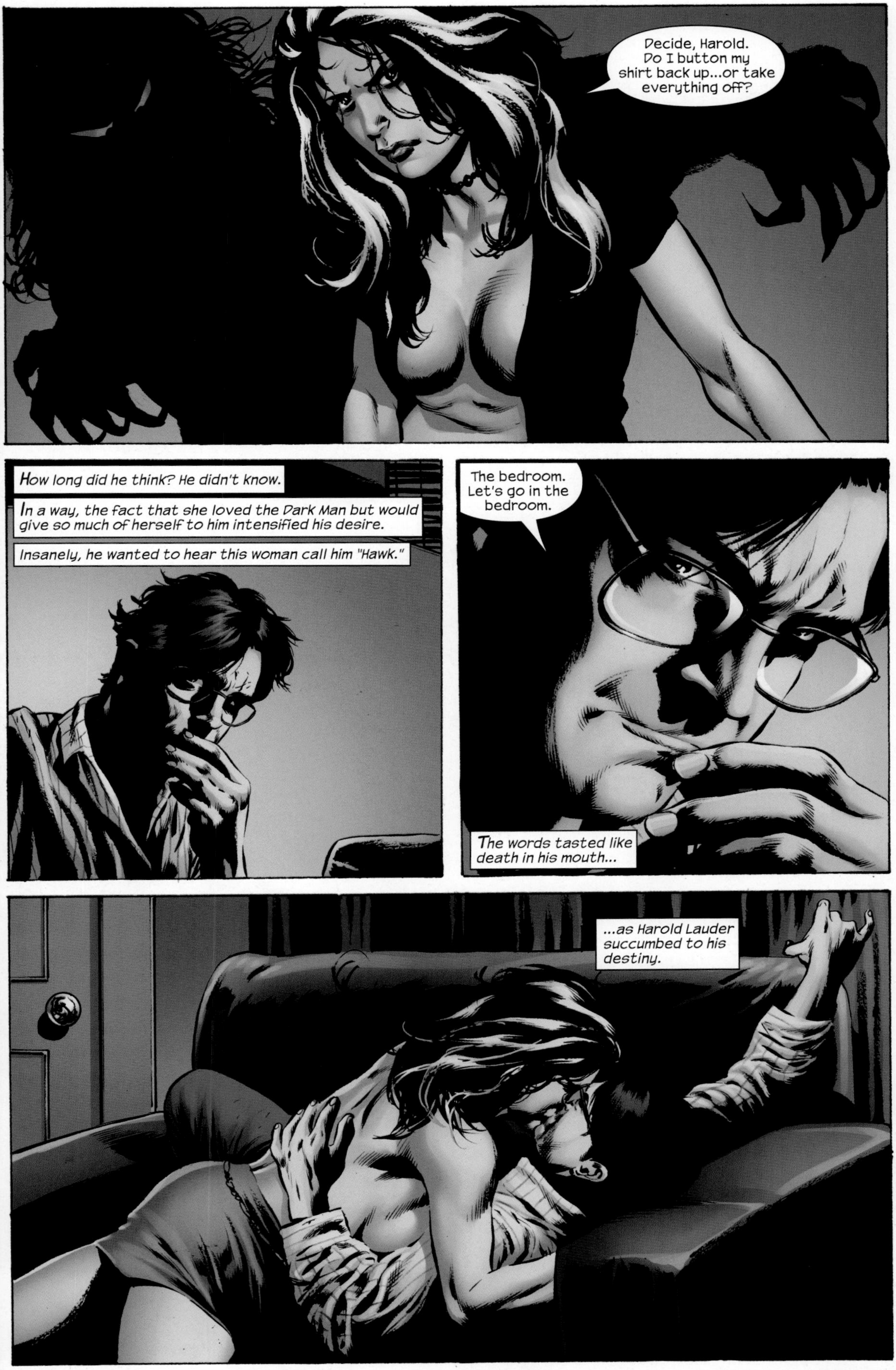

Decide, Harold. Do I button my shirt back up...or take everything off?
How long did he think? He didn't know.
In a way, the fact that she loved the Dark Man but would give so much of herself to him intensified his desire.
Insanely, he wanted to hear this woman call him "Hawk."
The bedroom. Let's go in the bedroom.
The words tasted like death in his mouth...
...as Harold Lauder succumbed to his destiny.

chapter TWO

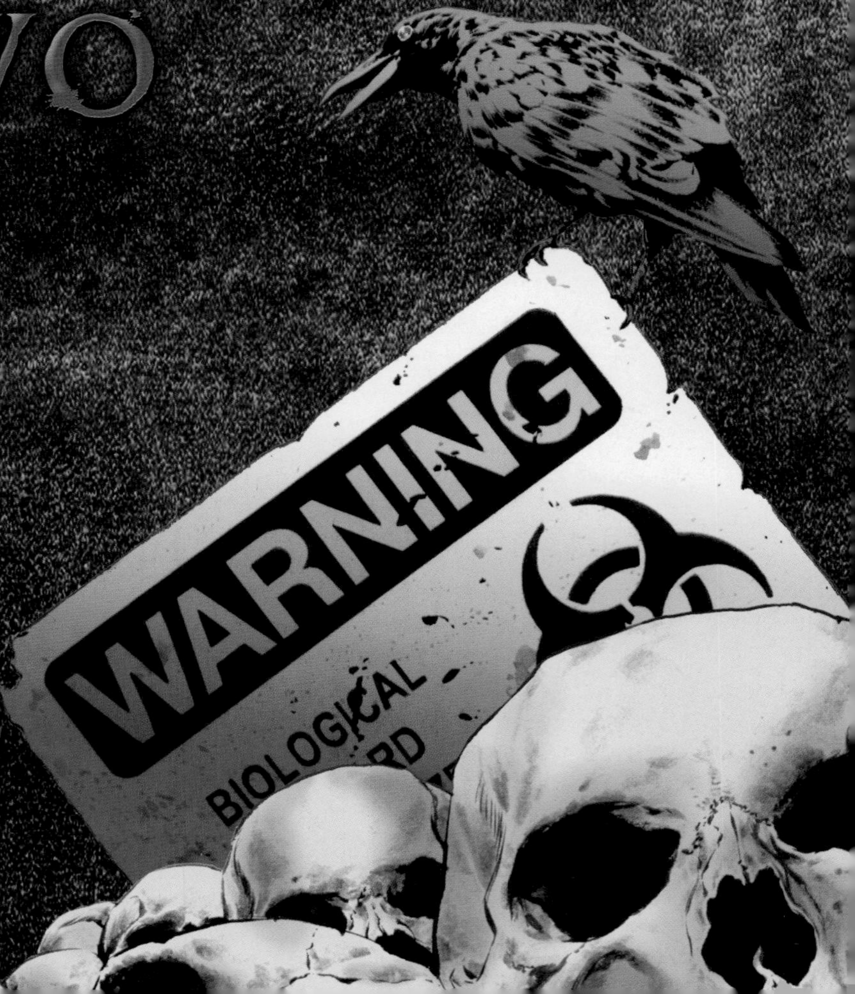
WARNING
BIOLOGICAL

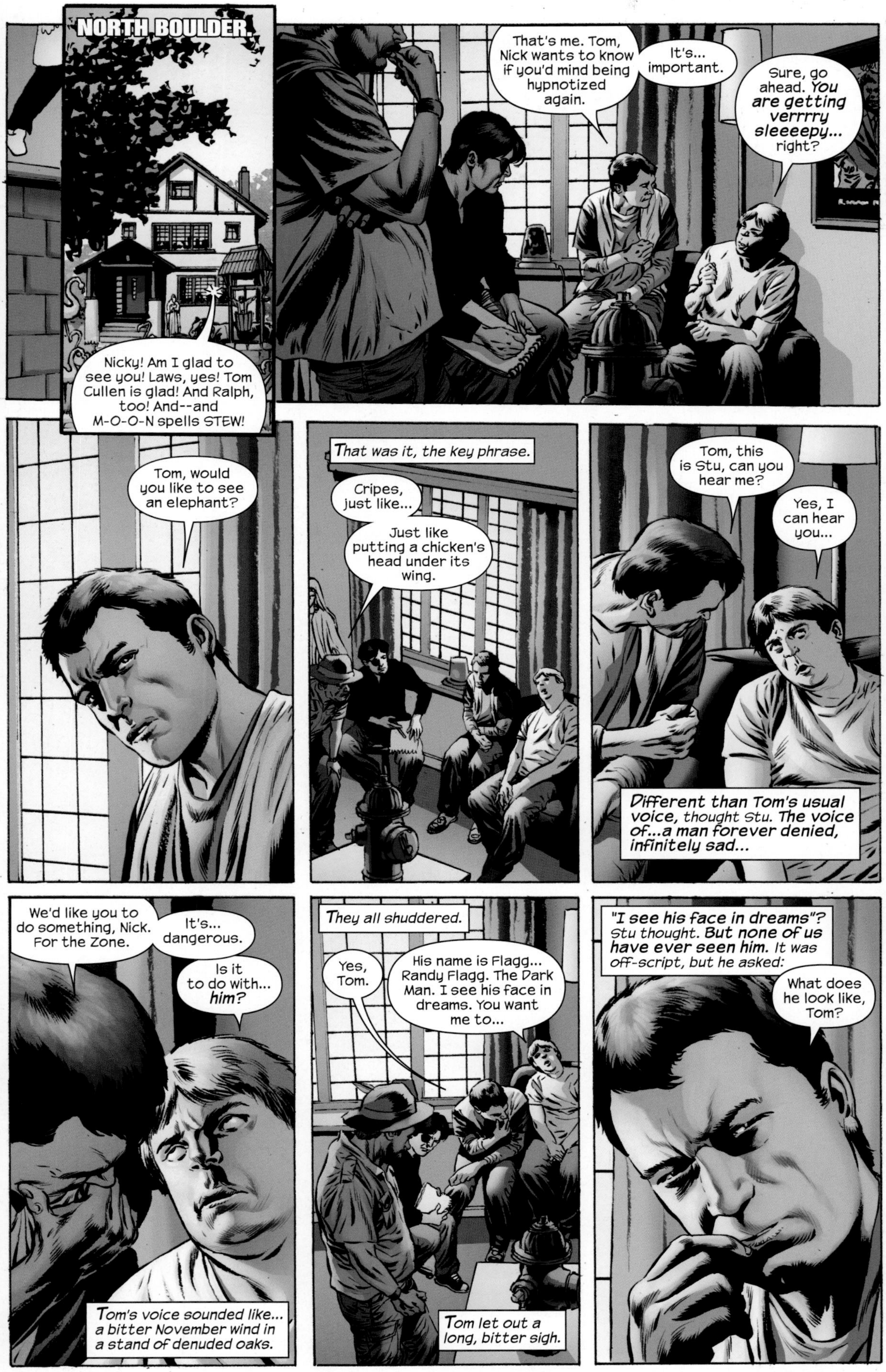
NORTH BOULDER.
Nicky! Am I glad to see you! Laws, yes! Tom Cullen is glad! And Ralph, too! And--and M-O-O-N spells STEW!
That's me. Tom, Nick wants to know if you'd mind being hypnotized again.
It's... important.
Sure, go ahead. You are getting verrrry sleeeepy... right?
Tom, would you like to see an elephant?
That was it, the key phrase.
Cripes, just like...
Just like putting a chicken's head under its wing.
Tom, this is Stu, can you hear me?
Yes, I can hear you...
Different than Tom's usual voice, thought Stu. The voice of...a man forever denied, infinitely sad...
We'd like you to do something, Nick. For the Zone.
It's... dangerous.
Is it to do with... him?
Tom's voice sounded like... a bitter November wind in a stand of denuded oaks.
They all shuddered.
Yes, Tom.
His name is Flagg... Randy Flagg. The Dark Man. I see his face in dreams. You want me to...
Tom let out a long, bitter sigh.
"I see his face in dreams"? Stu thought. But none of us have ever seen him. It was off-script, but he asked:
What does he look like, Tom?

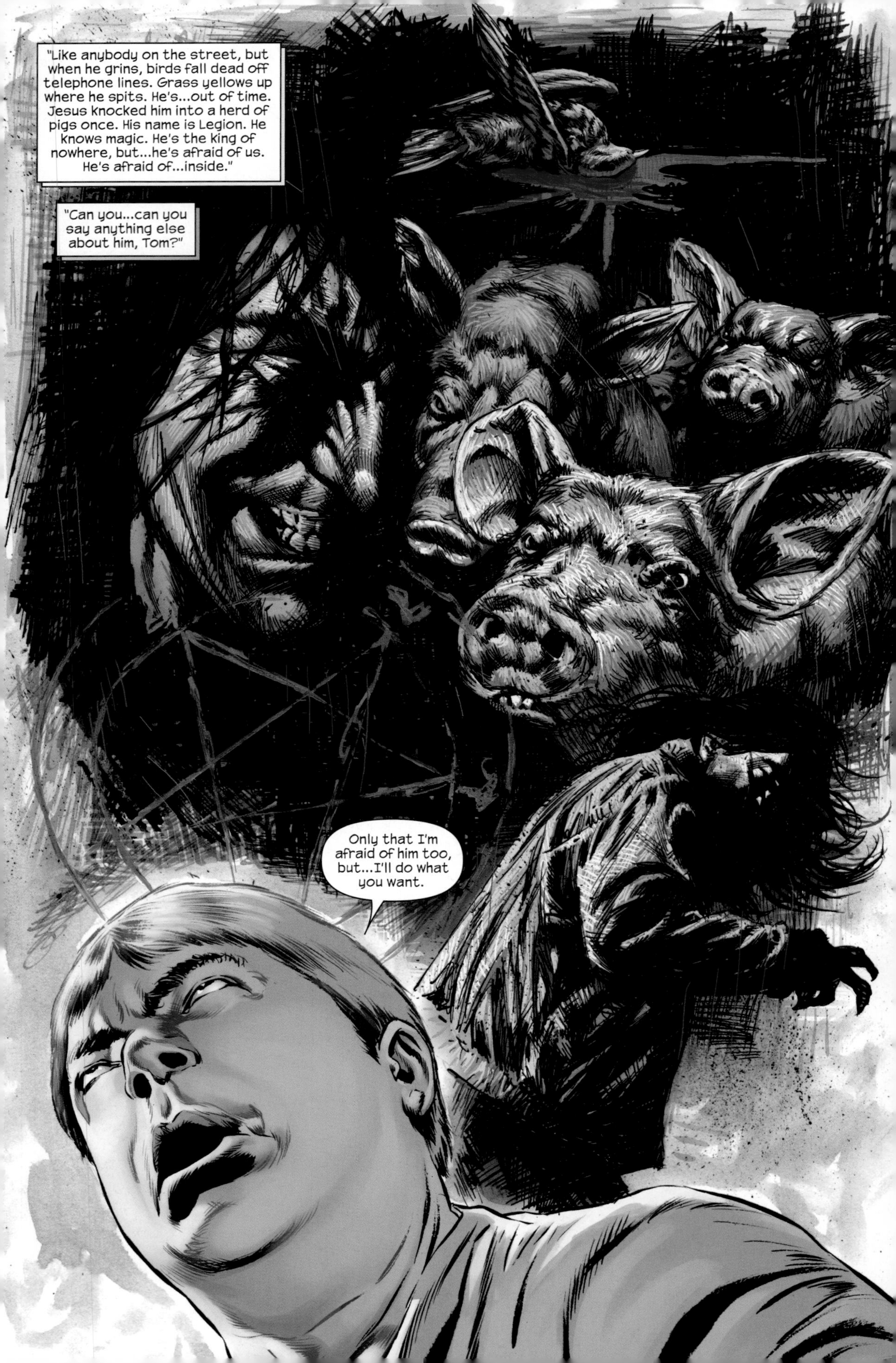
"Like anybody on the street, but when he grins, birds fall dead off telephone lines. Grass yellows up where he spits. He's...out of time. Jesus knocked him into a herd of pigs once. His name is Legion. He knows magic. He's the king of nowhere, but...he's afraid of us. He's afraid of...inside."
"Can you...can you say anything else about him, Tom?"
Only that I'm afraid of him too, but...I'll do what you want.

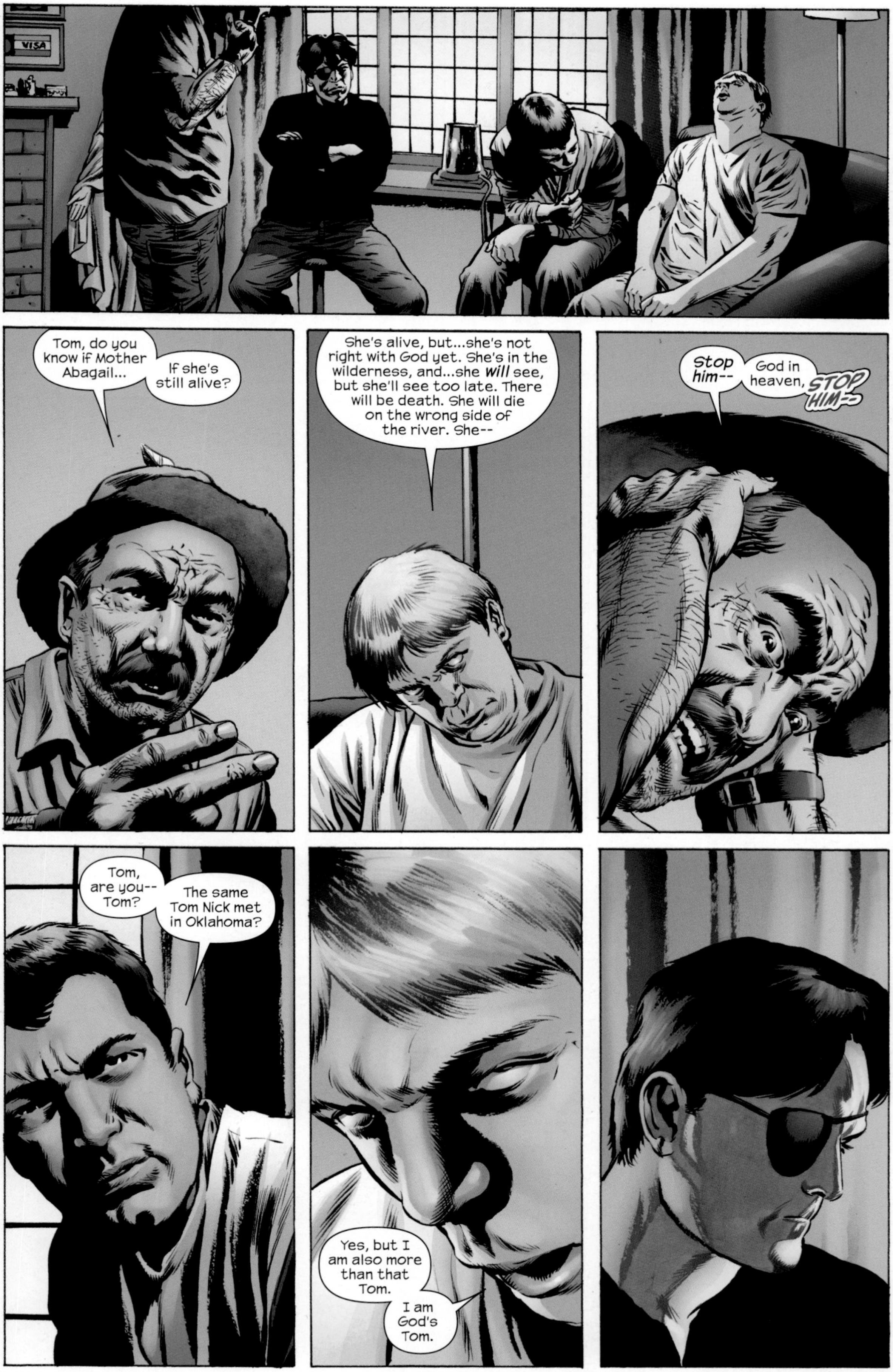
Tom, do you know if Mother Abagail...
If she's still alive?
She's alive, but...she's not right with God yet. She's in the wilderness, and...she *will* see, but she'll see too late. There will be death. She will die on the wrong side of the river. She--
Stop him--
God in heaven, STOP HIM--
Tom, are you--Tom?
The same Tom Nick met in Oklahoma?
Yes, but I am also more than that Tom.
I am God's Tom.

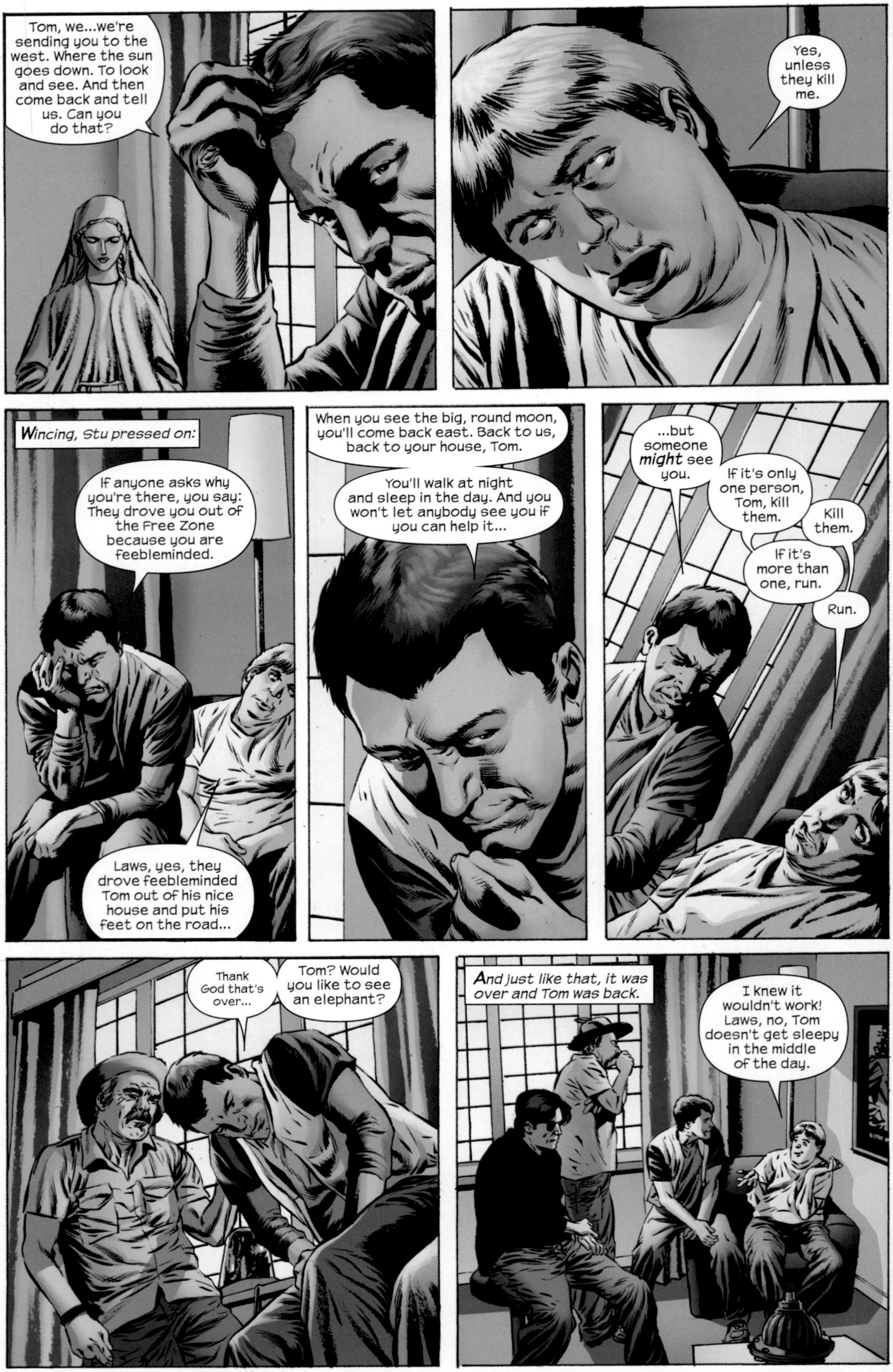

Tom, we...we're sending you to the west. Where the sun goes down. To look and see. And then come back and tell us. Can you do that?
Yes, unless they kill me.
Wincing, Stu pressed on:
If anyone asks why you're there, you say: They drove you out of the Free Zone because you are feebleminded.
Laws, yes, they drove feebleminded Tom out of his nice house and put his feet on the road...
When you see the big, round moon, you'll come back east. Back to us, back to your house, Tom.
You'll walk at night and sleep in the day. And you won't let anybody see you if you can help it...
...but someone *might* see you.
If it's only one person, Tom, kill them.
Kill them.
If it's more than one, run.
Run.
Thank God that's over...
Tom? Would you like to see an elephant?
And just like that, it was over and Tom was back.
I knew it wouldn't work! Laws, no, Tom doesn't get sleepy in the middle of the day.

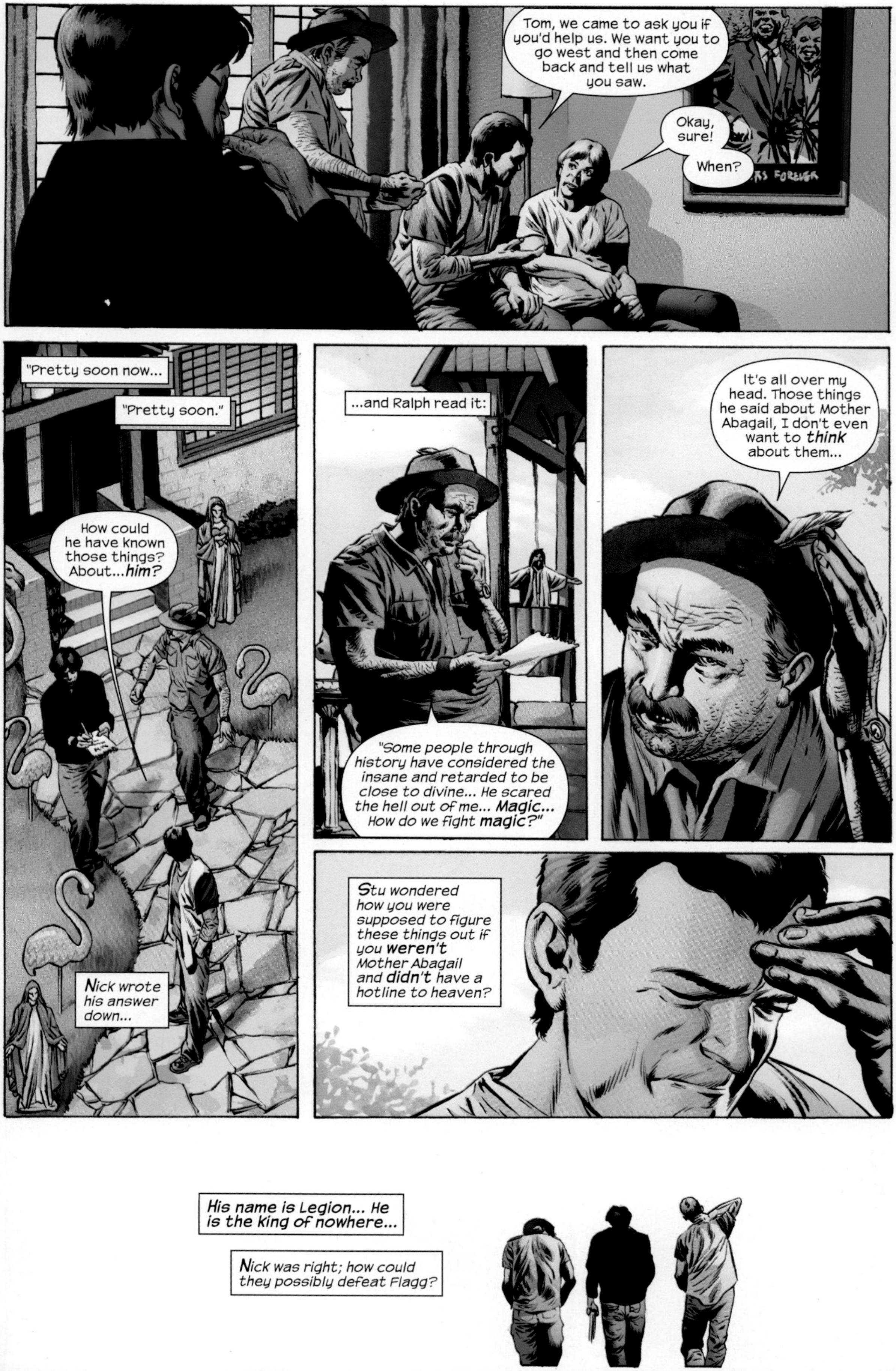
Tom, we came to ask you if you'd help us. We want you to go west and then come back and tell us what you saw.
Okay, sure!
When?
"Pretty soon now...
"Pretty soon."
How could he have known those things? About...*him*?
Nick wrote his answer down...
...and Ralph read it:
"Some people through history have considered the insane and retarded to be close to divine... He scared the hell out of me... **Magic...** How do we fight **magic**?"
It's all over my head. Those things he said about Mother Abagail, I don't even want to **think** about them...
Stu wondered how you were supposed to figure these things out if you **weren't** Mother Abagail and **didn't** have a hotline to heaven?
His name is Legion... He is the king of nowhere...
Nick was right; how could they possibly defeat Flagg?

THE JUDGE'S HOUSE.
OVERLOOKING THE CEMETERY.

When I was a boy, we lived near the finest boneyard in Illinois. Mount Hope. Whenever my father and I walked by it, he would ask, *"What do you think, Teddy? Is there any hope?"*

And I would answer, *"There's Mount Hope,"* and he would roar with laughter.

He died when I was a teenager, Larry...

Judge...

I know why you're here.

You want to send me west, don't you? To... spy out that land?

If that's it, I accept.

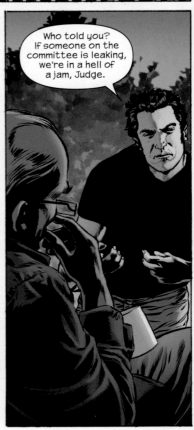

Who told you? If someone on the committee is leaking, we're in a hell of a jam, Judge.

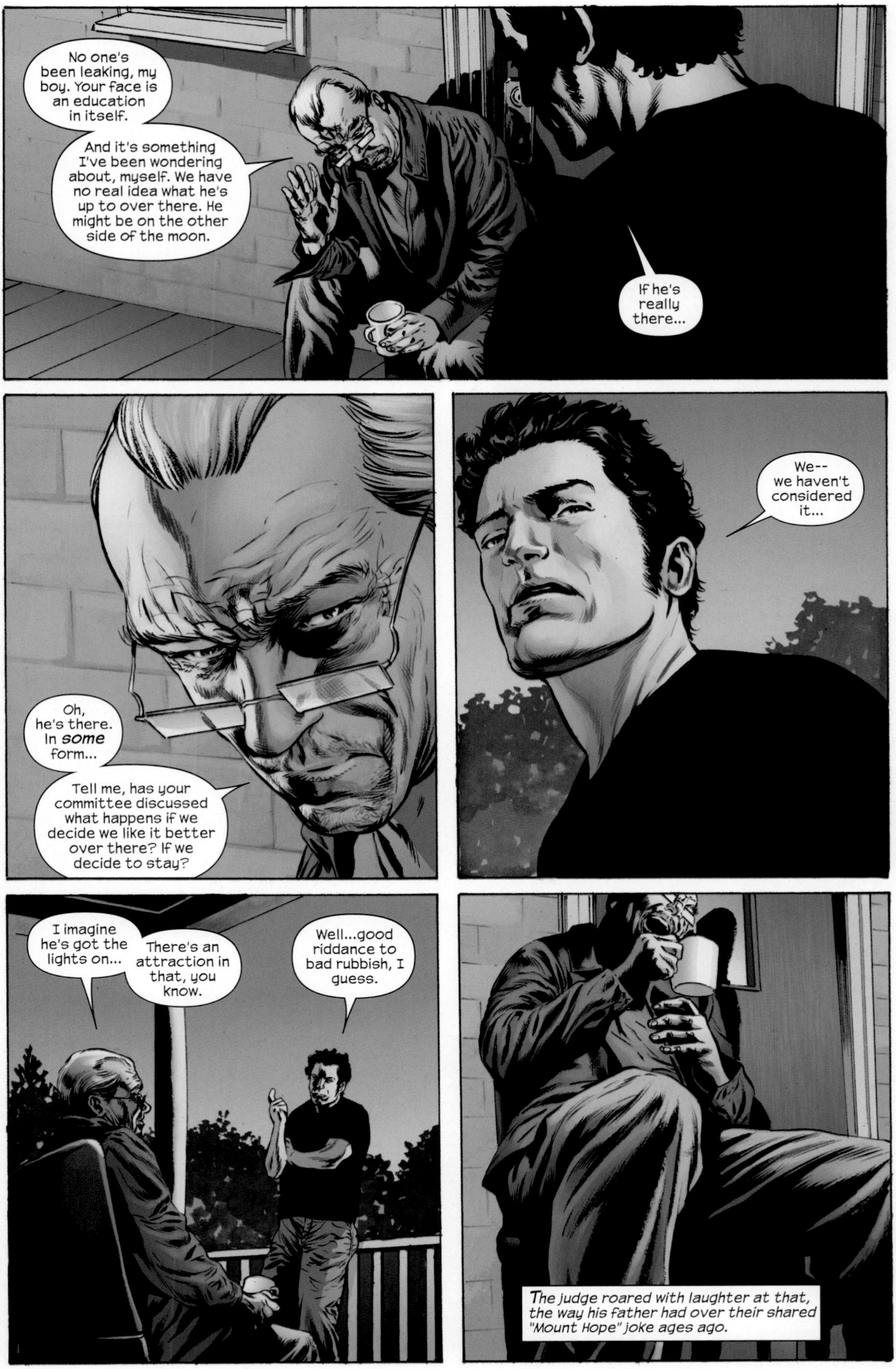
No one's been leaking, my boy. Your face is an education in itself.
And it's something I've been wondering about, myself. We have no real idea what he's up to over there. He might be on the other side of the moon.
If he's really there...
Oh, he's there. In *some* form...
Tell me, has your committee discussed what happens if we decide we like it better over there? If we decide to stay?
We-- we haven't considered it...
I imagine he's got the lights on...
There's an attraction in that, you know.
Well...good riddance to bad rubbish, I guess.
The judge roared with laughter at that, the way his father had over their shared "Mount Hope" joke ages ago.

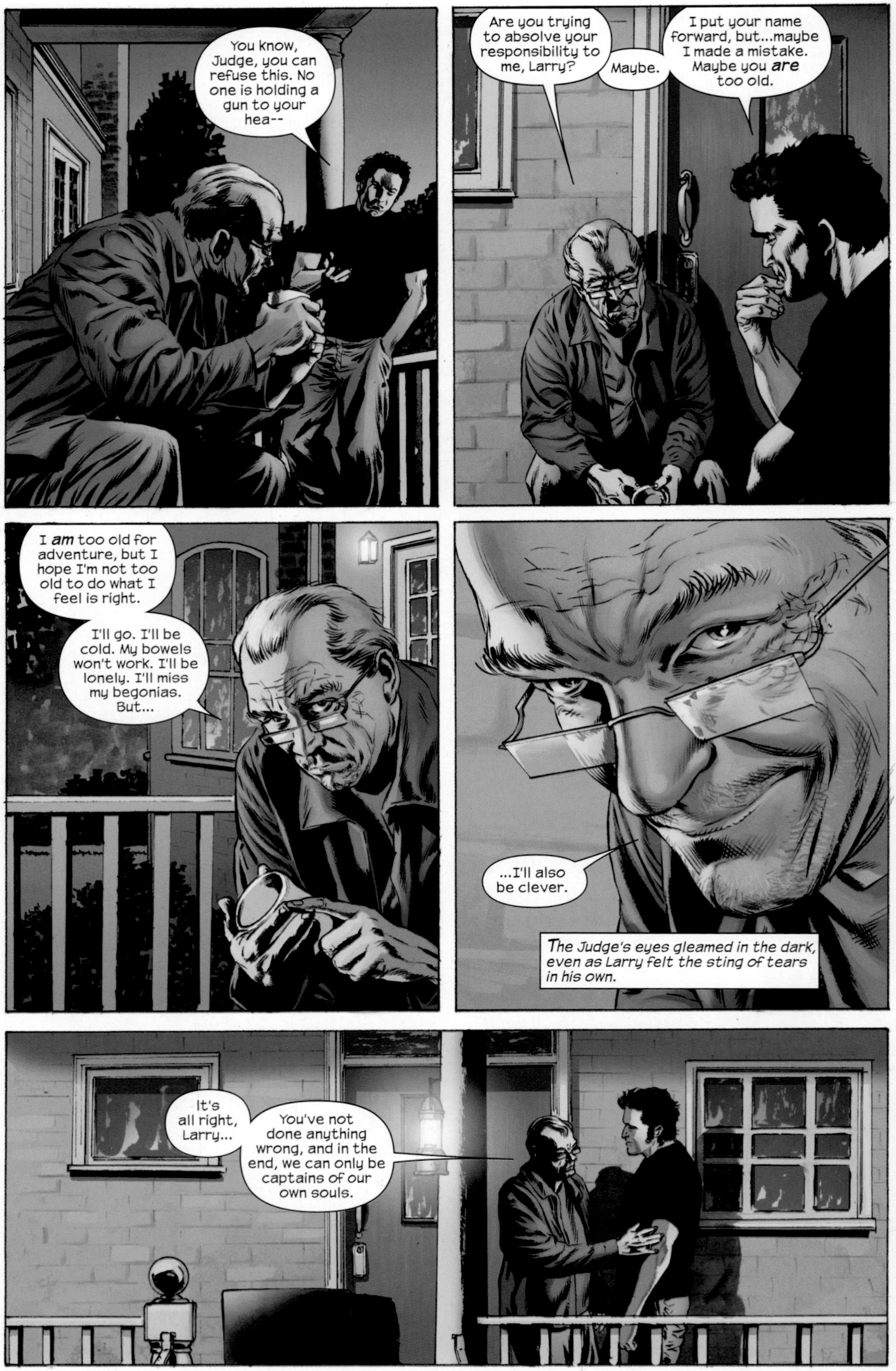
You know, Judge, you can refuse this. No one is holding a gun to your hea--
Are you trying to absolve your responsibility to me, Larry?
Maybe.
I put your name forward, but...maybe I made a mistake. Maybe you *are* too old.
I *am* too old for adventure, but I hope I'm not too old to do what I feel is right.
I'll go. I'll be cold. My bowels won't work. I'll be lonely. I'll miss my begonias. But...
...I'll also be clever.
The Judge's eyes gleamed in the dark, even as Larry felt the sting of tears in his own.
It's all right, Larry...
You've not done anything wrong, and in the end, we can only be captains of our own souls.

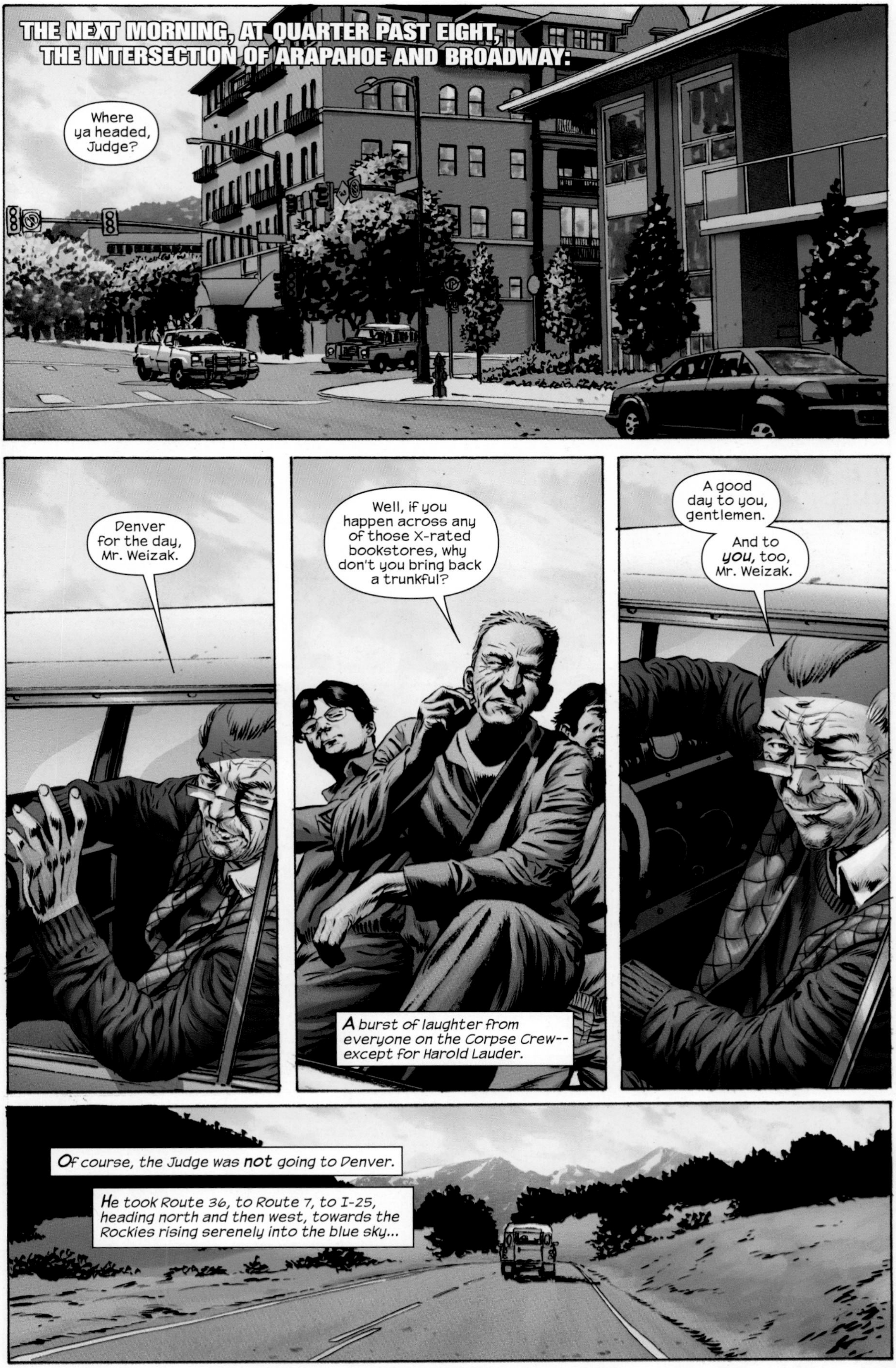
THE NEXT MORNING, AT QUARTER PAST EIGHT, THE INTERSECTION OF ARAPAHOE AND BROADWAY:
Where ya headed, Judge?
Denver for the day, Mr. Weizak.
Well, if you happen across any of those X-rated bookstores, why don't you bring back a trunkful?
A burst of laughter from everyone on the Corpse Crew--except for Harold Lauder.
A good day to you, gentlemen.
And to you, too, Mr. Weizak.
Of course, the Judge was not going to Denver.
He took Route 36, to Route 7, to I-25, heading north and then west, towards the Rockies rising serenely into the blue sky...

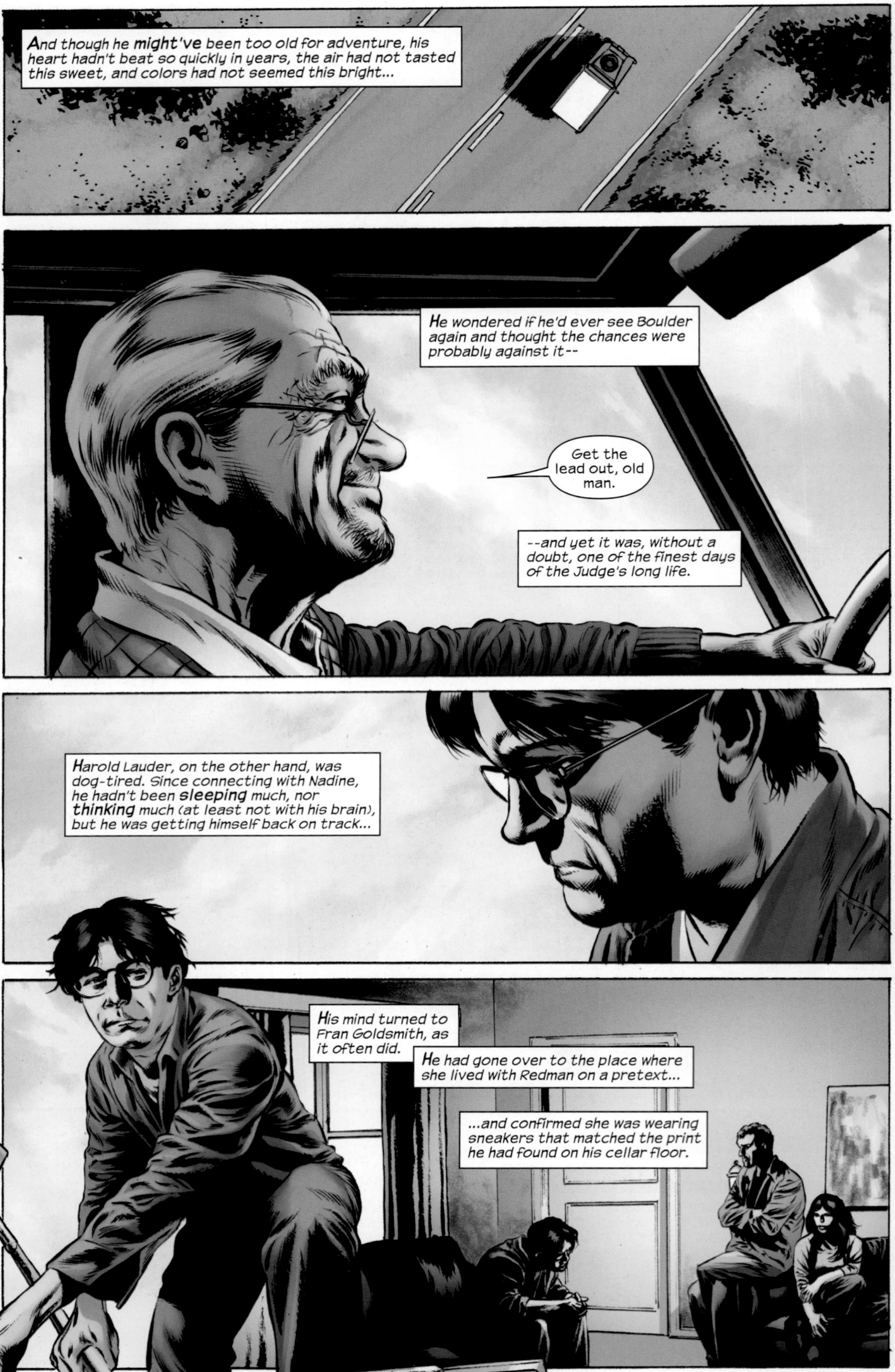
And though he might've been too old for adventure, his heart hadn't beat so quickly in years, the air had not tasted this sweet, and colors had not seemed this bright...
He wondered if he'd ever see Boulder again and thought the chances were probably against it--
Get the lead out, old man.
--and yet it was, without a doubt, one of the finest days of the Judge's long life.
Harold Lauder, on the other hand, was dog-tired. Since connecting with Nadine, he hadn't been sleeping much, nor thinking much (at least not with his brain), but he was getting himself back on track...
His mind turned to Fran Goldsmith, as it often did.
He had gone over to the place where she lived with Redman on a pretext...
...and confirmed she was wearing sneakers that matched the print he had found on his cellar floor.

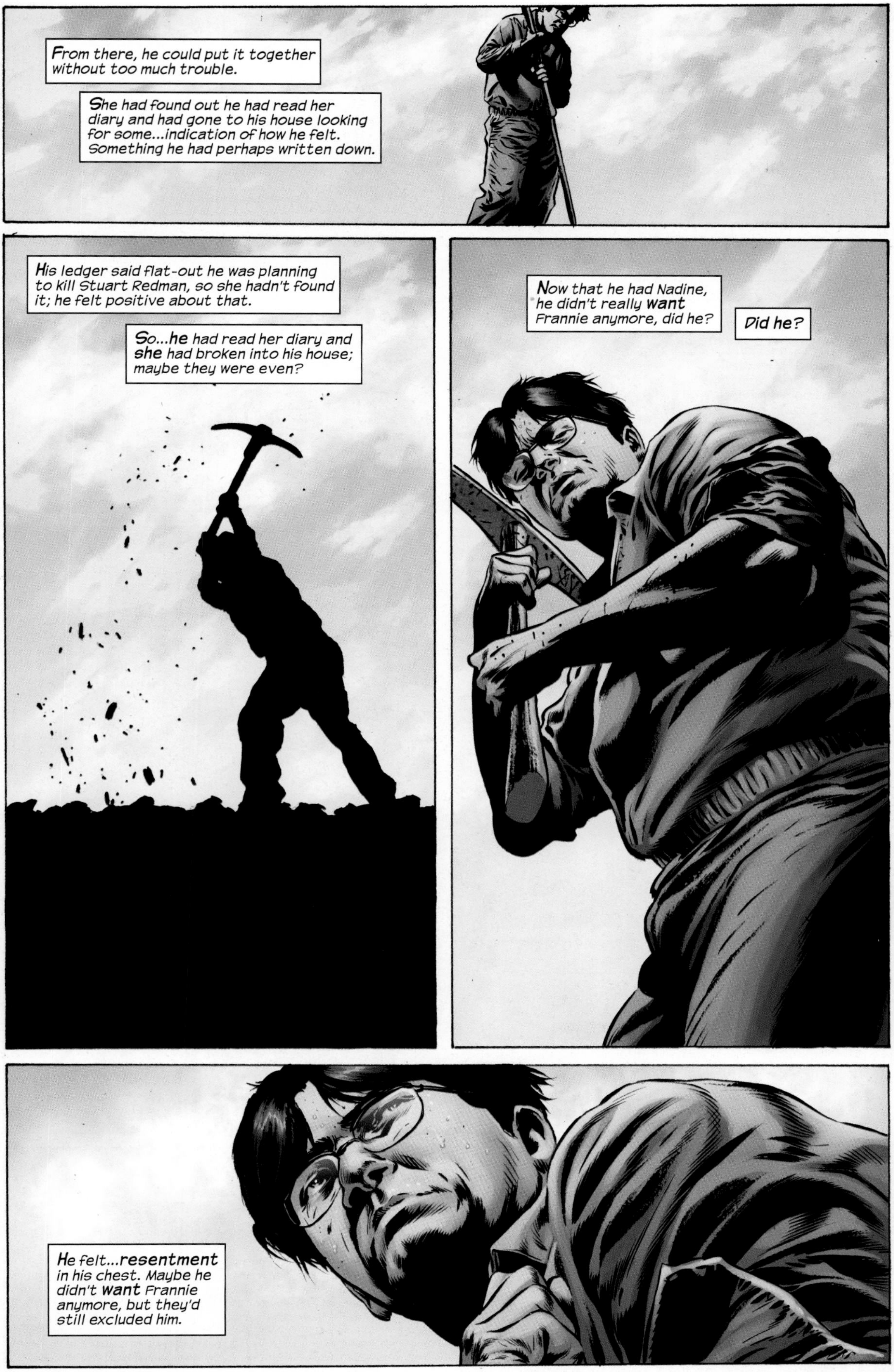
From there, he could put it together without too much trouble.
She had found out he had read her diary and had gone to his house looking for some...indication of how he felt. Something he had perhaps written down.
His ledger said flat-out he was planning to kill Stuart Redman, so she hadn't found it; he felt positive about that.
So...he had read her diary and she had broken into his house; maybe they were even?
Now that he had Nadine, he didn't really want Frannie anymore, did he?
Did he?
He felt...resentment in his chest. Maybe he didn't want Frannie anymore, but they'd still excluded him.

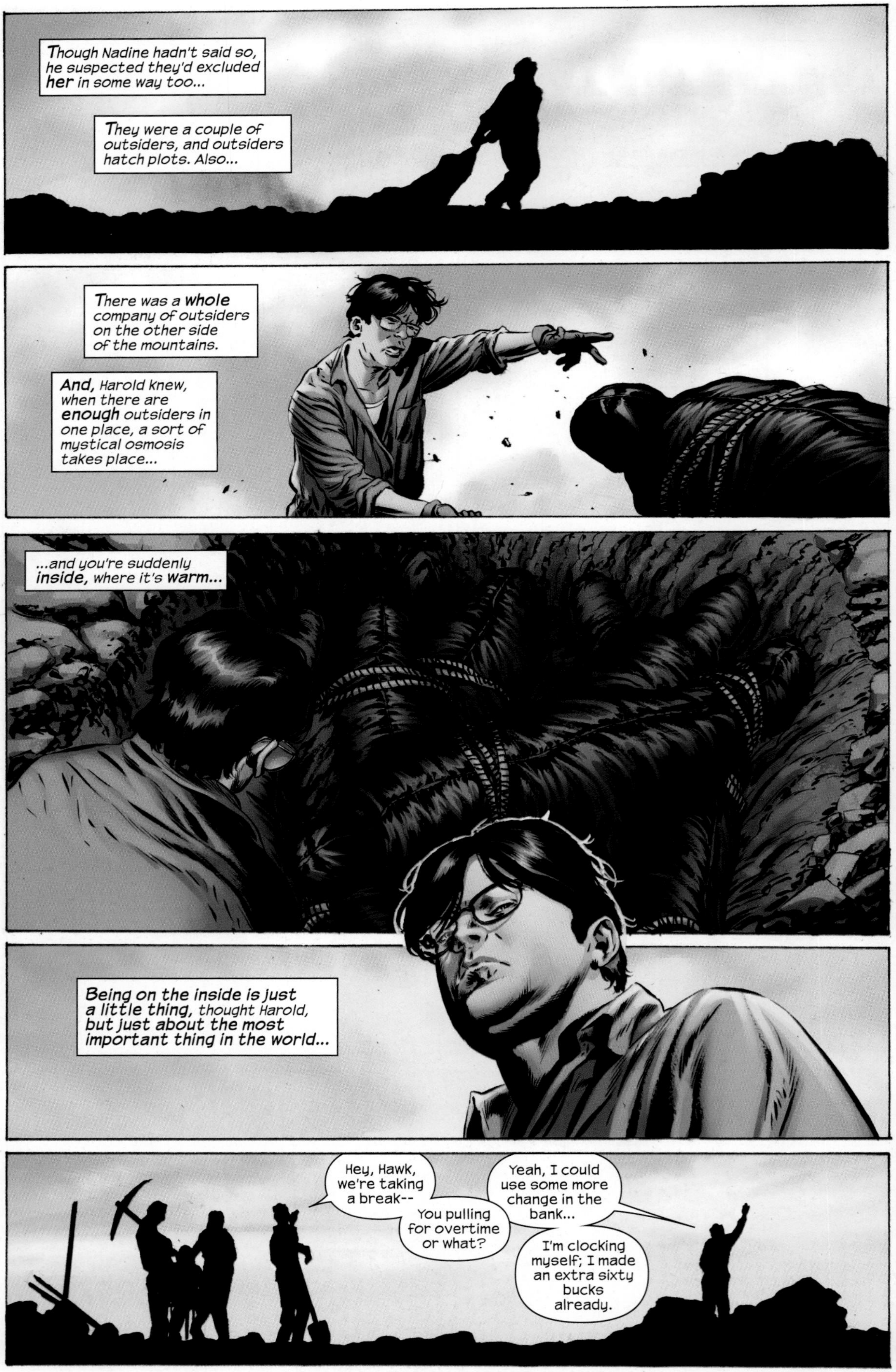
Though Nadine hadn't said so, he suspected they'd excluded her in some way too...
They were a couple of outsiders, and outsiders hatch plots. Also...
There was a whole company of outsiders on the other side of the mountains.
And, Harold knew, when there are enough outsiders in one place, a sort of mystical osmosis takes place...
...and you're suddenly inside, where it's warm...
Being on the inside is just a little thing, thought Harold, but just about the most important thing in the world...
Hey, Hawk, we're taking a break--
You pulling for overtime or what?
Yeah, I could use some more change in the bank...
I'm clocking myself; I made an extra sixty bucks already.

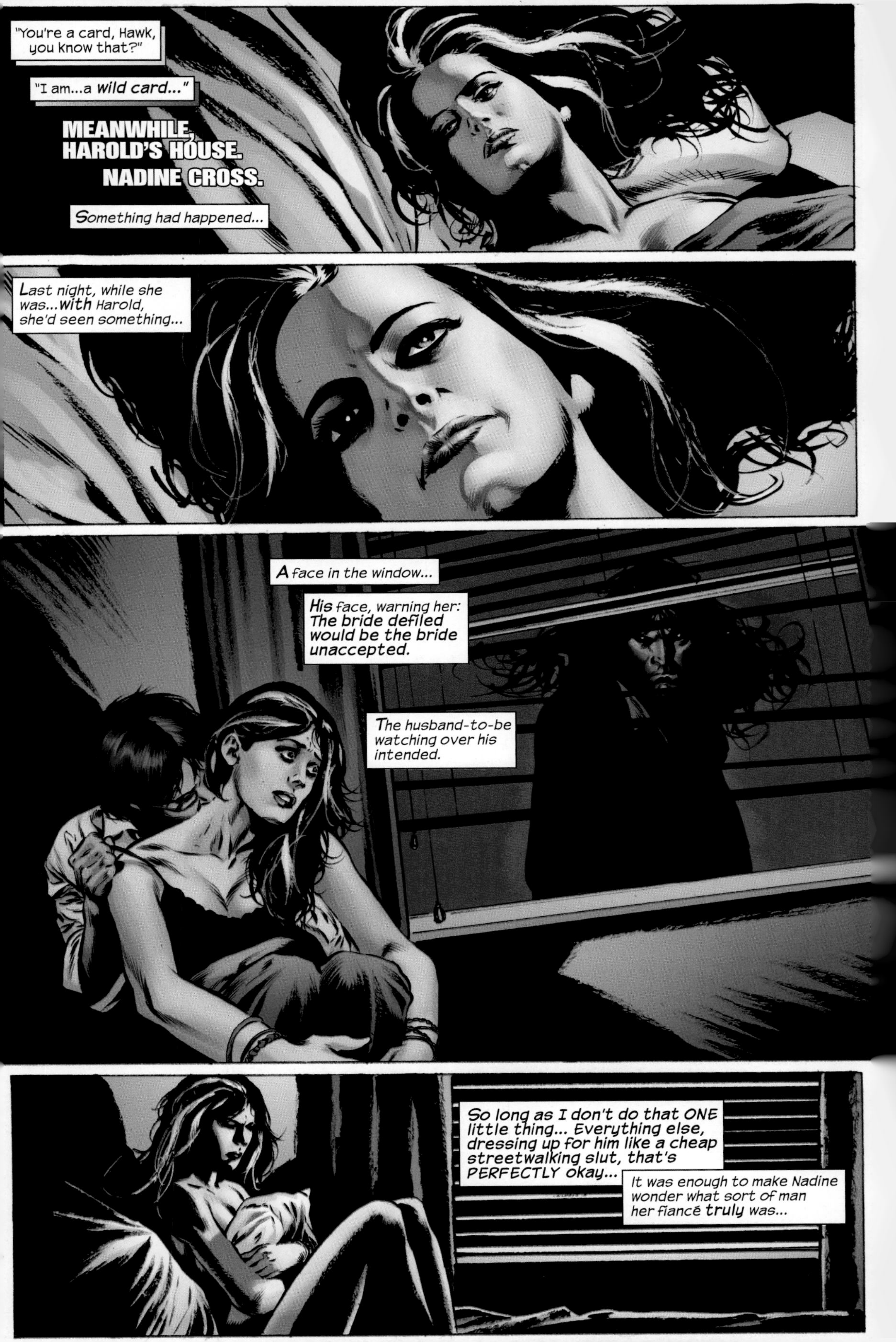
"You're a card, Hawk, you know that?"
"I am...a wild card..."
MEANWHILE, HAROLD'S HOUSE. NADINE CROSS.
Something had happened...
Last night, while she was...with Harold, she'd seen something...
A face in the window...
His face, warning her: The bride defiled would be the bride unaccepted.
The husband-to-be watching over his intended.
So long as I don't do that ONE little thing... Everything else, dressing up for him like a cheap streetwalking slut, that's PERFECTLY okay...
It was enough to make Nadine wonder what sort of man her fiancé truly was...

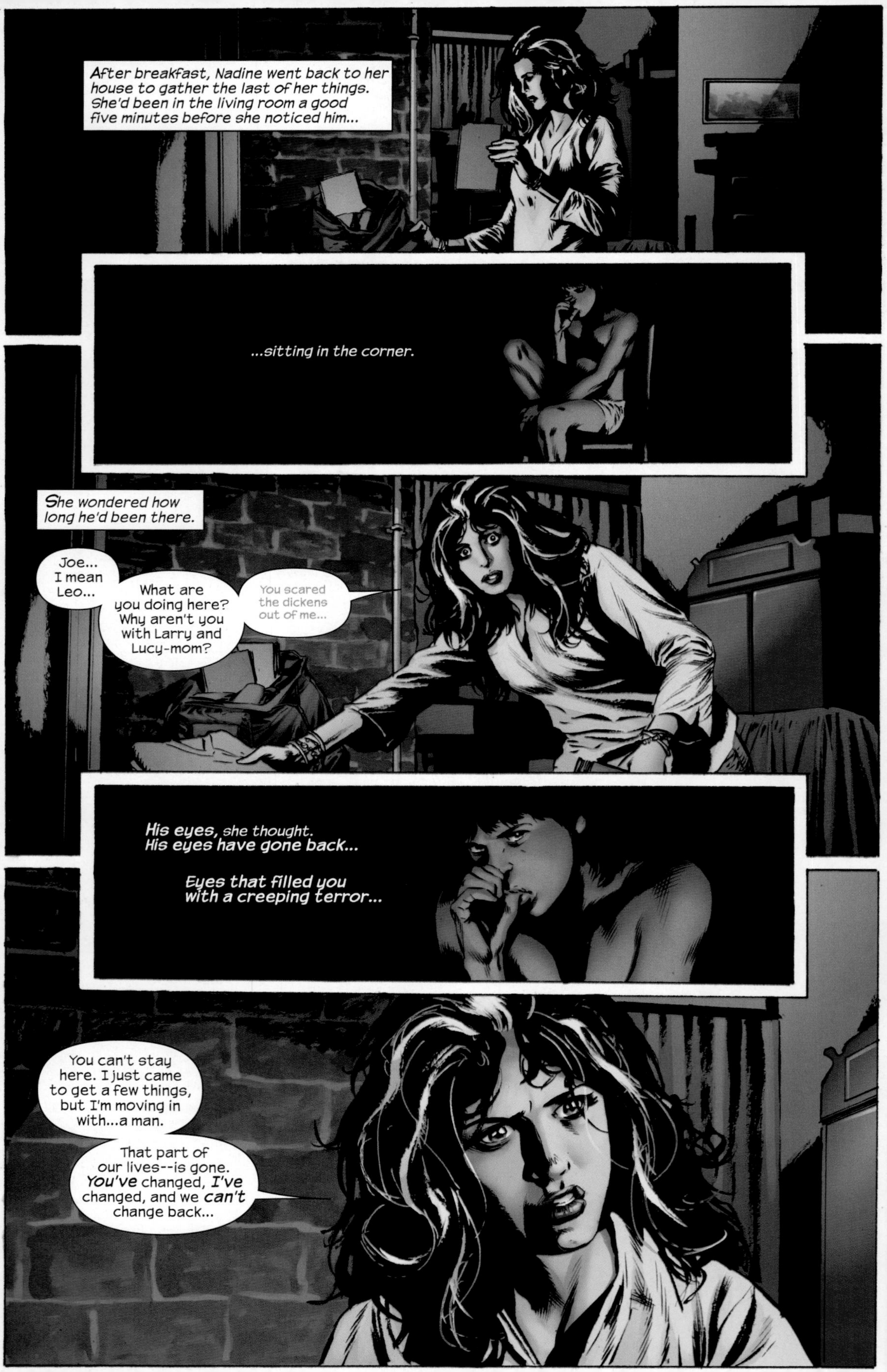
After breakfast, Nadine went back to her house to gather the last of her things. She'd been in the living room a good five minutes before she noticed him...
...sitting in the corner.
She wondered how long he'd been there.
Joe... I mean Leo...
What are you doing here? Why aren't you with Larry and Lucy-mom?
You scared the dickens out of me...
His eyes, she thought. His eyes have gone back...
Eyes that filled you with a creeping terror...
You can't stay here. I just came to get a few things, but I'm moving in with...a man.
That part of our lives--is gone. You've changed, I've changed, and we can't change back...

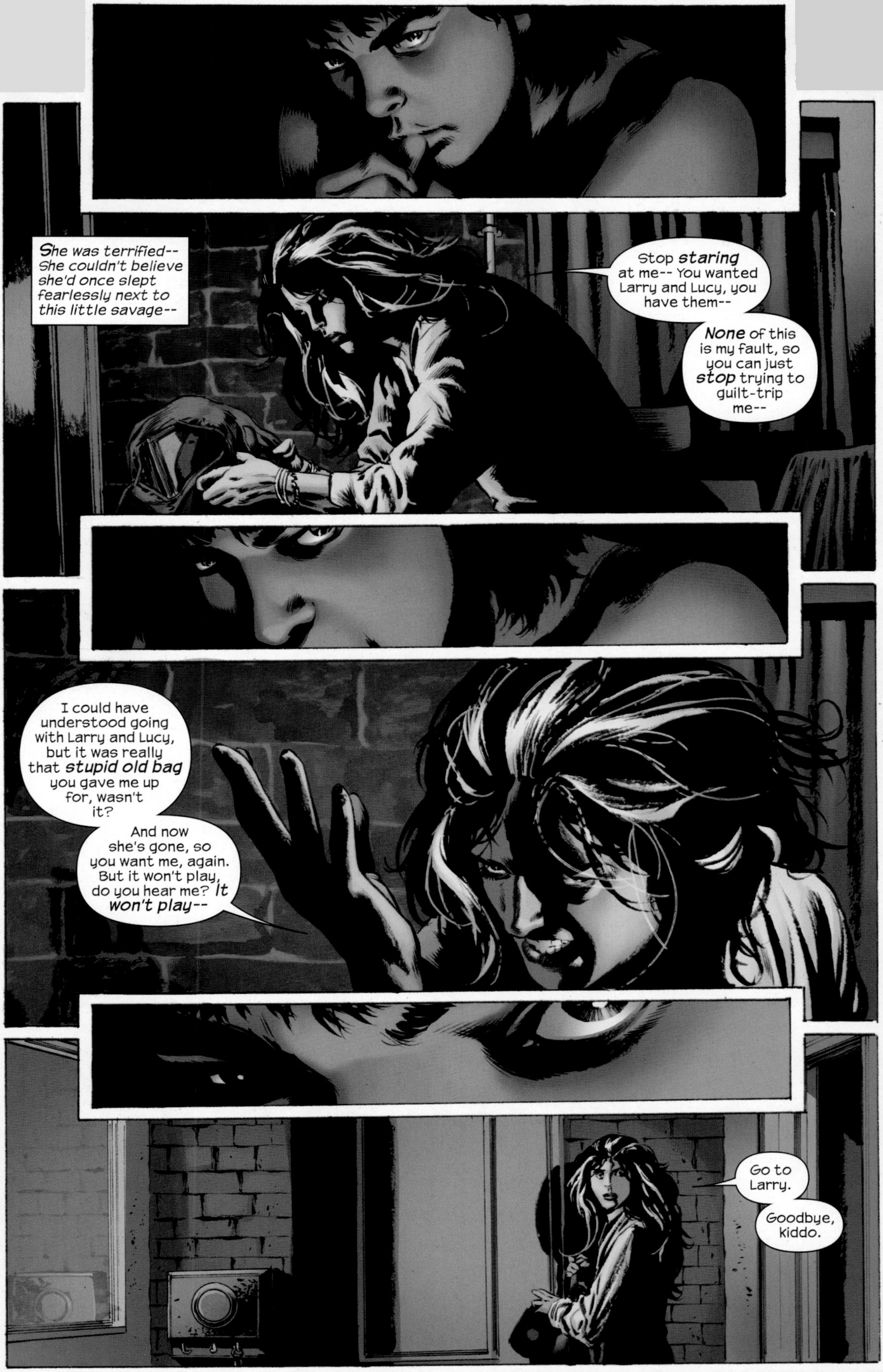
She was terrified--
She couldn't believe she'd once slept fearlessly next to this little savage--
Stop staring at me-- You wanted Larry and Lucy, you have them--
None of this is my fault, so you can just stop trying to guilt-trip me--
I could have understood going with Larry and Lucy, but it was really that stupid old bag you gave me up for, wasn't it?
And now she's gone, so you want me, again. But it won't play, do you hear me? It won't play--
Go to Larry.
Goodbye, kiddo.

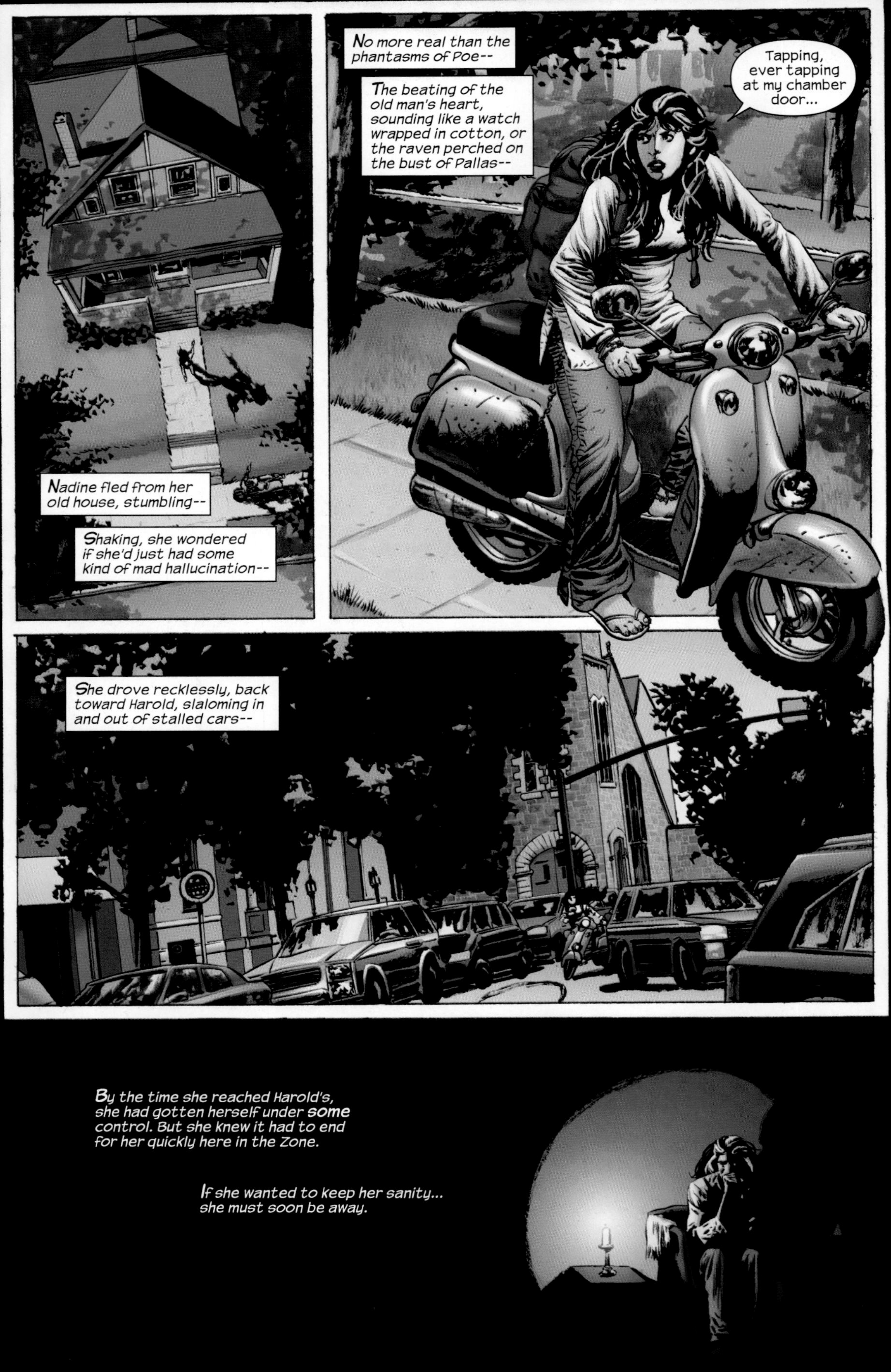
Nadine fled from her old house, stumbling--
Shaking, she wondered if she'd just had some kind of mad hallucination--
No more real than the phantasms of Poe--
The beating of the old man's heart, sounding like a watch wrapped in cotton, or the raven perched on the bust of Pallas--
Tapping, ever tapping at my chamber door...
She drove recklessly, back toward Harold, slaloming in and out of stalled cars--
By the time she reached Harold's, she had gotten herself under **some** control. But she knew it had to end for her quickly here in the Zone.
If she wanted to keep her sanity... she must soon be away.

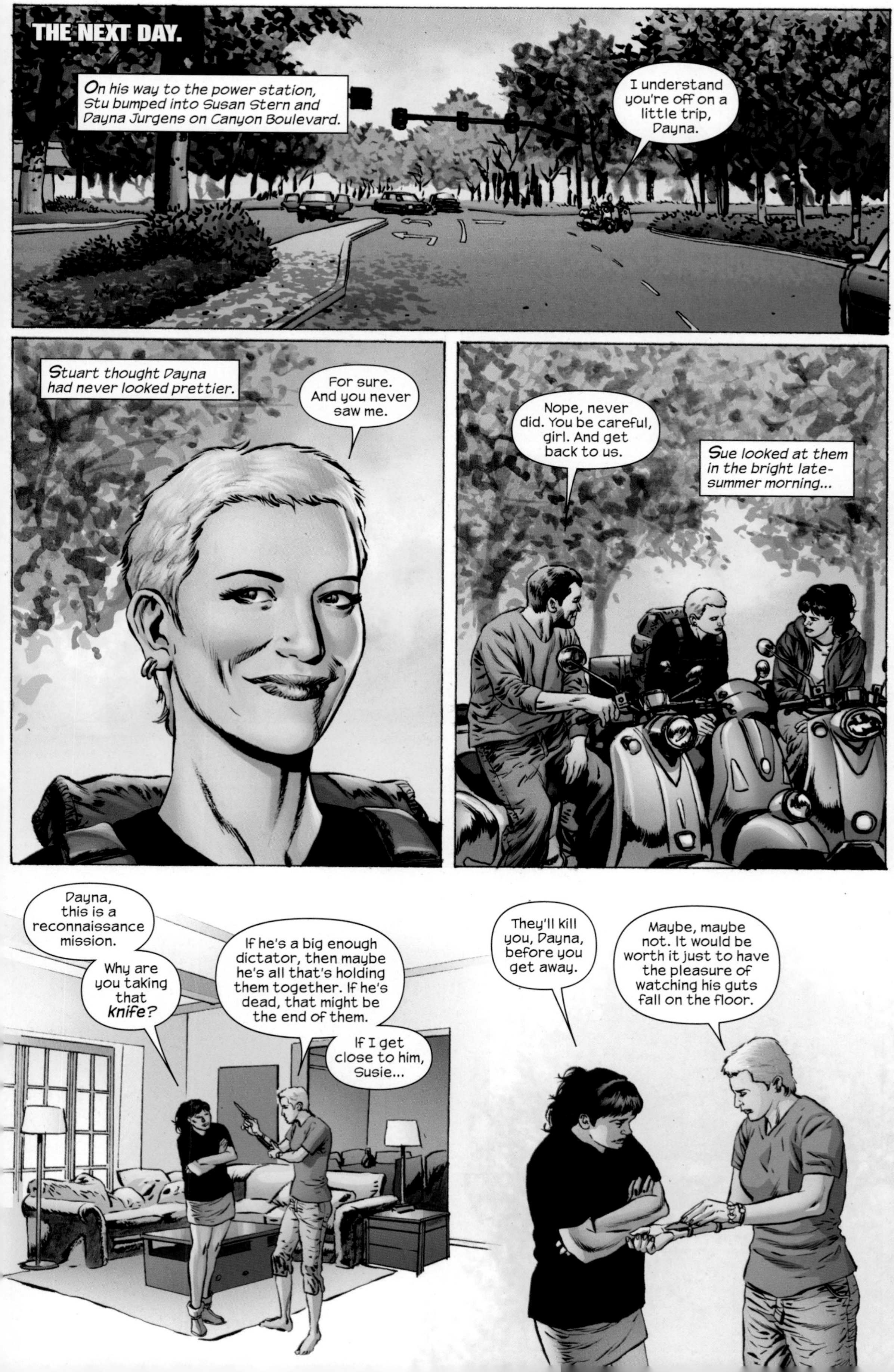
THE NEXT DAY.
On his way to the power station, Stu bumped into Susan Stern and Dayna Jurgens on Canyon Boulevard.
I understand you're off on a little trip, Dayna.
Stuart thought Dayna had never looked prettier.
For sure. And you never saw me.
Nope, never did. You be careful, girl. And get back to us.
Sue looked at them in the bright late-summer morning...
Dayna, this is a reconnaissance mission.
Why are you taking that *knife*?
If he's a big enough dictator, then maybe he's all that's holding them together. If he's dead, that might be the end of them.
If I get close to him, Susie...
They'll kill you, Dayna, before you get away.
Maybe, maybe not. It would be worth it just to have the pleasure of watching his guts fall on the floor.

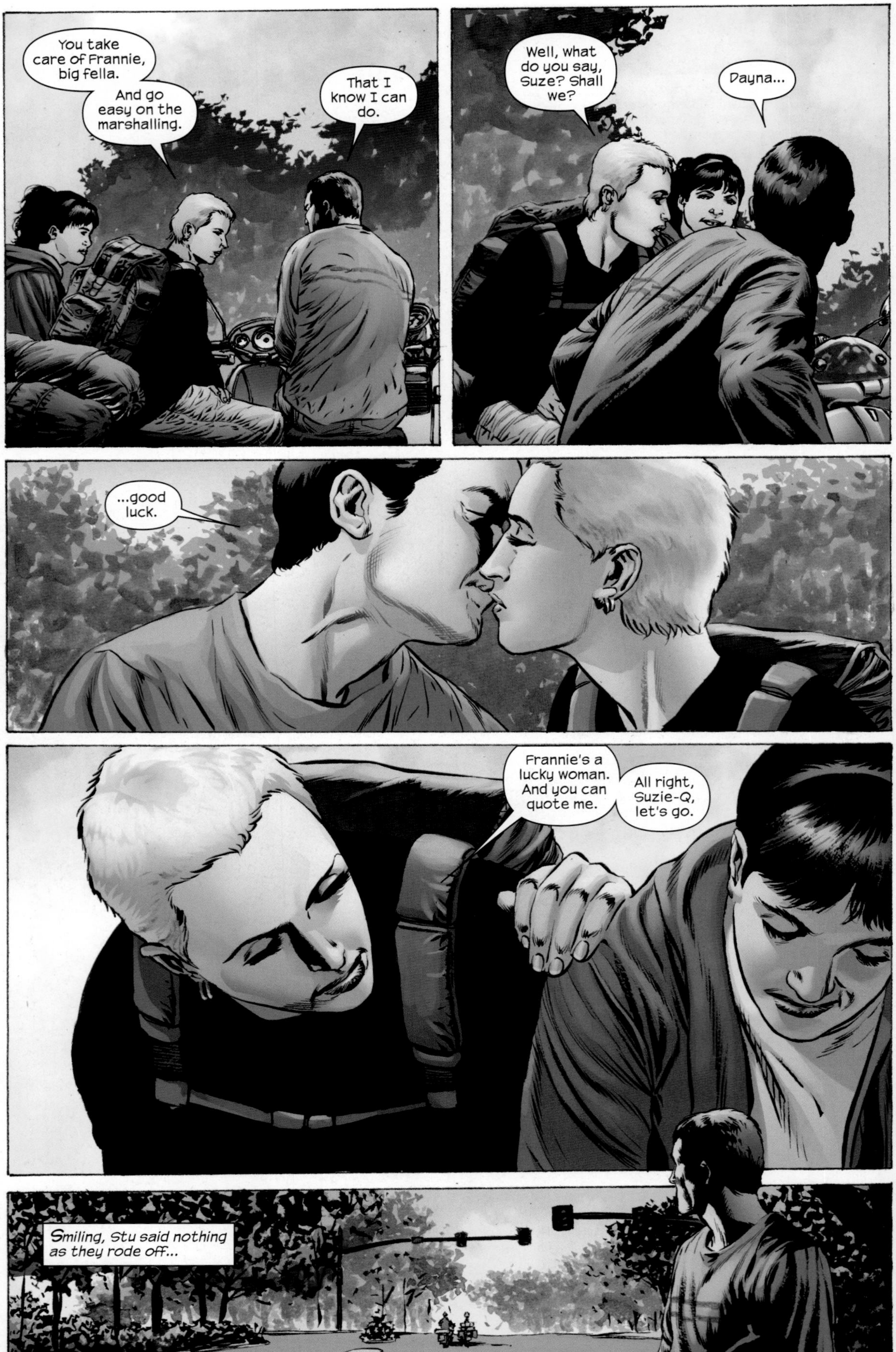
You take care of Frannie, big fella.
And go easy on the marshalling.
That I know I can do.
Well, what do you say, Suze? Shall we?
Dayna...
...good luck.
Frannie's a lucky woman. And you can quote me.
All right, Suzie-Q, let's go.
Smiling, Stu said nothing as they rode off...

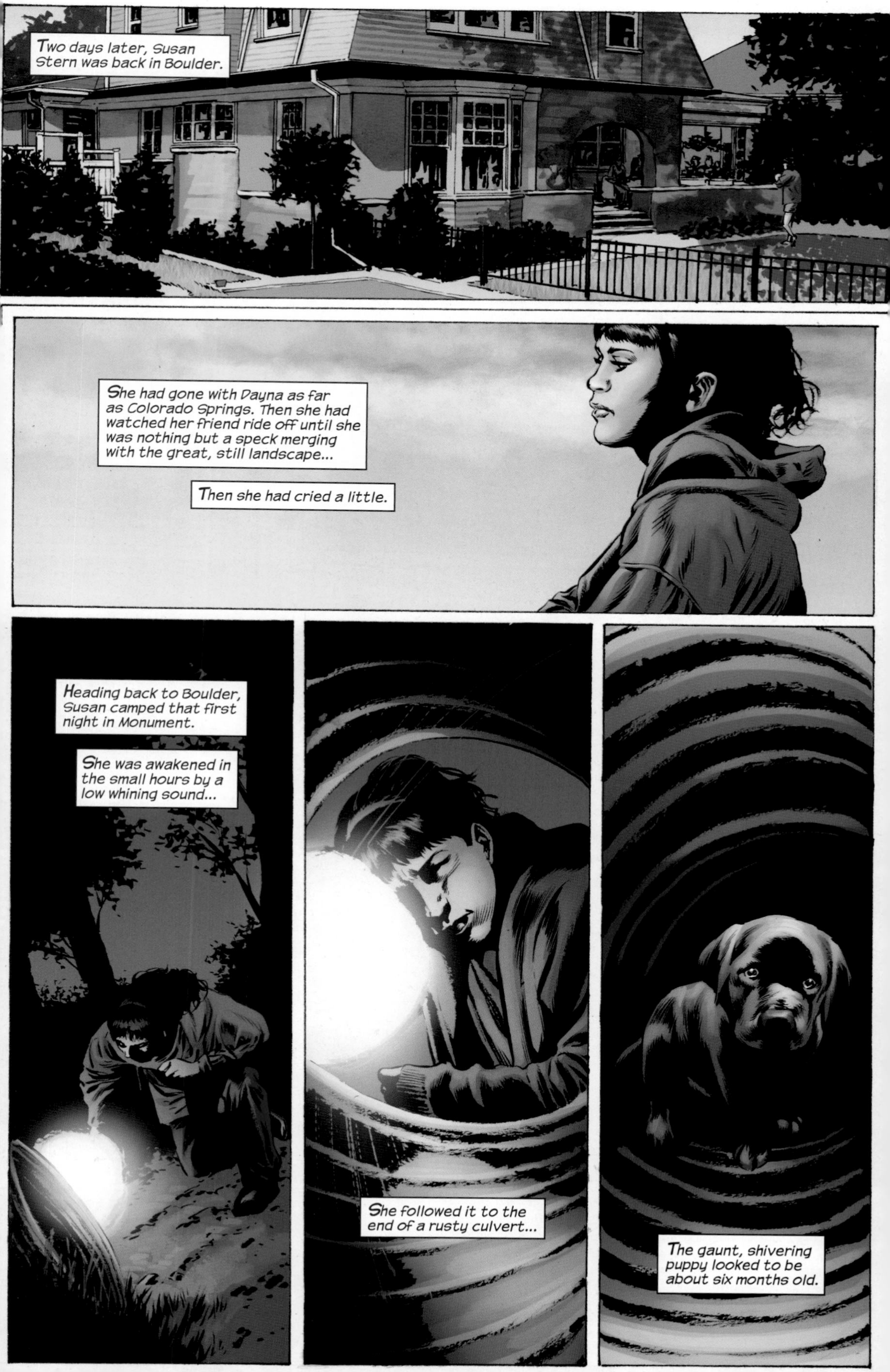
Two days later, Susan Stern was back in Boulder.
She had gone with Dayna as far as Colorado Springs. Then she had watched her friend ride off until she was nothing but a speck merging with the great, still landscape...
Then she had cried a little.
Heading back to Boulder, Susan camped that first night in Monument.
She was awakened in the small hours by a low whining sound...
She followed it to the end of a rusty culvert...
The gaunt, shivering puppy looked to be about six months old.

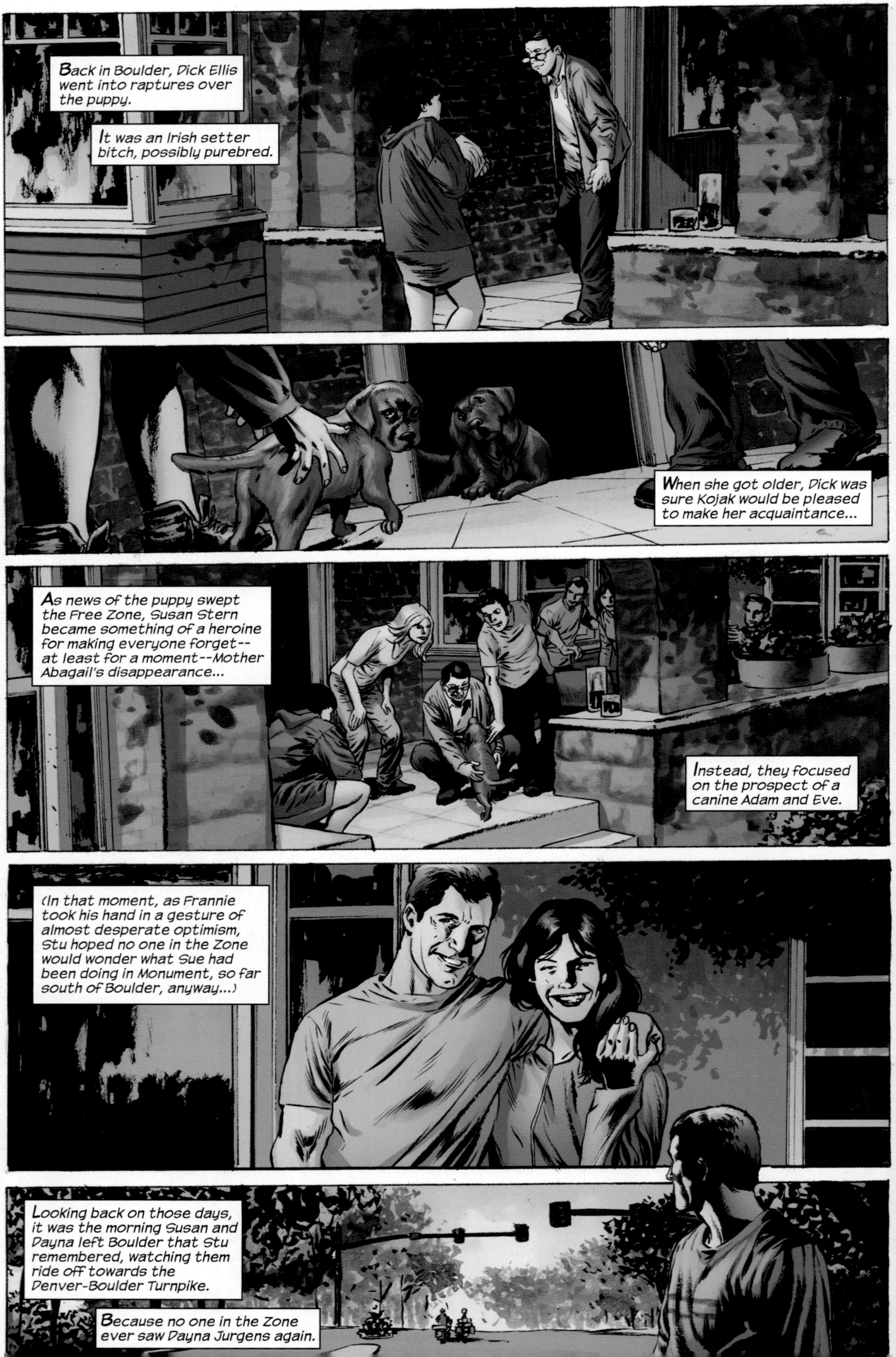
Back in Boulder, Dick Ellis went into raptures over the puppy.
It was an Irish setter bitch, possibly purebred.
When she got older, Dick was sure Kojak would be pleased to make her acquaintance...
As news of the puppy swept the Free Zone, Susan Stern became something of a heroine for making everyone forget--at least for a moment--Mother Abagail's disappearance...
Instead, they focused on the prospect of a canine Adam and Eve.
(In that moment, as Frannie took his hand in a gesture of almost desperate optimism, Stu hoped no one in the Zone would wonder what Sue had been doing in Monument, so far south of Boulder, anyway...)
Looking back on those days, it was the morning Susan and Dayna left Boulder that Stu remembered, watching them ride off towards the Denver-Boulder Turnpike.
Because no one in the Zone ever saw Dayna Jurgens again.

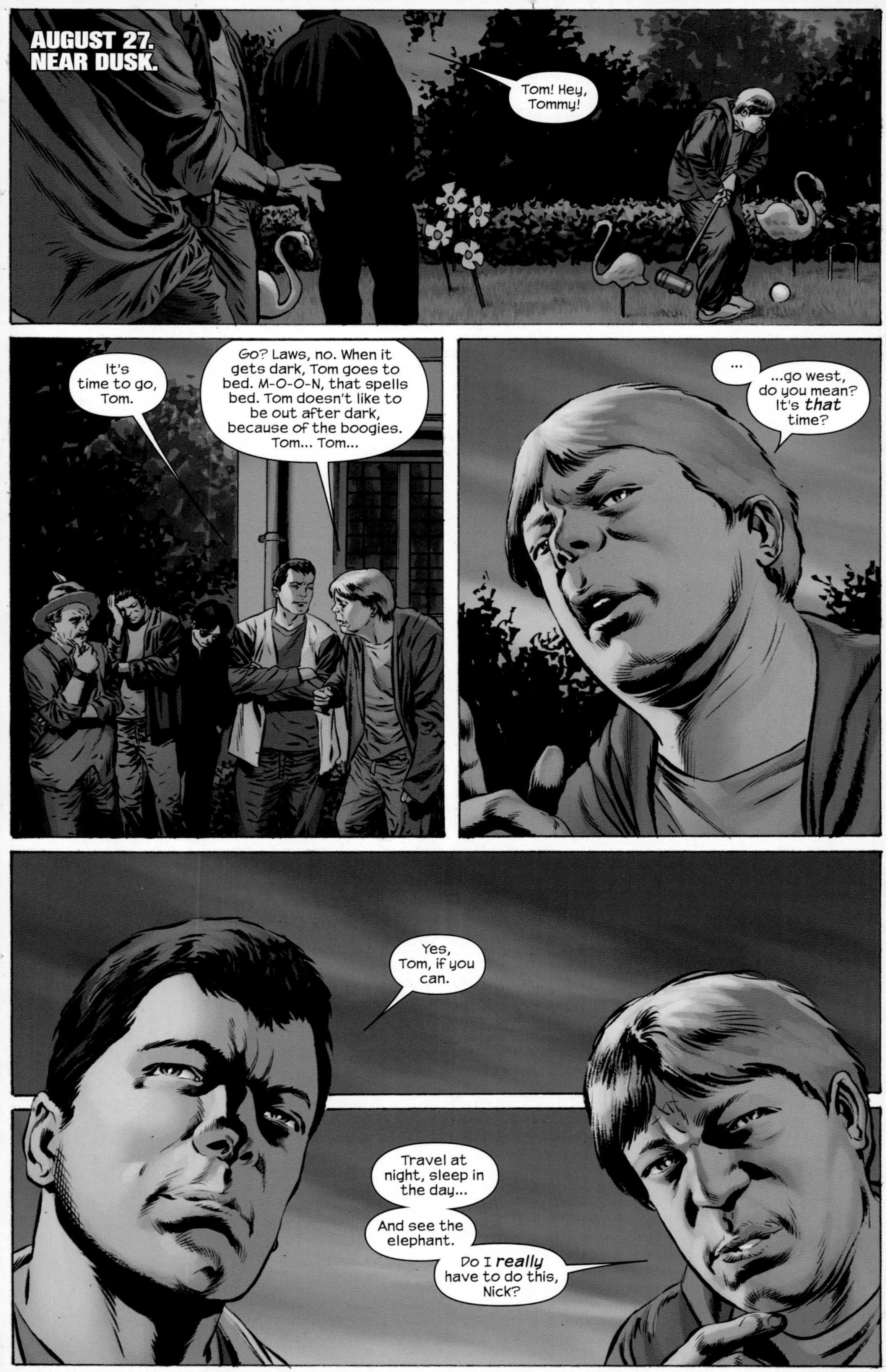
AUGUST 27. NEAR DUSK.
Tom! Hey, Tommy!
It's time to go, Tom.
Go? Laws, no. When it gets dark, Tom goes to bed. M-O-O-N, that spells bed. Tom doesn't like to be out after dark, because of the boogies. Tom... Tom...
...
...go west, do you mean? It's *that* time?
Yes, Tom, if you can.
Travel at night, sleep in the day...
And see the elephant.
Do I *really* have to do this, Nick?

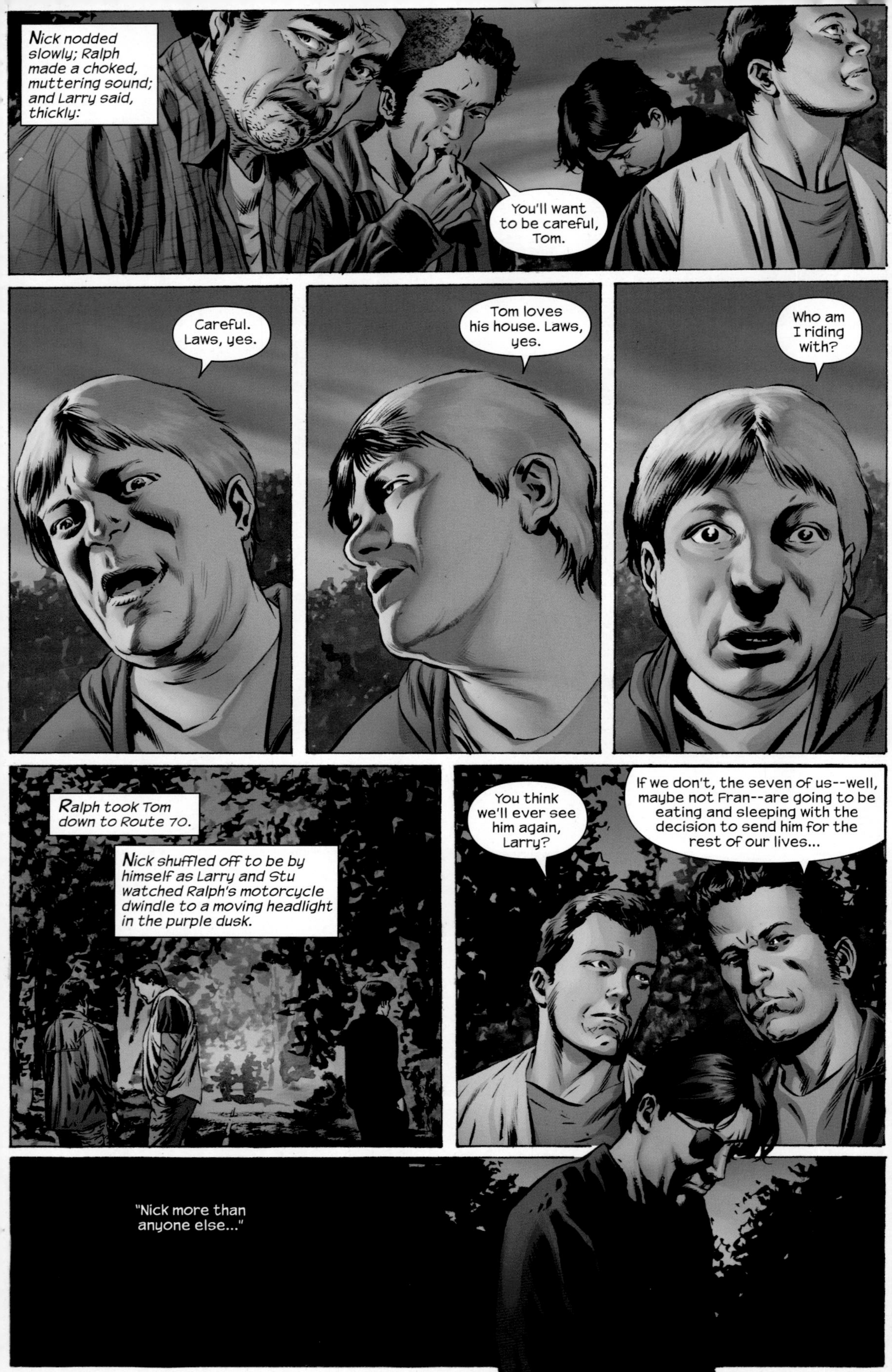
Nick nodded slowly; Ralph made a choked, muttering sound; and Larry said, thickly:
You'll want to be careful, Tom.
Careful. Laws, yes.
Tom loves his house. Laws, yes.
Who am I riding with?
Ralph took Tom down to Route 70.
Nick shuffled off to be by himself as Larry and Stu watched Ralph's motorcycle dwindle to a moving headlight in the purple dusk.
You think we'll ever see him again, Larry?
If we don't, the seven of us--well, maybe not Fran--are going to be eating and sleeping with the decision to send him for the rest of our lives...
"Nick more than anyone else..."

chapter THREE

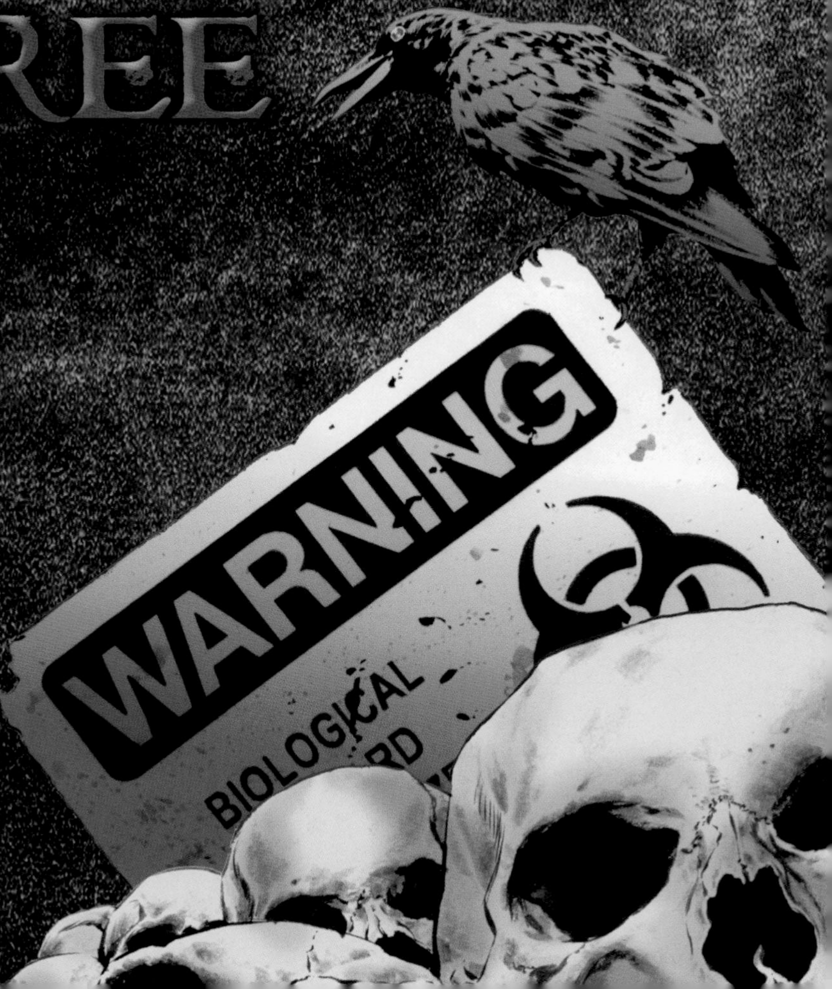
WARNING
BIOLOGICAL

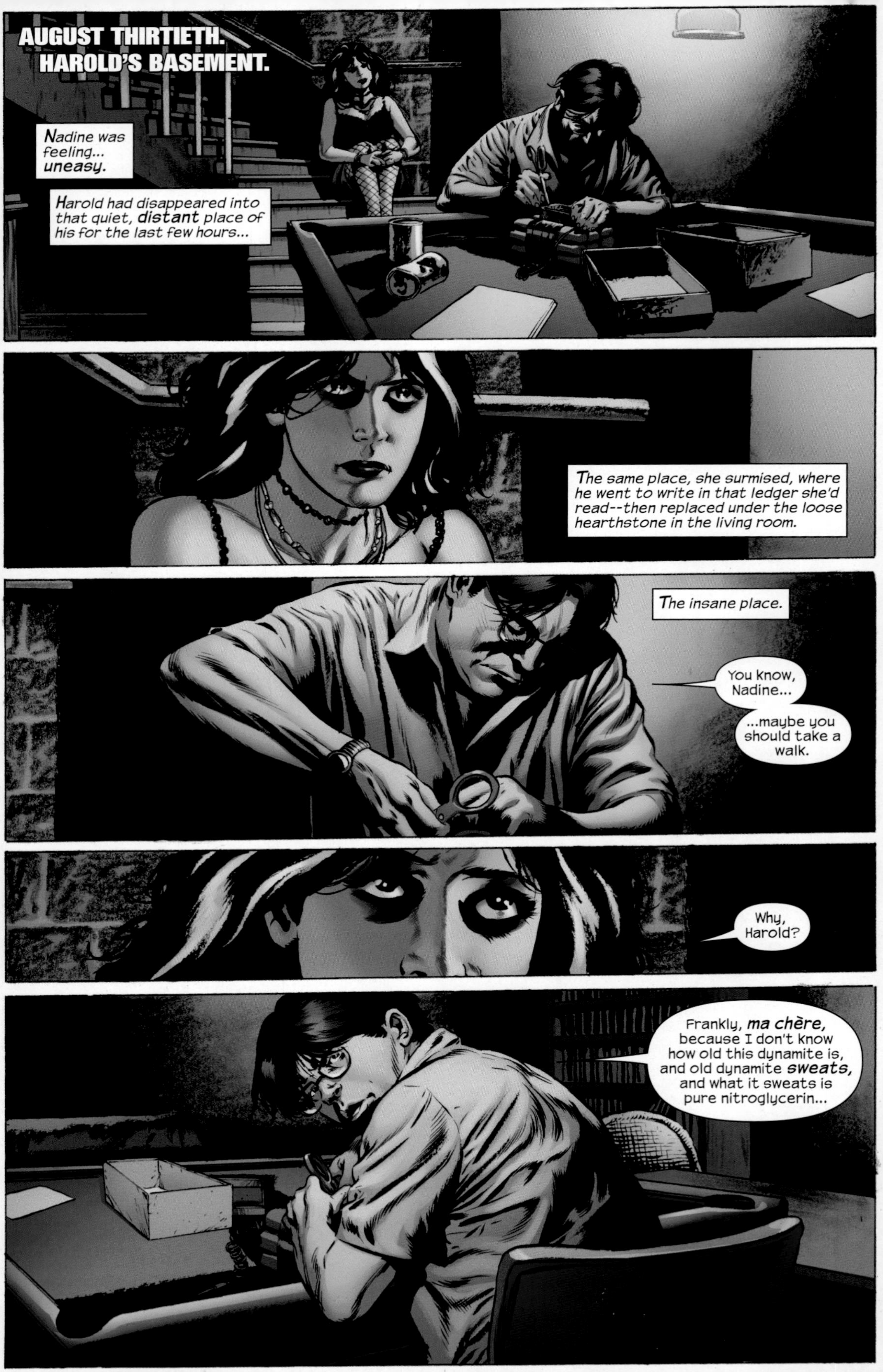
AUGUST THIRTIETH. HAROLD'S BASEMENT.
Nadine was feeling... uneasy.
Harold had disappeared into that quiet, distant place of his for the last few hours...
The same place, she surmised, where he went to write in that ledger she'd read--then replaced under the loose hearthstone in the living room.
The insane place.
You know, Nadine...
...maybe you should take a walk.
Why, Harold?
Frankly, ma chère, because I don't know how old this dynamite is, and old dynamite sweats, and what it sweats is pure nitroglycerin...

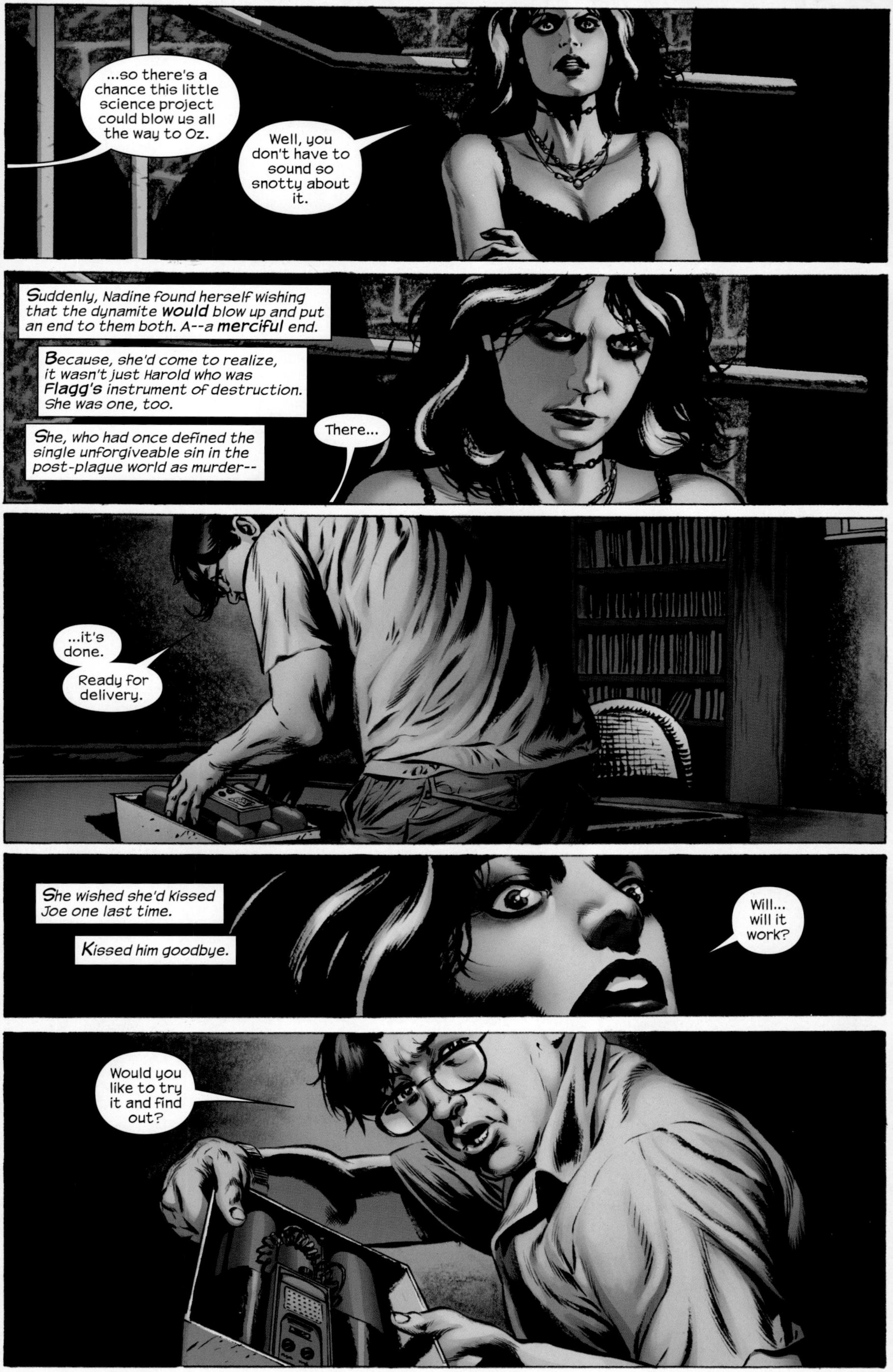
...so there's a chance this little science project could blow us all the way to Oz.
Well, you don't have to sound so snotty about it.
Suddenly, Nadine found herself wishing that the dynamite **would** blow up and put an end to them both. A--a **merciful** end.
Because, she'd come to realize, it wasn't just Harold who was **Flagg's** instrument of destruction. She was one, too.
She, who had once defined the single unforgiveable sin in the post-plague world as murder--
There...
...it's done.
Ready for delivery.
She wished she'd kissed Joe one last time.
Kissed him goodbye.
Will... will it work?
Would you like to try it and find out?

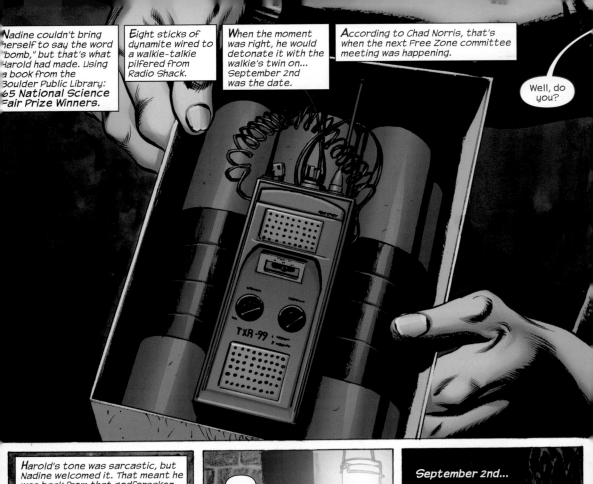

Nadine couldn't bring herself to say the word "bomb," but that's what Harold had made. Using a book from the Boulder Public Library: 65 National Science Fair Prize Winners.

Eight sticks of dynamite wired to a walkie-talkie pilfered from Radio Shack.

When the moment was right, he would detonate it with the walkie's twin on... September 2nd was the date.

According to Chad Norris, that's when the next Free Zone committee meeting was happening.

Well, do you?

TXR-99

Harold's tone was sarcastic, but Nadine welcomed it. That meant he was back from that godforsaken place. His talk was just talk again, and she could handle him.

Or...we could go upstairs and play for a bit.

Like we did last night.

...

Yeah. Okay. Good.

September 2nd...

Harold could hardly wait...

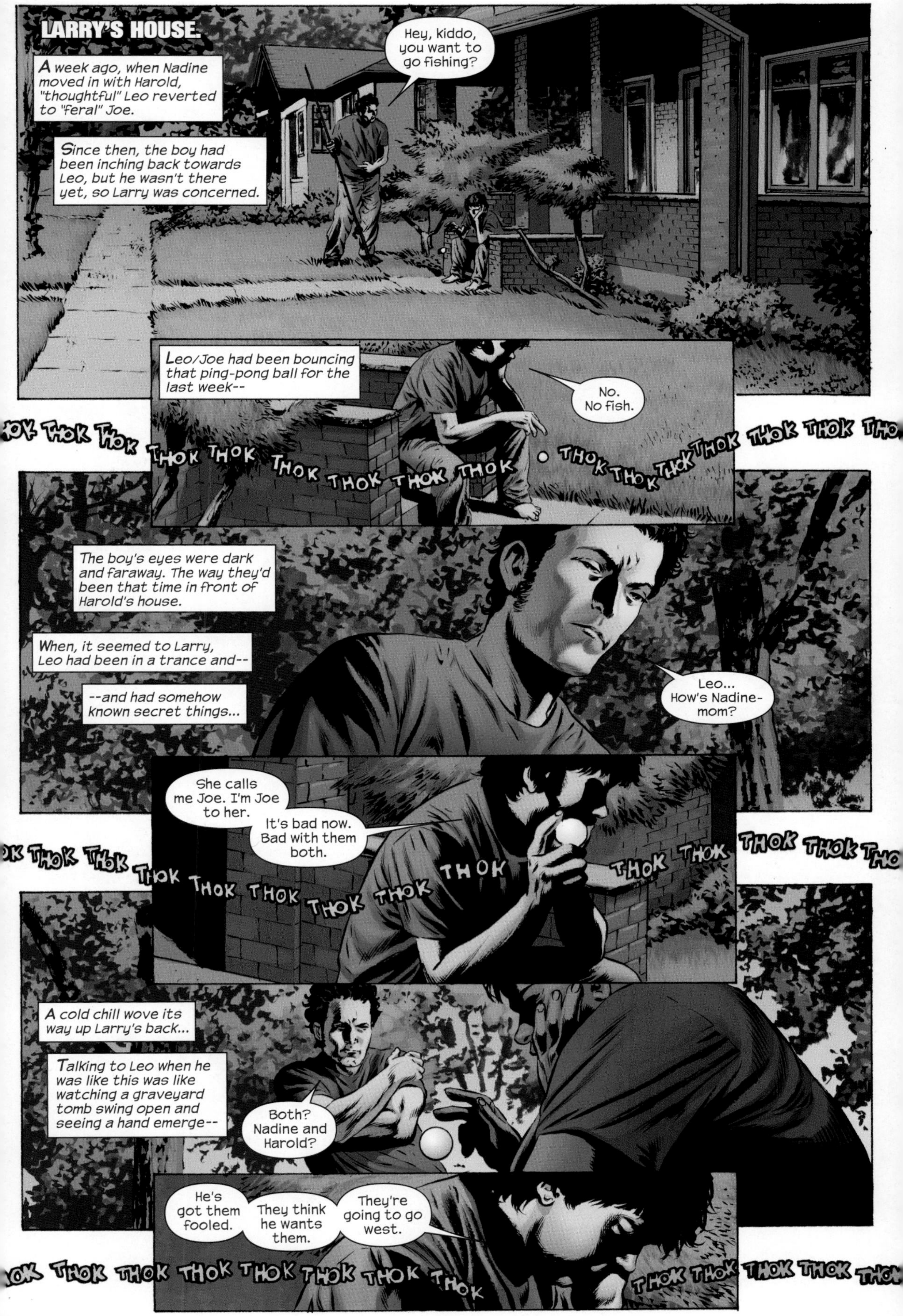

LARRY'S HOUSE.
A week ago, when Nadine moved in with Harold, "thoughtful" Leo reverted to "feral" Joe.
Since then, the boy had been inching back towards Leo, but he wasn't there yet, so Larry was concerned.
Hey, kiddo, you want to go fishing?
Leo/Joe had been bouncing that ping-pong ball for the last week--
No. No fish.
THOK THOK THOK THOK THOK THOK THOK THOK THOK THOK THOK THOK THOK THOK THOK THOK
The boy's eyes were dark and faraway. The way they'd been that time in front of Harold's house.
When, it seemed to Larry, Leo had been in a trance and--
--and had somehow known secret things...
Leo... How's Nadine-mom?
She calls me Joe. I'm Joe to her.
It's bad now. Bad with them both.
THOK THOK THOK THOK THOK THOK THOK THOK THOK THOK THOK THOK
A cold chill wove its way up Larry's back...
Talking to Leo when he was like this was like watching a graveyard tomb swing open and seeing a hand emerge--
Both? Nadine and Harold?
He's got them fooled.
They think he wants them.
They're going to go west.
THOK THOK THOK THOK THOK THOK THOK THOK THOK THOK THOK THOK THOK

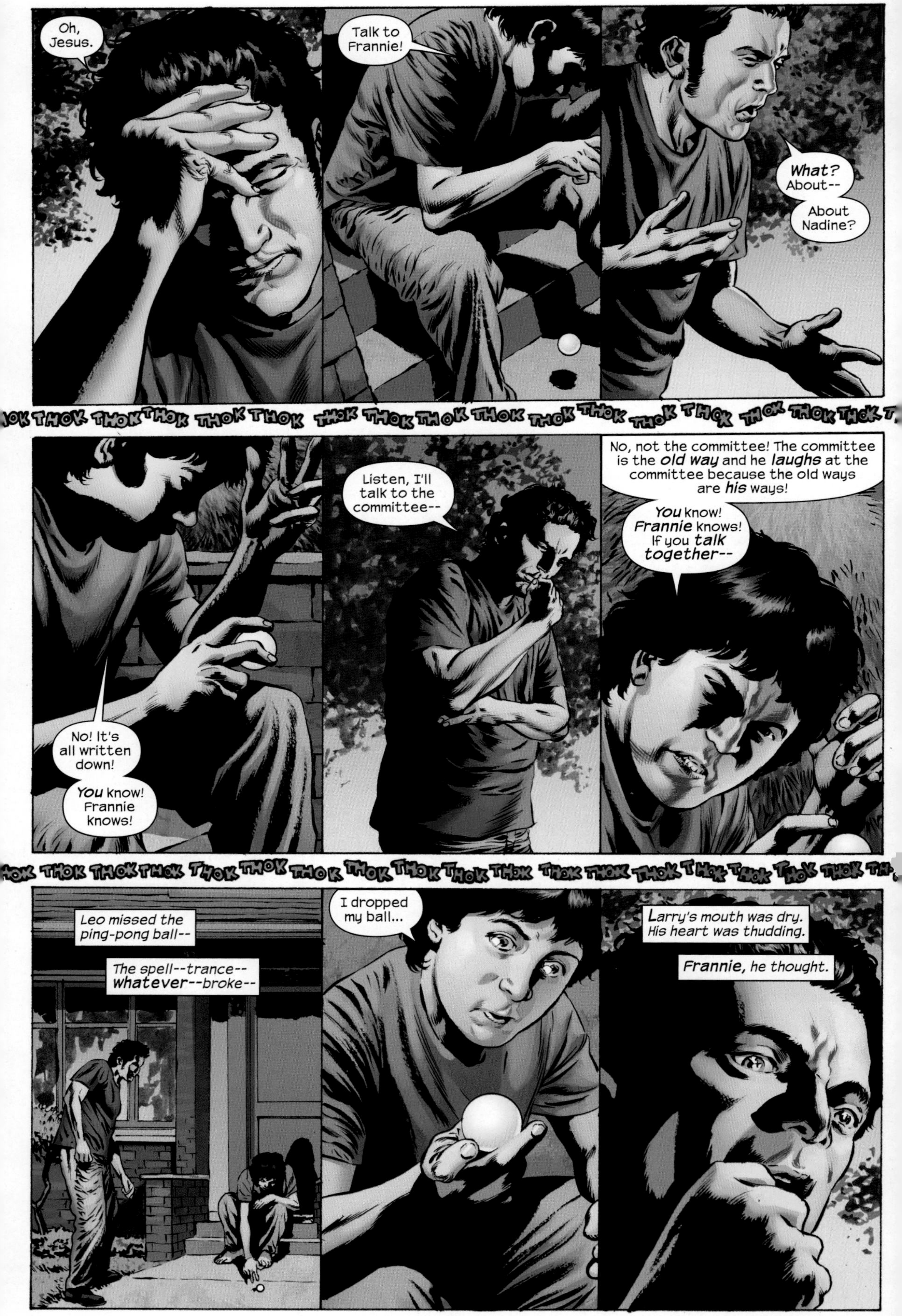
Oh, Jesus.
Talk to Frannie!
What? About--
About Nadine?
THOK THOK THOK THOK THOK THOK THOK THOK THOK THOK THOK THOK THOK THOK
No! It's all written down!
You know! Frannie knows!
Listen, I'll talk to the committee--
No, not the committee! The committee is the old way and he laughs at the committee because the old ways are his ways!
You know! Frannie knows! If you talk together--
THOK THOK THOK THOK THOK THOK THOK THOK THOK THOK THOK THOK THOK THOK
Leo missed the ping-pong ball--
The spell--trance--whatever--broke--
I dropped my ball...
Larry's mouth was dry. His heart was thudding.
Frannie, he thought.

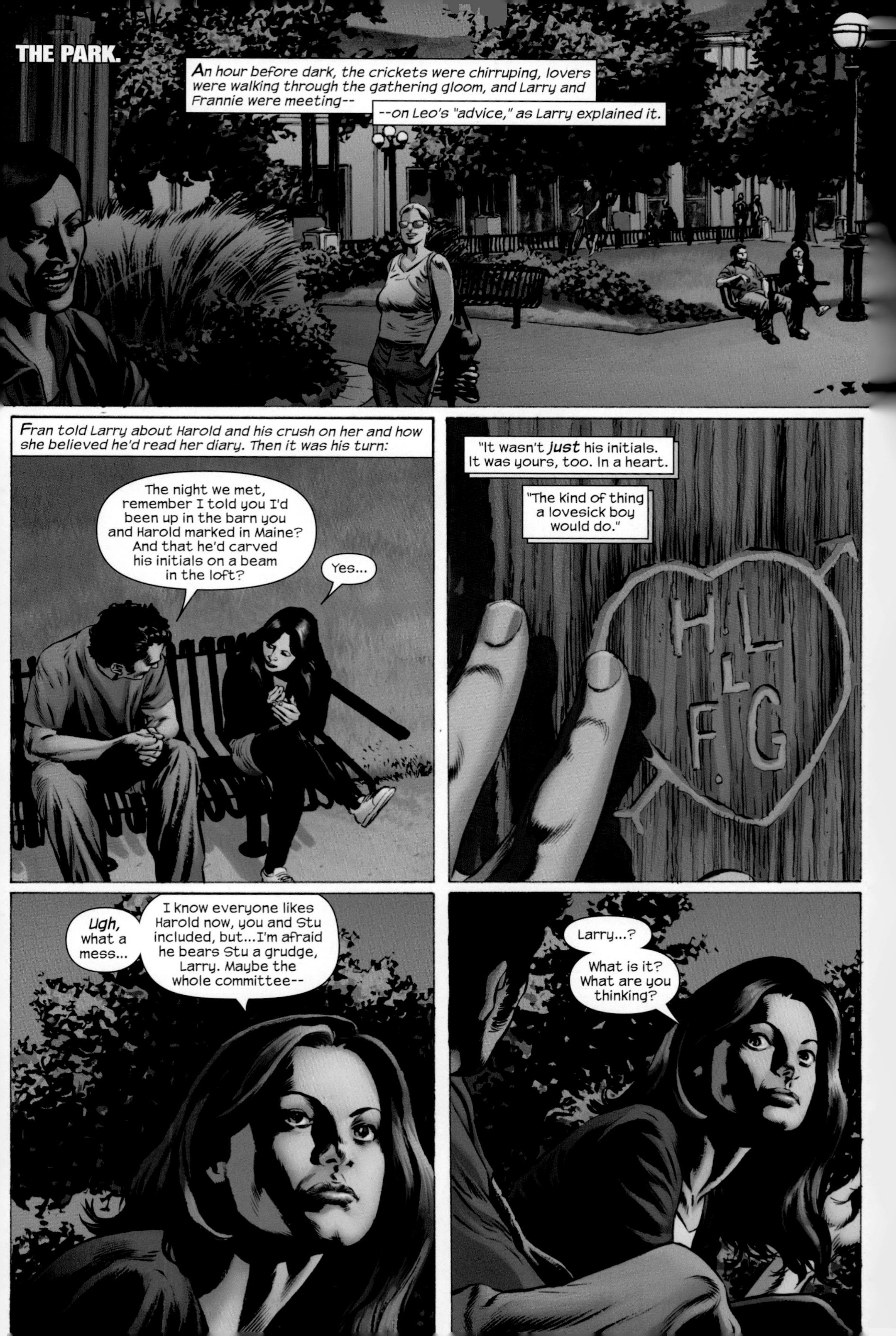
THE PARK.
An hour before dark, the crickets were chirruping, lovers were walking through the gathering gloom, and Larry and Frannie were meeting--
--on Leo's "advice," as Larry explained it.
Fran told Larry about Harold and his crush on her and how she believed he'd read her diary. Then it was his turn:
The night we met, remember I told you I'd been up in the barn you and Harold marked in Maine? And that he'd carved his initials on a beam in the loft?
Yes...
"It wasn't just his initials. It was yours, too. In a heart.
"The kind of thing a lovesick boy would do."
HL
LL
FG
Ugh, what a mess...
I know everyone likes Harold now, you and Stu included, but...I'm afraid he bears Stu a grudge, Larry. Maybe the whole committee--
Larry...?
What is it? What are you thinking?

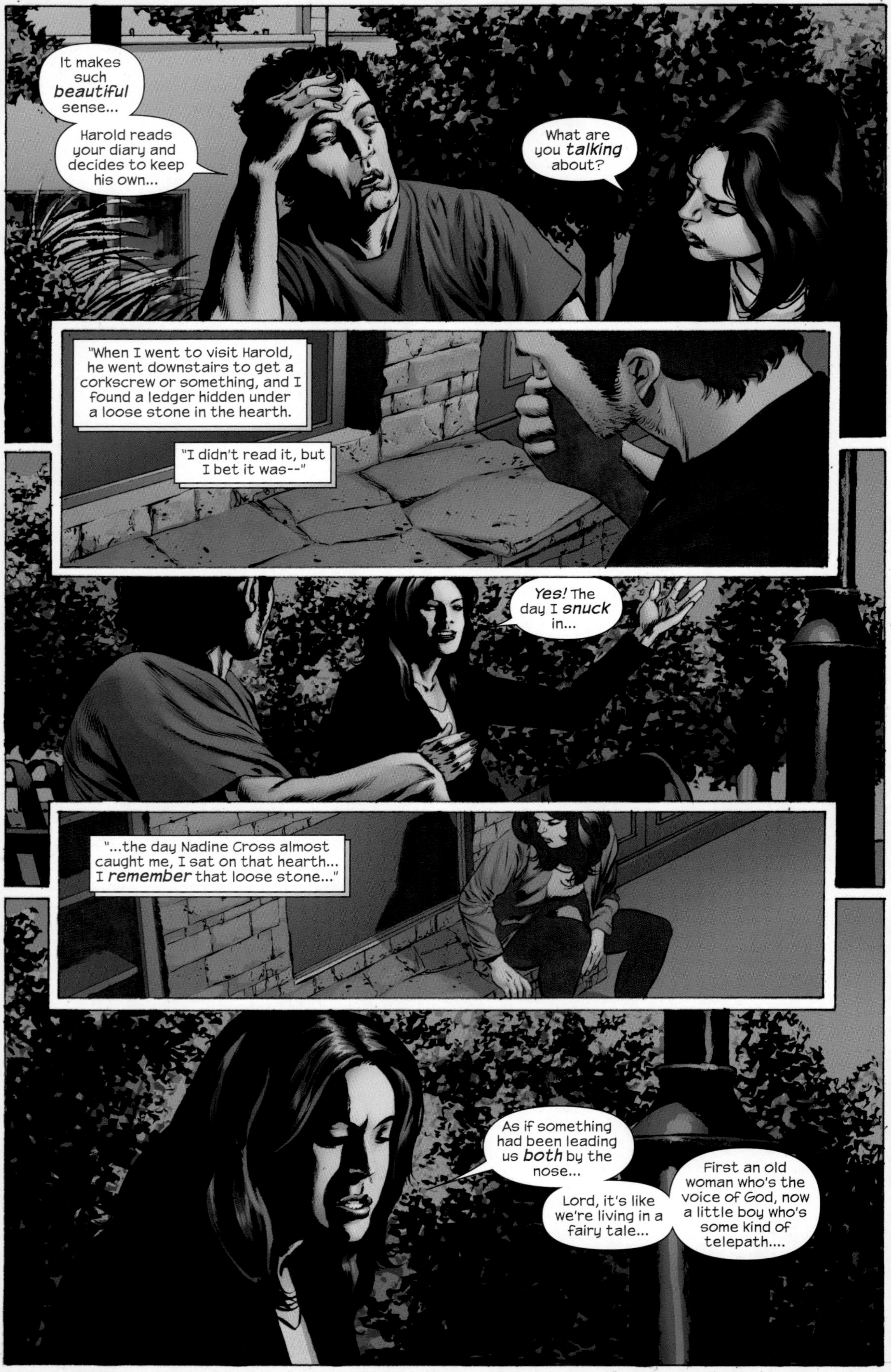

It makes such *beautiful* sense...
Harold reads your diary and decides to keep his own...
What are you *talking* about?
"When I went to visit Harold, he went downstairs to get a corkscrew or something, and I found a ledger hidden under a loose stone in the hearth.
"I didn't read it, but I bet it was--"
Yes! The day I *snuck* in...
"...the day Nadine Cross almost caught me, I sat on that hearth... I *remember* that loose stone..."
As if something had been leading us *both* by the nose...
Lord, it's like we're living in a fairy tale...
First an old woman who's the voice of God, now a little boy who's some kind of telepath....

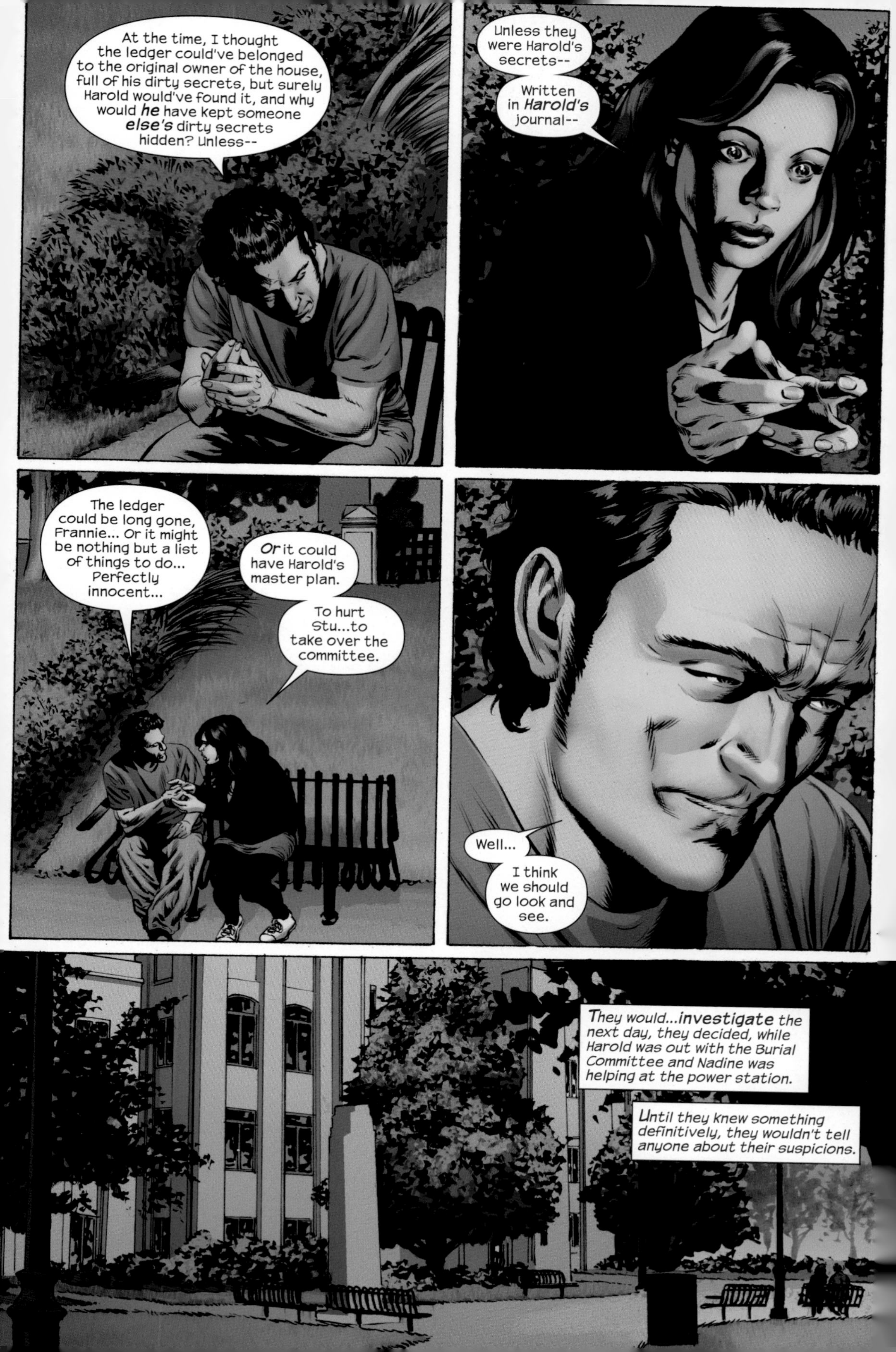
At the time, I thought the ledger could've belonged to the original owner of the house, full of his dirty secrets, but surely Harold would've found it, and why would *he* have kept someone *else's* dirty secrets hidden? Unless--
Unless they were Harold's secrets--
Written in *Harold's* journal--
The ledger could be long gone, Frannie... Or it might be nothing but a list of things to do... Perfectly innocent...
Or it could have Harold's master plan.
To hurt Stu...to take over the committee.
Well...
I think we should go look and see.
They would...*investigate* the next day, they decided, while Harold was out with the Burial Committee and Nadine was helping at the power station.
Until they knew something definitively, they wouldn't tell anyone about their suspicions.

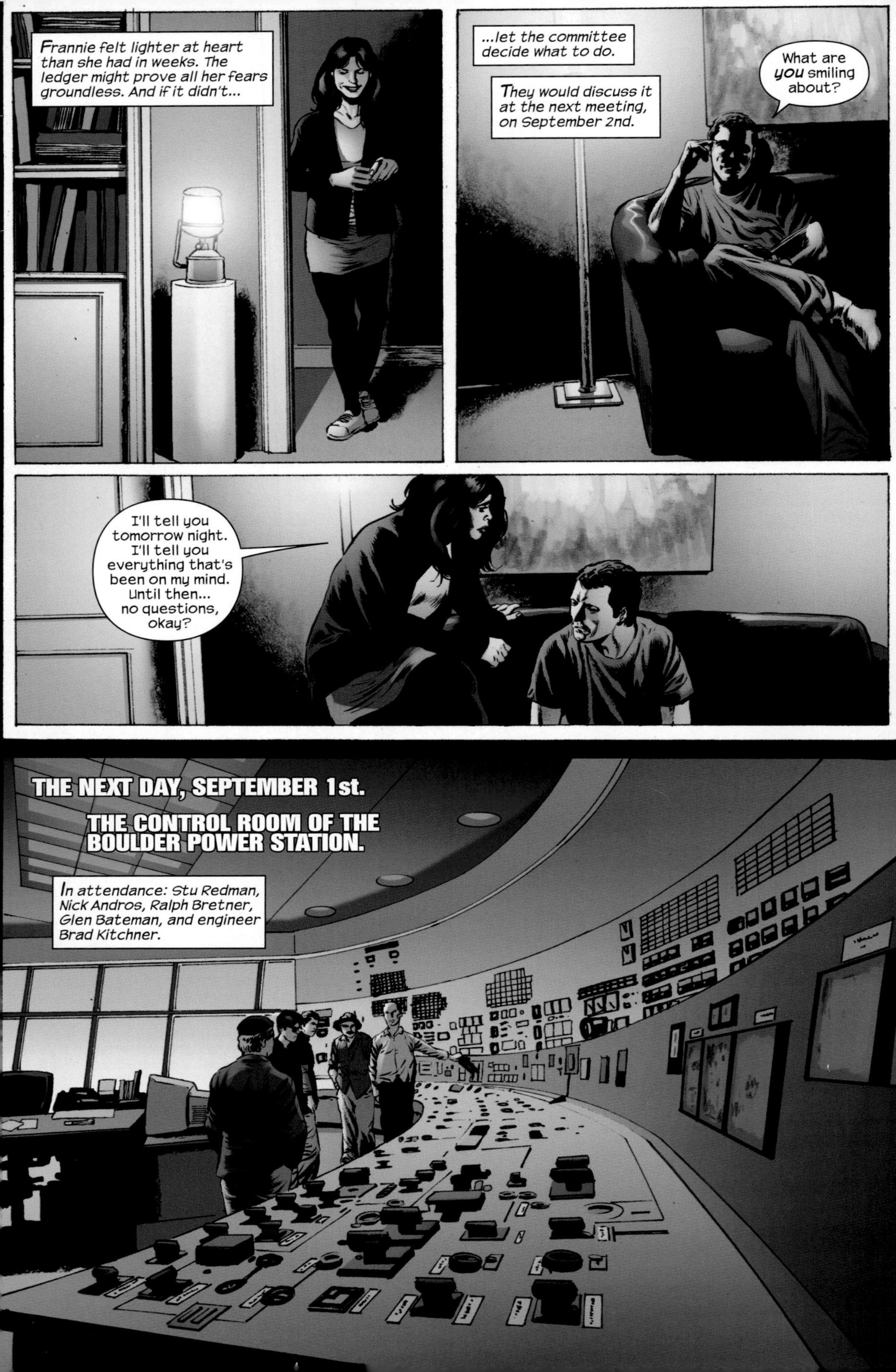
Frannie felt lighter at heart than she had in weeks. The ledger might prove all her fears groundless. And if it didn't...
...let the committee decide what to do.
They would discuss it at the next meeting, on September 2nd.
What are **you** smiling about?
I'll tell you tomorrow night. I'll tell you everything that's been on my mind. Until then... no questions, okay?
THE NEXT DAY, SEPTEMBER 1st.
THE CONTROL ROOM OF THE BOULDER POWER STATION.
In attendance: Stu Redman, Nick Andros, Ralph Bretner, Glen Bateman, and engineer Brad Kitchner.

Hail Mary, fulla grace, help me win this stock car race--

--Brad prayed, as he yanked two switches down hard.

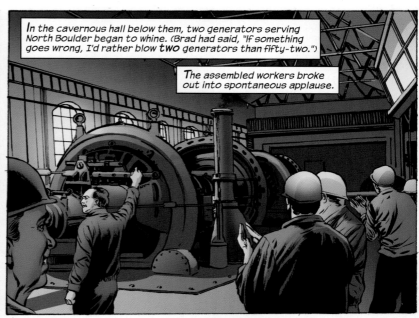

In the cavernous hall below them, two generators serving North Boulder began to whine. (Brad had said, "If something goes wrong, I'd rather blow *two* generators than fifty-two.")

The assembled workers broke out into spontaneous applause.

Above them, the fluorescents had begun to glow.

Nick elbowed Stu. For him, the feeling was the exact *opposite* of the dread he had known when the lights went out in Shoyo--not one of entombment now, but of resurrection.

And all over North Boulder...

TV sets went on in blares of snow...

In a house on Spruce, a blender whirred to life, mixing a long-congealed cheese-and-egg mixture....

In a garage on Maple, a power saw buzzed sawdust from its guts...

Stove burners began to glow...

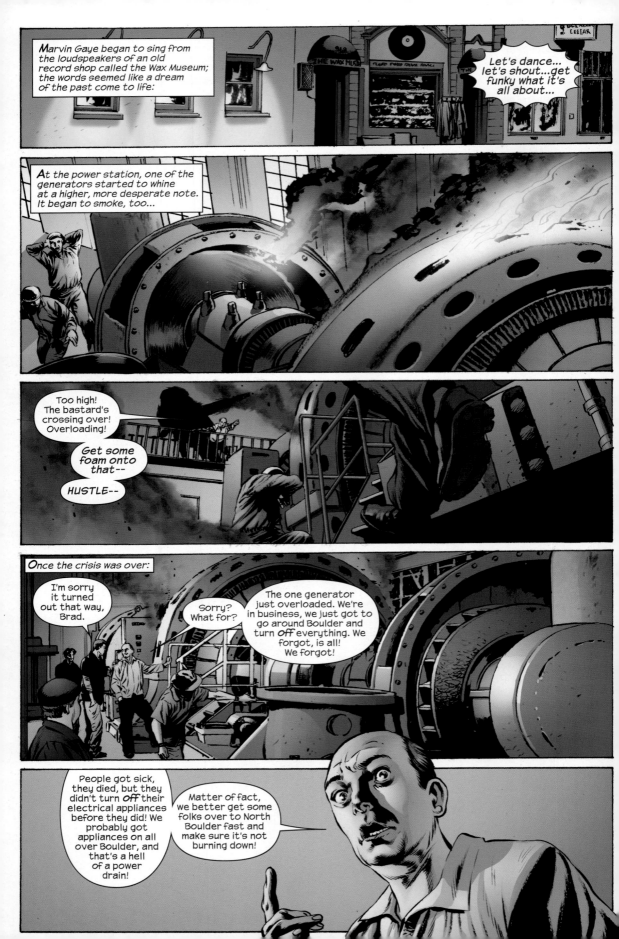

Marvin Gaye began to sing from the loudspeakers of an old record shop called the Wax Museum; the words seemed like a dream of the past come to life:

Let's dance... let's shout...get funky what it's all about...

At the power station, one of the generators started to whine at a higher, more desperate note. It began to smoke, too...

Too high! The bastard's crossing over! Overloading!

Get some foam onto that--

HUSTLE--

Once the crisis was over:

I'm sorry it turned out that way, Brad.

Sorry? What for?

The one generator just overloaded. We're in business, we just got to go around Boulder and turn off everything. We forgot, is all! We forgot!

People got sick, they died, but they didn't turn off their electrical appliances before they did! We probably got appliances on all over Boulder, and that's a hell of a power drain!

Matter of fact, we better get some folks over to North Boulder fast and make sure it's not burning down!

What **most** people in the Zone remembered about the first of September was that it was the day the power came back on, if only for 30 seconds or so.

Not Frannie and Larry, though.

They remembered it as the day they broke into Harold's house--and everything changed.

There's a good chance he's moved the ledger, anyway...

And Harold had. But Nadine had replaced it.

Well...are we going to admire it or read it?

You, Larry, I don't even wanna touch it.

They read:

To follow one's star is to concede the power of some greater force... YOUR **GOD**, your **DEVIL**, owns the keys to the lighthouse, but to each of us, he has given the responsibility of **NAVIGATION** ...

HAROLD EMERY LAUDER

It's Harold's way of saying following is as honorable as leading, I guess, but as a motto, it's not gonna replace "Waste not, want not"--

Whoo, look at this entry, Frannie!

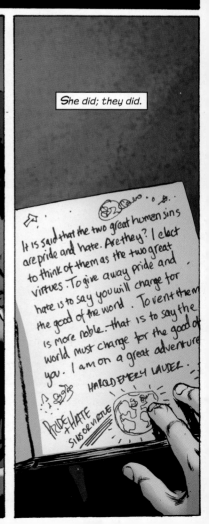

She did; they did.

It is said that the two great human sins are pride and hate. Are they? I elect to think of them as the two great virtues. To give away pride and hate is to say you will change for the good of the world. To vent them is more noble...that is to say the world must change for the good of you. I am on a great adventure.

HAROLD EMERY LAUDER

PRIDE/HATE
SINS OR VIRTUE

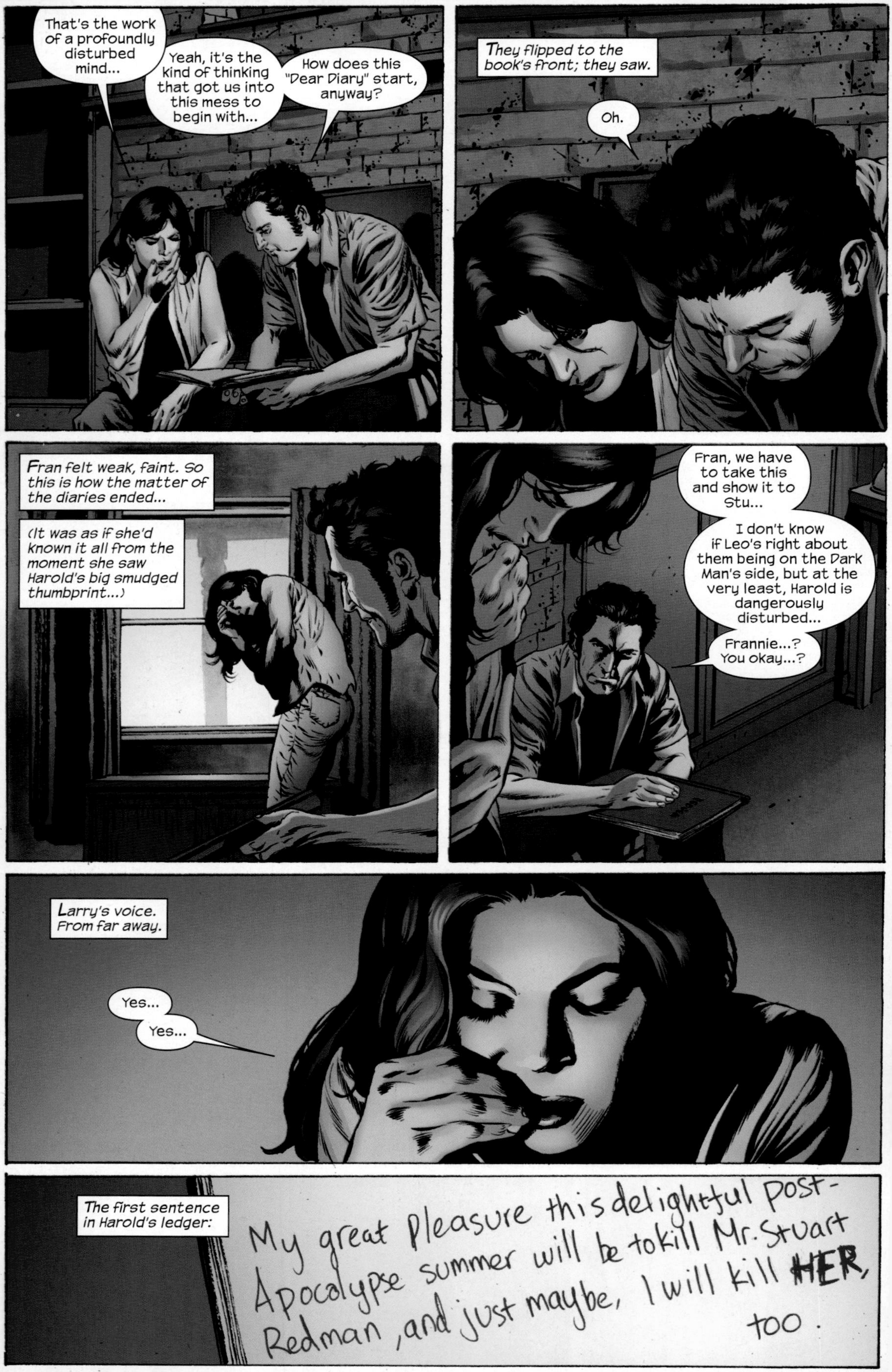
That's the work of a profoundly disturbed mind...
Yeah, it's the kind of thinking that got us into this mess to begin with...
How does this "Dear Diary" start, anyway?
They flipped to the book's front; they saw.
Oh.
Fran felt weak, faint. So this is how the matter of the diaries ended...
(It was as if she'd known it all from the moment she saw Harold's big smudged thumbprint...)
Fran, we have to take this and show it to Stu...
I don't know if Leo's right about them being on the Dark Man's side, but at the very least, Harold is dangerously disturbed...
Frannie...? You okay...?
Larry's voice. From far away.
Yes...
Yes...
The first sentence in Harold's ledger:
My great Pleasure this delightful post-Apocalypse summer will be to kill Mr. Stuart Redman, and just maybe, I will kill HER, too.

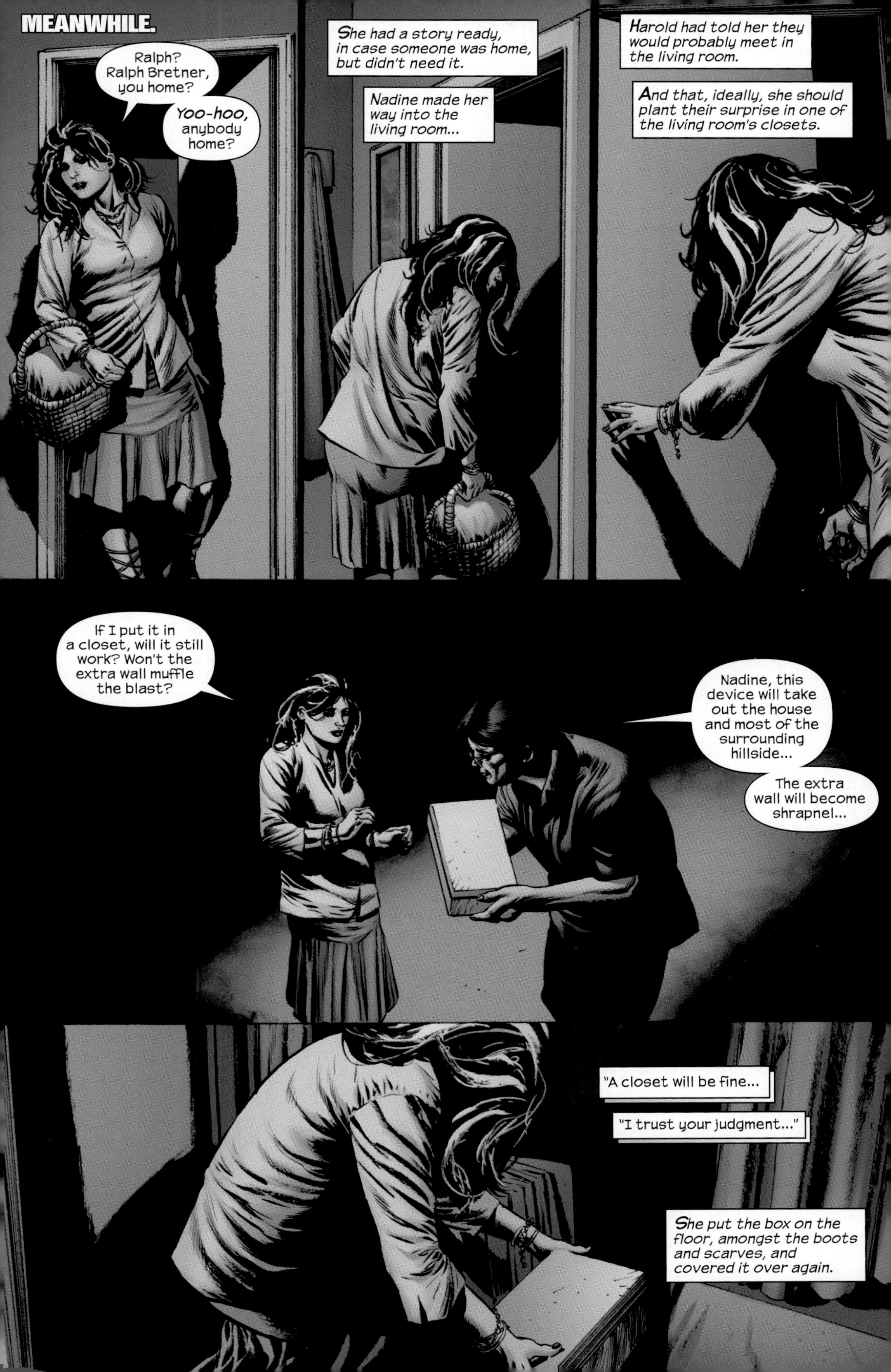
MEANWHILE.
Ralph? Ralph Bretner, you home?
Yoo-hoo, anybody home?
She had a story ready, in case someone was home, but didn't need it.
Nadine made her way into the living room...
Harold had told her they would probably meet in the living room.
And that, ideally, she should plant their surprise in one of the living room's closets.
If I put it in a closet, will it still work? Won't the extra wall muffle the blast?
Nadine, this device will take out the house and most of the surrounding hillside...
The extra wall will become shrapnel...
"A closet will be fine...
"I trust your judgment..."
She put the box on the floor, amongst the boots and scarves, and covered it over again.

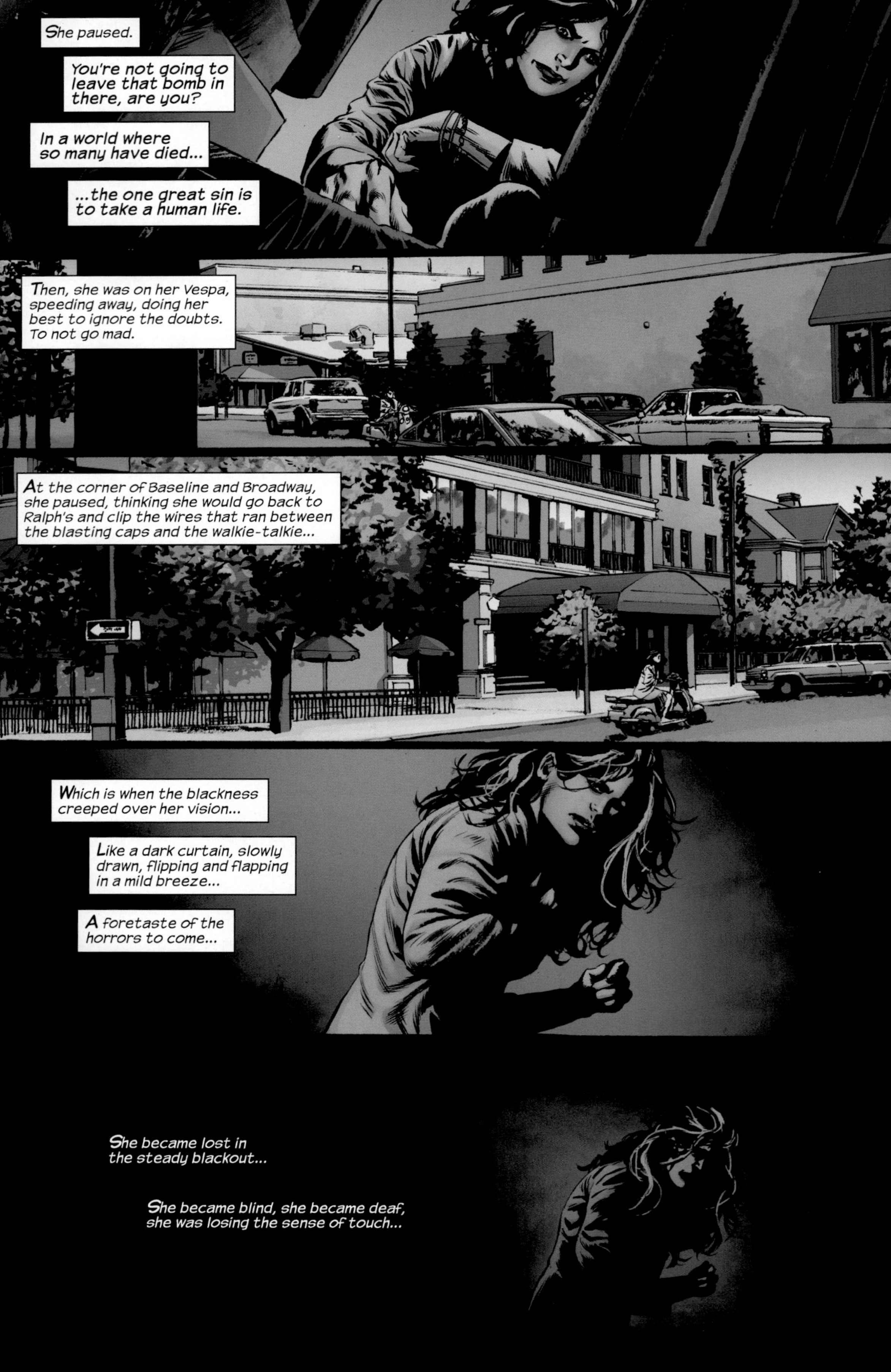

She paused.
You're not going to leave that bomb in there, are you?
In a world where so many have died...
...the one great sin is to take a human life.
Then, she was on her Vespa, speeding away, doing her best to ignore the doubts. To not go mad.
At the corner of Baseline and Broadway, she paused, thinking she would go back to Ralph's and clip the wires that ran between the blasting caps and the walkie-talkie...
Which is when the blackness creeped over her vision...
Like a dark curtain, slowly drawn, flipping and flapping in a mild breeze...
A foretaste of the horrors to come...
She became lost in the steady blackout...
She became blind, she became deaf, she was losing the sense of touch...

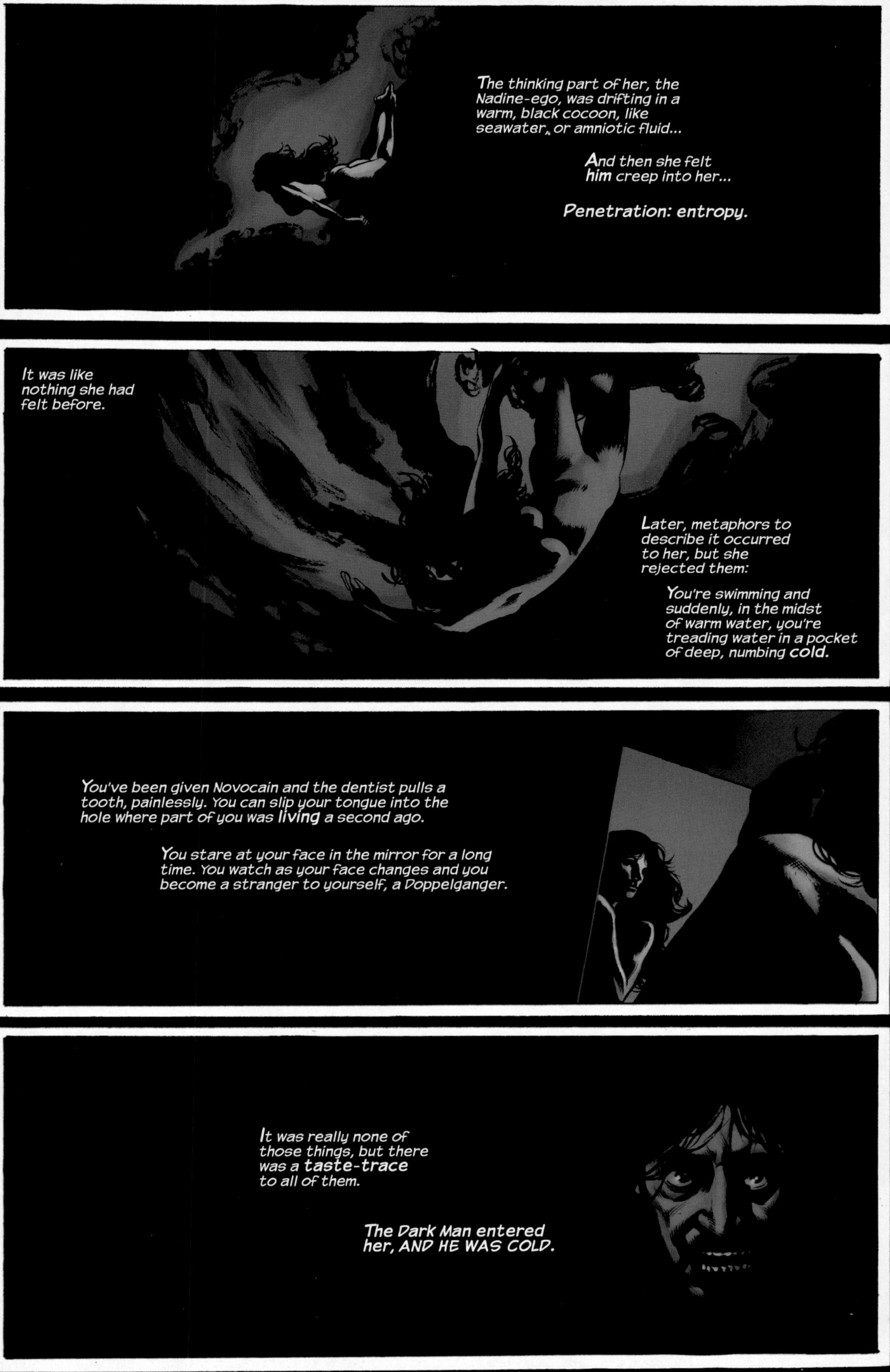
The thinking part of her, the Nadine-ego, was drifting in a warm, black cocoon, like seawater, or amniotic fluid...
And then she felt him creep into her...
Penetration: entropy.
It was like nothing she had felt before.
Later, metaphors to describe it occurred to her, but she rejected them:
You're swimming and suddenly, in the midst of warm water, you're treading water in a pocket of deep, numbing cold.
You've been given Novocain and the dentist pulls a tooth, painlessly. You can slip your tongue into the hole where part of you was living a second ago.
You stare at your face in the mirror for a long time. You watch as your face changes and you become a stranger to yourself, a Doppelganger.
It was really none of those things, but there was a taste-trace to all of them.
The Dark Man entered her, AND HE WAS COLD.

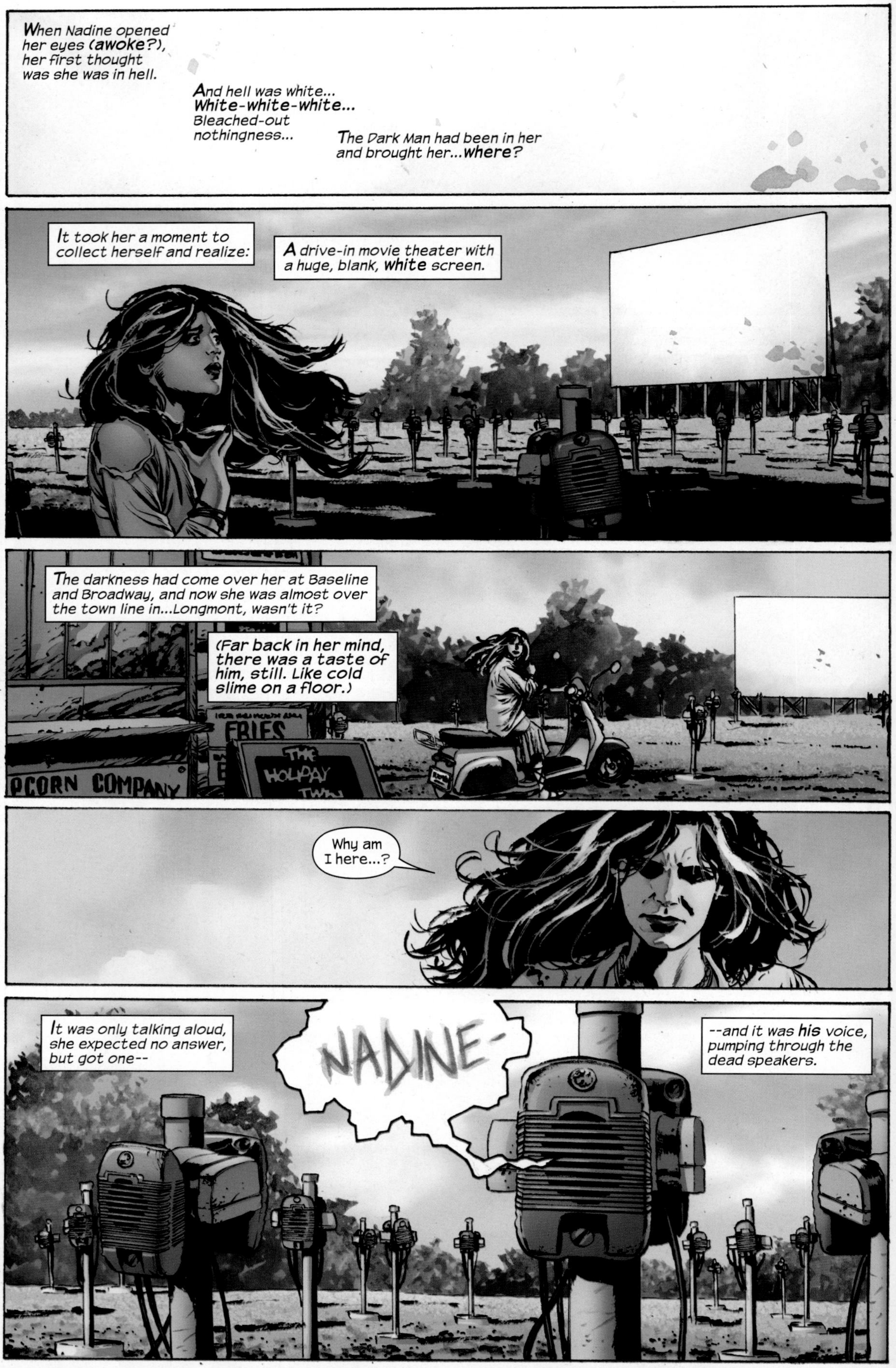
When Nadine opened her eyes (awoke?), her first thought was she was in hell.
And hell was white... White-white-white... Bleached-out nothingness...
The Dark Man had been in her and brought her...where?
It took her a moment to collect herself and realize:
A drive-in movie theater with a huge, blank, white screen.
The darkness had come over her at Baseline and Broadway, and now she was almost over the town line in...Longmont, wasn't it?
(Far back in her mind, there was a taste of him, still. Like cold slime on a floor.)
FRIES
PCORN COMPANY
THE HOLIDAY TWIN
Why am I here...?
It was only talking aloud, she expected no answer, but got one--
NADINE-
--and it was his voice, pumping through the dead speakers.

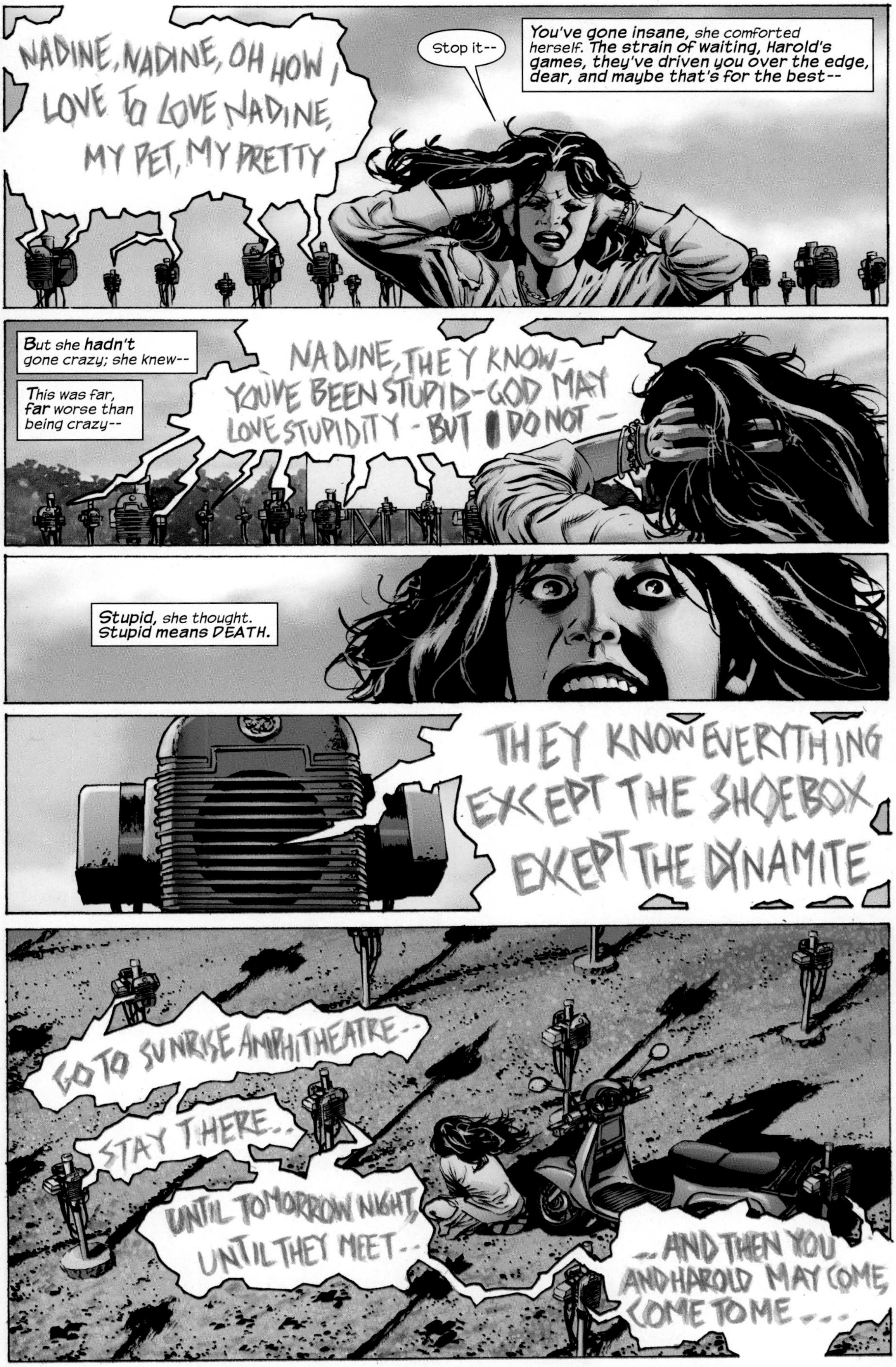
NADINE, NADINE, OH HOW I LOVE TO LOVE NADINE, MY PET, MY PRETTY
Stop it--
You've gone insane, she comforted herself. The strain of waiting, Harold's games, they've driven you over the edge, dear, and maybe that's for the best--
But she hadn't gone crazy; she knew--
This was far, far worse than being crazy--
NADINE, THEY KNOW-YOU'VE BEEN STUPID-GOD MAY LOVE STUPIDITY - BUT I DO NOT -
Stupid, she thought. Stupid means DEATH.
THEY KNOW EVERYTHING EXCEPT THE SHOEBOX EXCEPT THE DYNAMITE
GO TO SUNRISE AMPHITHEATRE--
STAY THERE...
UNTIL TOMORROW NIGHT, UNTIL THEY MEET--
--AND THEN YOU AND HAROLD MAY COME, COME TO ME...

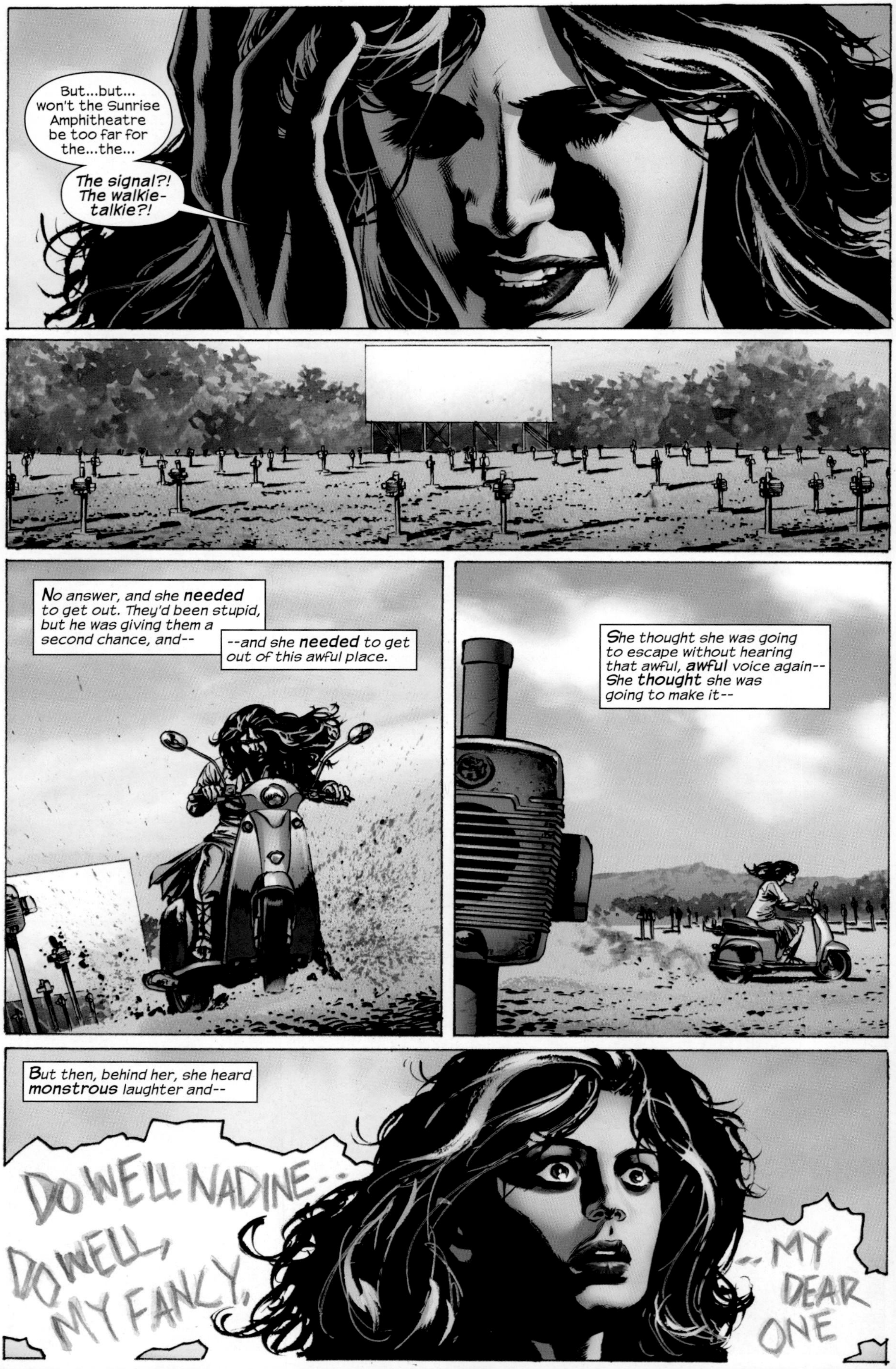
But...but... won't the Sunrise Amphitheatre be too far for the...the...
The signal?! The walkie-talkie?!
No answer, and she needed to get out. They'd been stupid, but he was giving them a second chance, and--
--and she needed to get out of this awful place.
She thought she was going to escape without hearing that awful, awful voice again-- She thought she was going to make it--
But then, behind her, she heard monstrous laughter and--
DO WELL NADINE...
DO WELL, MY FANCY,
...MY DEAR ONE

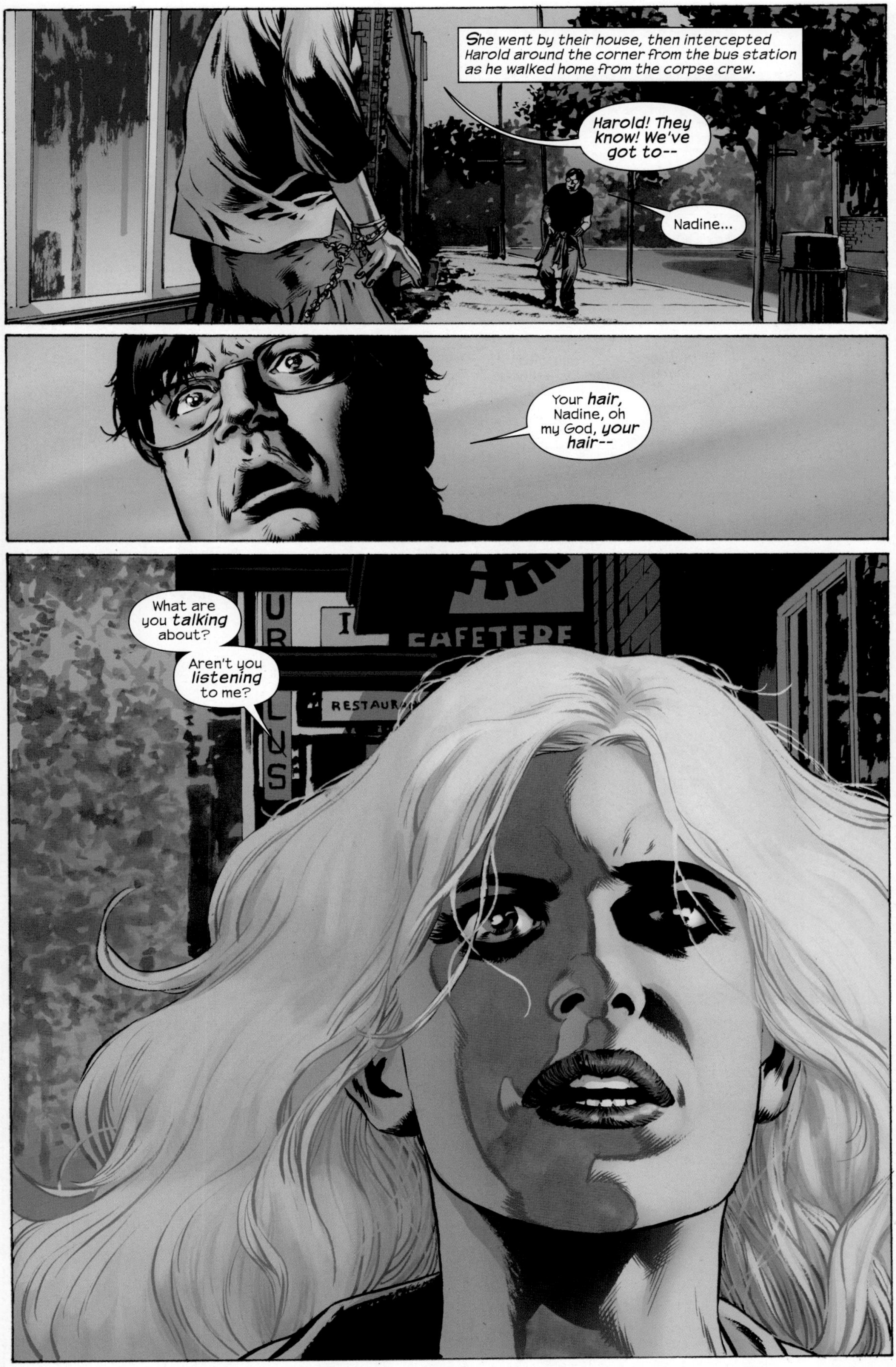
She went by their house, then intercepted Harold around the corner from the bus station as he walked home from the corpse crew.
Harold! They know! We've got to--
Nadine...
Your hair, Nadine, oh my God, your hair--
What are you talking about?
Aren't you listening to me?
RESTAURA

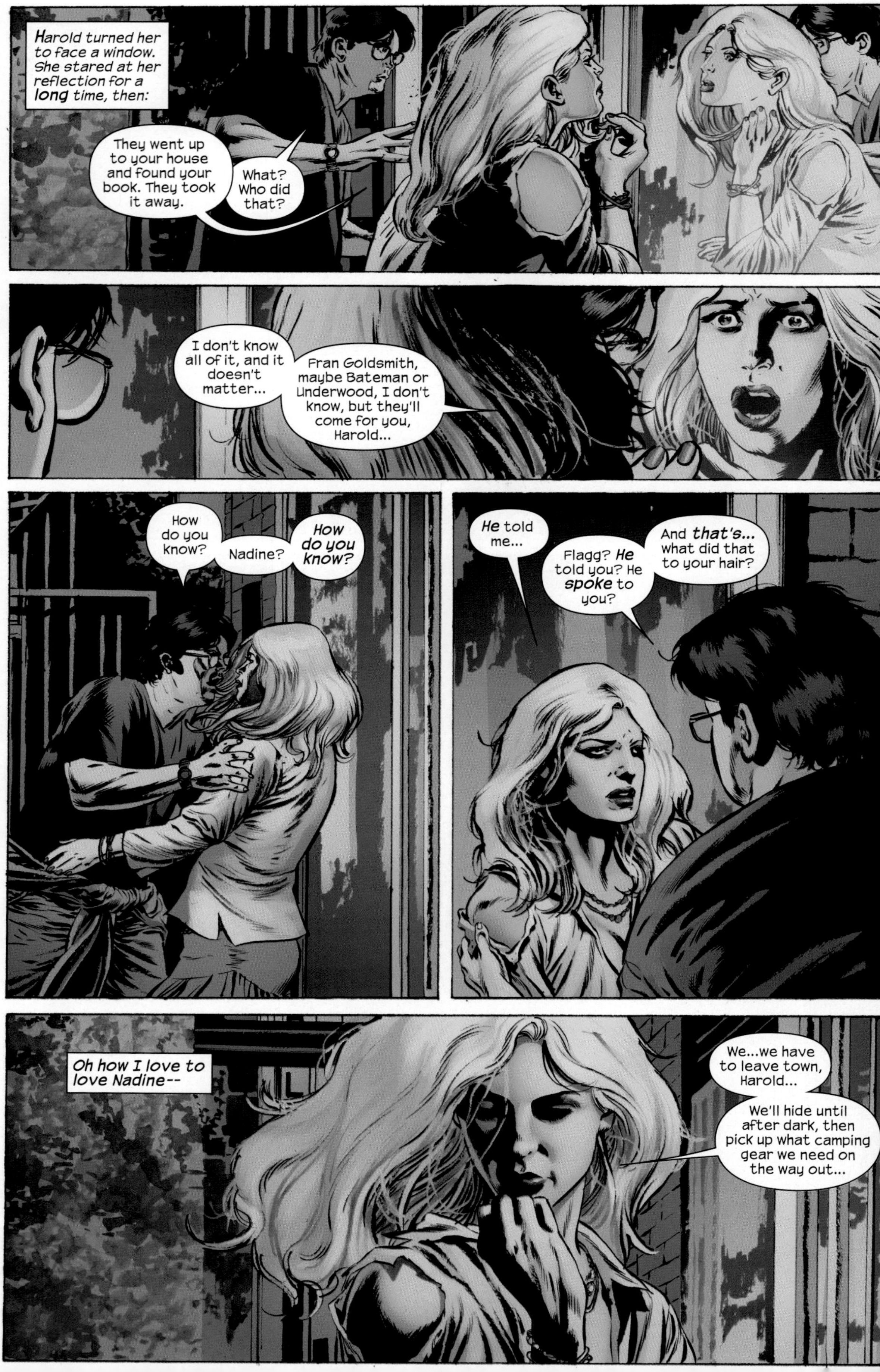
Harold turned her to face a window. She stared at her reflection for a **long** time, then:
They went up to your house and found your book. They took it away.
What? Who did that?
I don't know all of it, and it doesn't matter...
Fran Goldsmith, maybe Bateman or Underwood, I don't know, but they'll come for you, Harold...
How do you know?
Nadine?
How do you know?
He told me...
Flagg? *He* told you? He *spoke* to you?
And *that's...* what did that to your hair?
Oh how I love to love Nadine--
We...we have to leave town, Harold...
We'll hide until after dark, then pick up what camping gear we need on the way out...

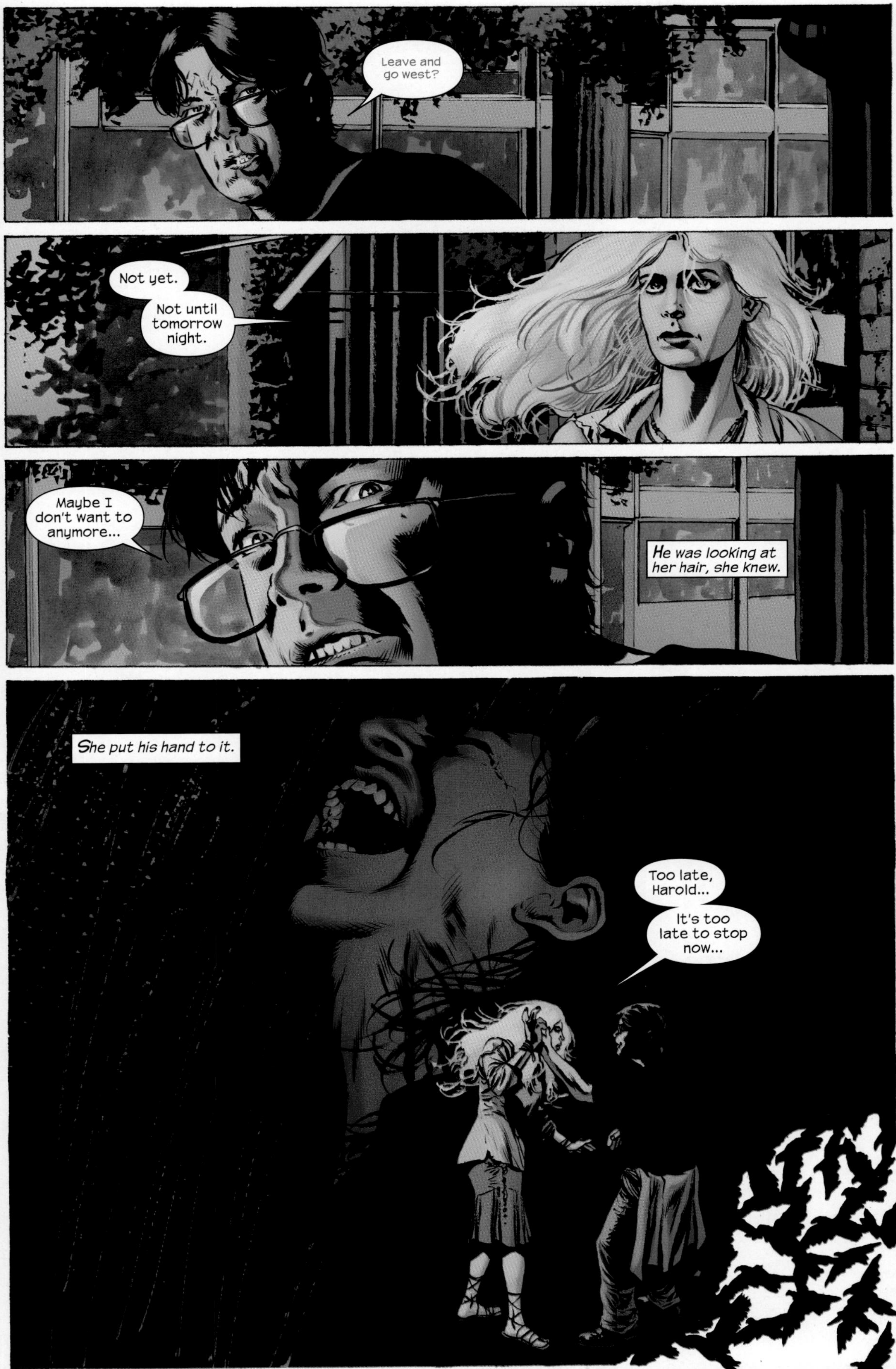
Leave and go west?
Not yet.
Not until tomorrow night.
Maybe I don't want to anymore...
He was looking at her hair, she knew.
She put his hand to it.
Too late, Harold...
It's too late to stop now...

chapter FOUR

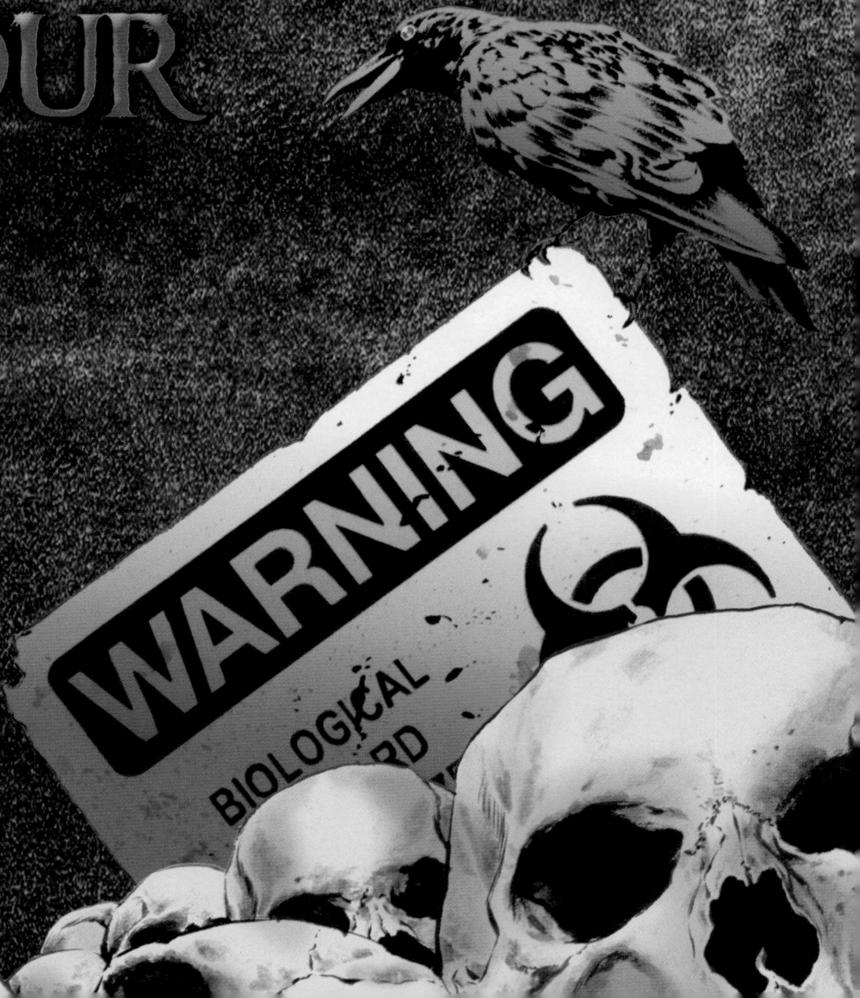
WARNING
BIOLOGICAL

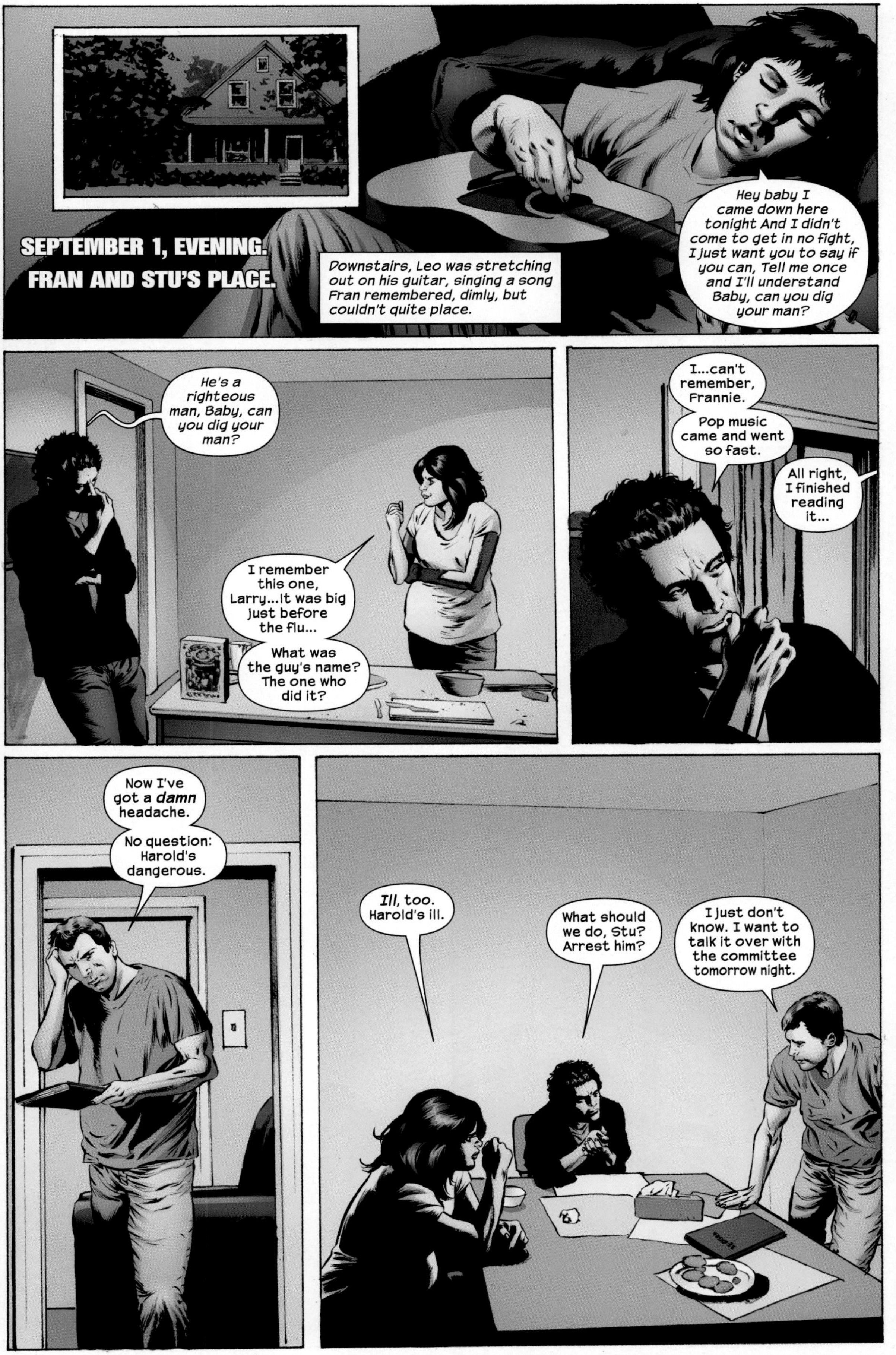

SEPTEMBER 1, EVENING.
FRAN AND STU'S PLACE.
Downstairs, Leo was stretching out on his guitar, singing a song Fran remembered, dimly, but couldn't quite place.
Hey baby I came down here tonight And I didn't come to get in no fight, I just want you to say if you can, Tell me once and I'll understand Baby, can you dig your man?
He's a righteous man, Baby, can you dig your man?
I remember this one, Larry...It was big just before the flu...
What was the guy's name? The one who did it?
I...can't remember, Frannie.
Pop music came and went so fast.
All right, I finished reading it...
Now I've got a *damn* headache.
No question: Harold's dangerous.
Ill, too. Harold's ill.
What should we do, Stu? Arrest him?
I just don't know. I want to talk it over with the committee tomorrow night.

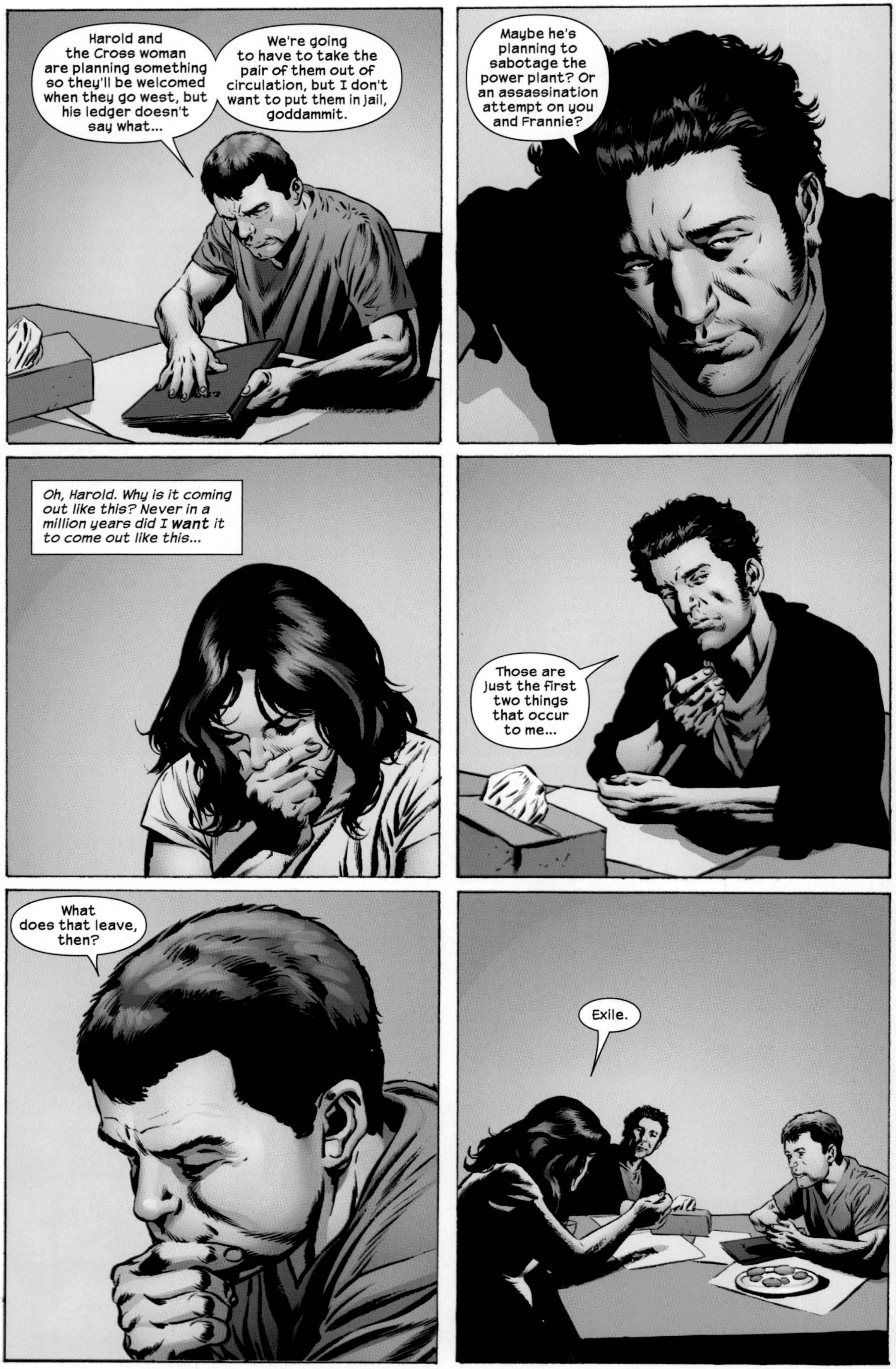
Harold and the Cross woman are planning something so they'll be welcomed when they go west, but his ledger doesn't say what...
We're going to have to take the pair of them out of circulation, but I don't want to put them in jail, goddammit.
Maybe he's planning to sabotage the power plant? Or an assassination attempt on you and Frannie?
Oh, Harold. Why is it coming out like this? Never in a million years did I want it to come out like this...
Those are just the first two things that occur to me...
What does that leave, then?
Exile.

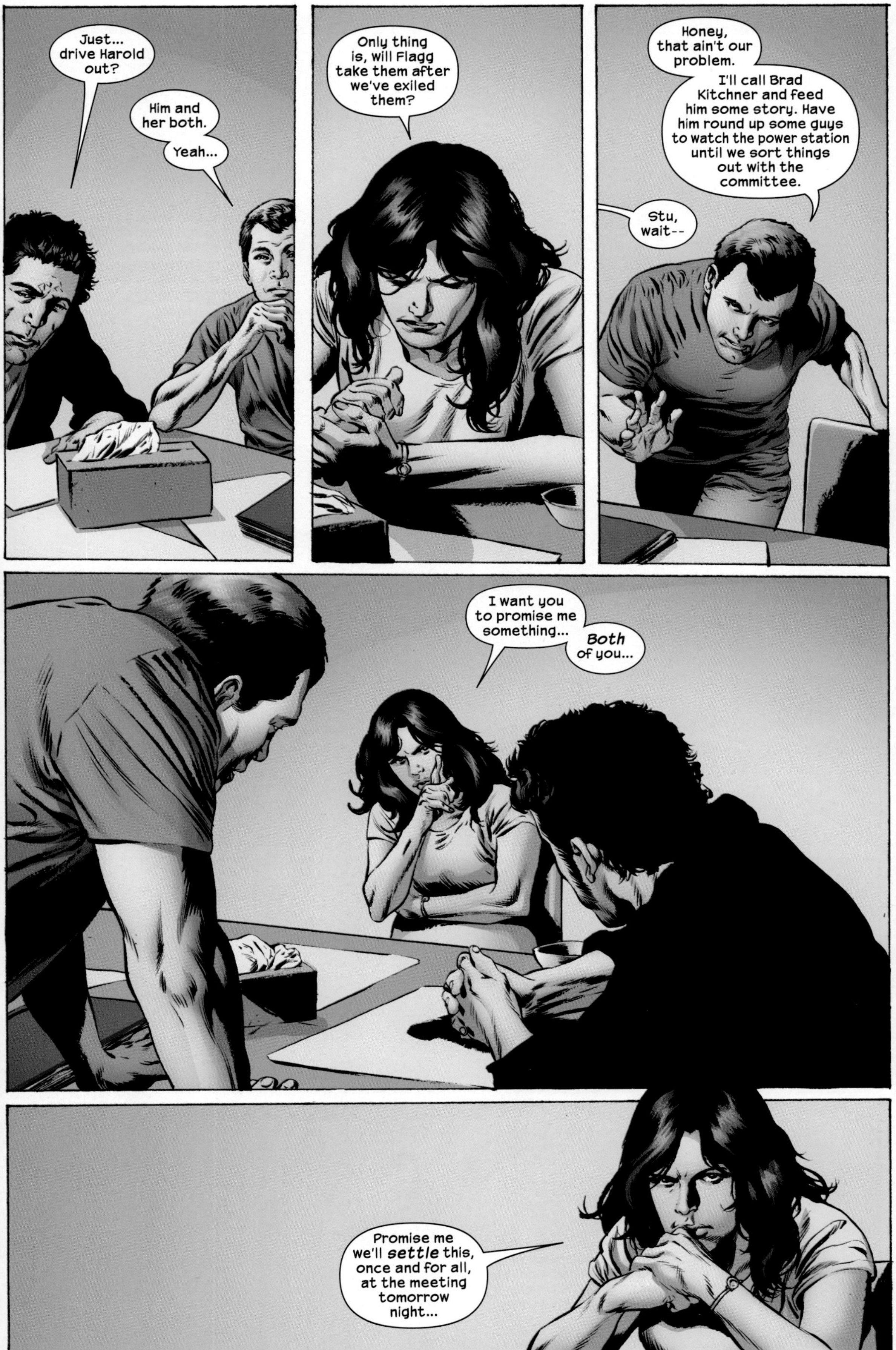
Just... drive Harold out?
Him and her both.
Yeah...
Only thing is, will Flagg take them after we've exiled them?
Honey, that ain't our problem.
I'll call Brad Kitchner and feed him some story. Have him round up some guys to watch the power station until we sort things out with the committee.
Stu, wait--
I want you to promise me something... *Both* of you...
Promise me we'll *settle* this, once and for all, at the meeting tomorrow night...

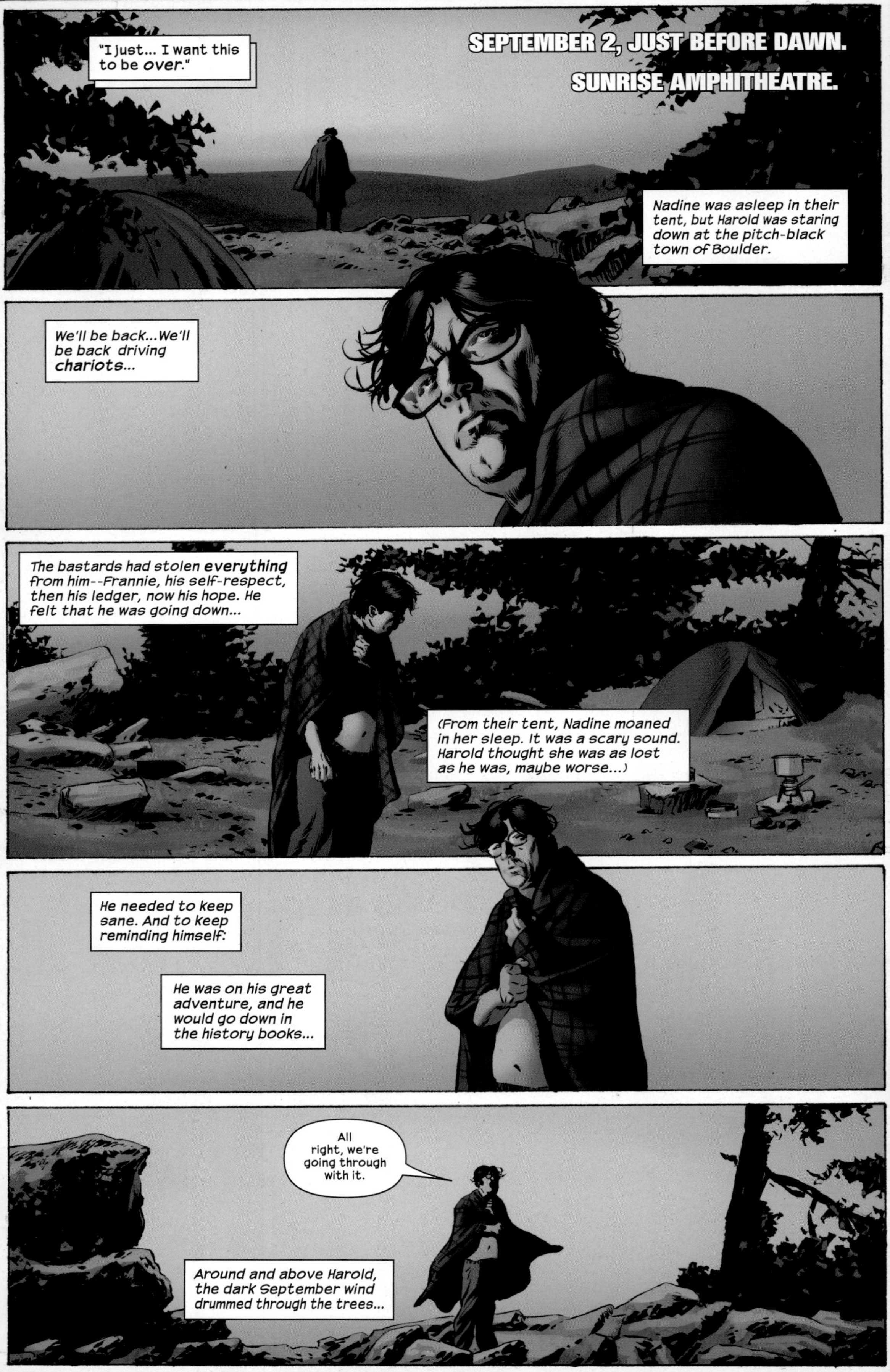
SEPTEMBER 2, JUST BEFORE DAWN.
SUNRISE AMPHITHEATRE.
"I just... I want this to be *over*."
Nadine was asleep in their tent, but Harold was staring down at the pitch-black town of Boulder.
We'll be back...We'll be back driving **chariots**...
The bastards had stolen **everything** from him--Frannie, his self-respect, then his ledger, now his hope. He felt that he was going down...
(From their tent, Nadine moaned in her sleep. It was a scary sound. Harold thought she was as lost as he was, maybe worse...)
He needed to keep sane. And to keep reminding himself:
He was on his great adventure, and he would go down in the history books...
All right, we're going through with it.
Around and above Harold, the dark September wind drummed through the trees...

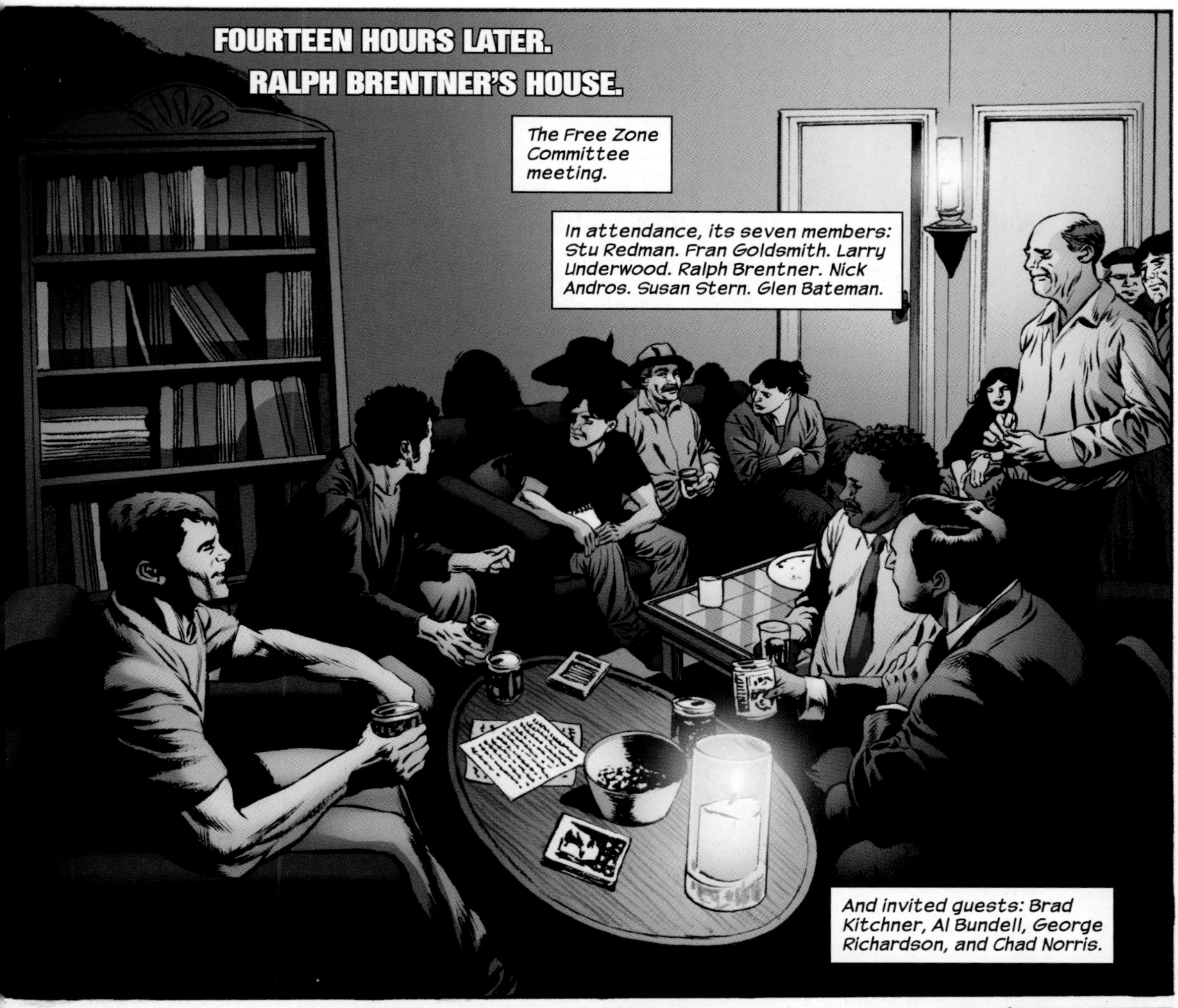
FOURTEEN HOURS LATER.
RALPH BRENTNER'S HOUSE.
The Free Zone Committee meeting.
In attendance, its seven members: Stu Redman. Fran Goldsmith. Larry Underwood. Ralph Brentner. Nick Andros. Susan Stern. Glen Bateman.
And invited guests: Brad Kitchner, Al Bundell, George Richardson, and Chad Norris.

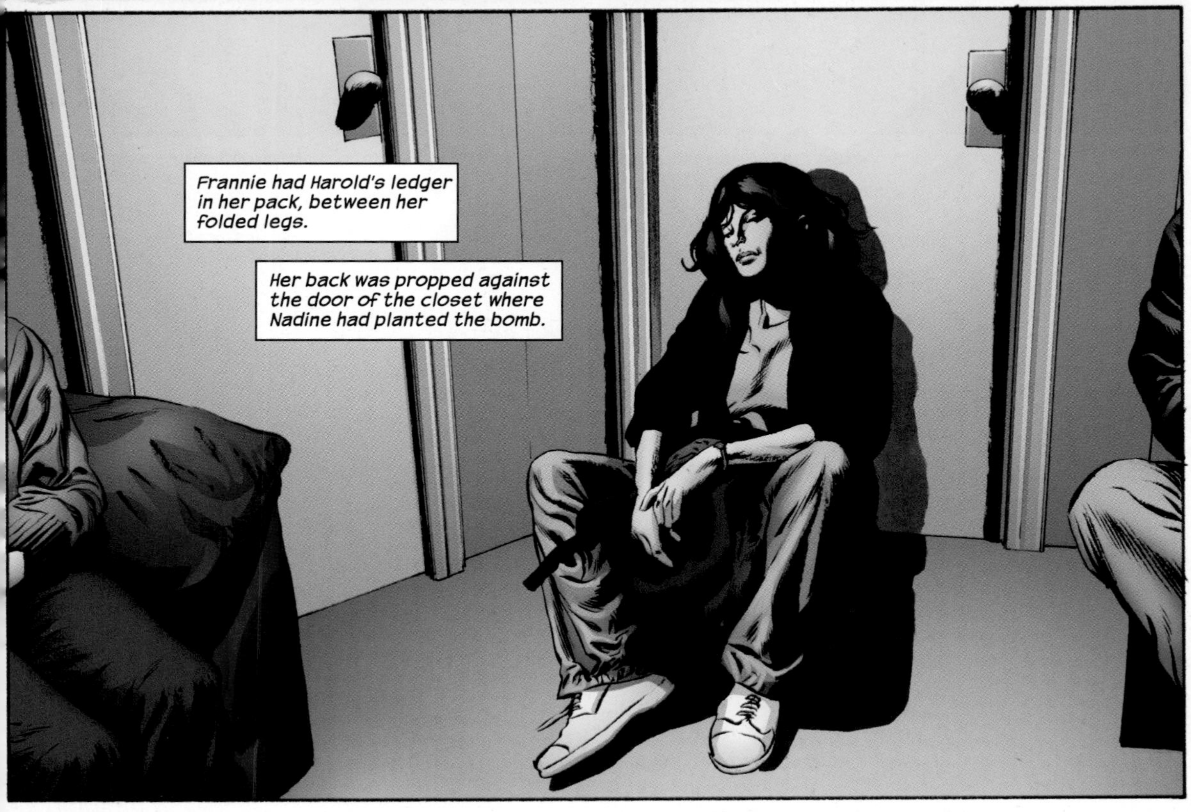
Frannie had Harold's ledger in her pack, between her folded legs.
Her back was propped against the door of the closet where Nadine had planted the bomb.

Stu turned the meeting over to a blushing, nervous Kitchner:

I'm. Real. Happy. To be. Here.

The...ah... power!

Right! The power is almost on!

The fire Ralph had kindled snapped comfortably...

Brad was lobbying for a crew to turn off all the appliances that might have been left on post-plague, so that his generators wouldn't overload again...

...and Fran was thinking, *It's going to be all right.*

Harold and Nadine had taken off without any prompting, so *that* problem was solved; Stu was safe from them.

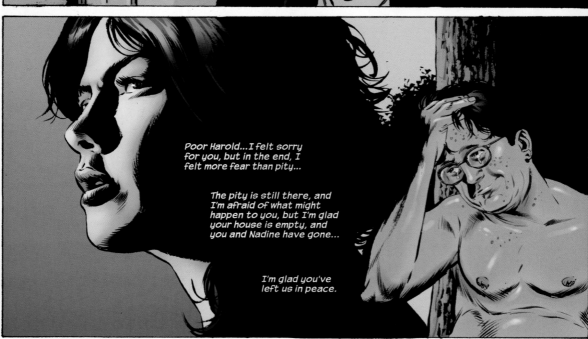

Poor Harold...I felt sorry for you, but in the end, I felt more fear than pity...

The pity is still there, and I'm afraid of what might happen to you, but I'm glad your house is empty, and you and Nadine have gone...

I'm glad you've left us in peace.

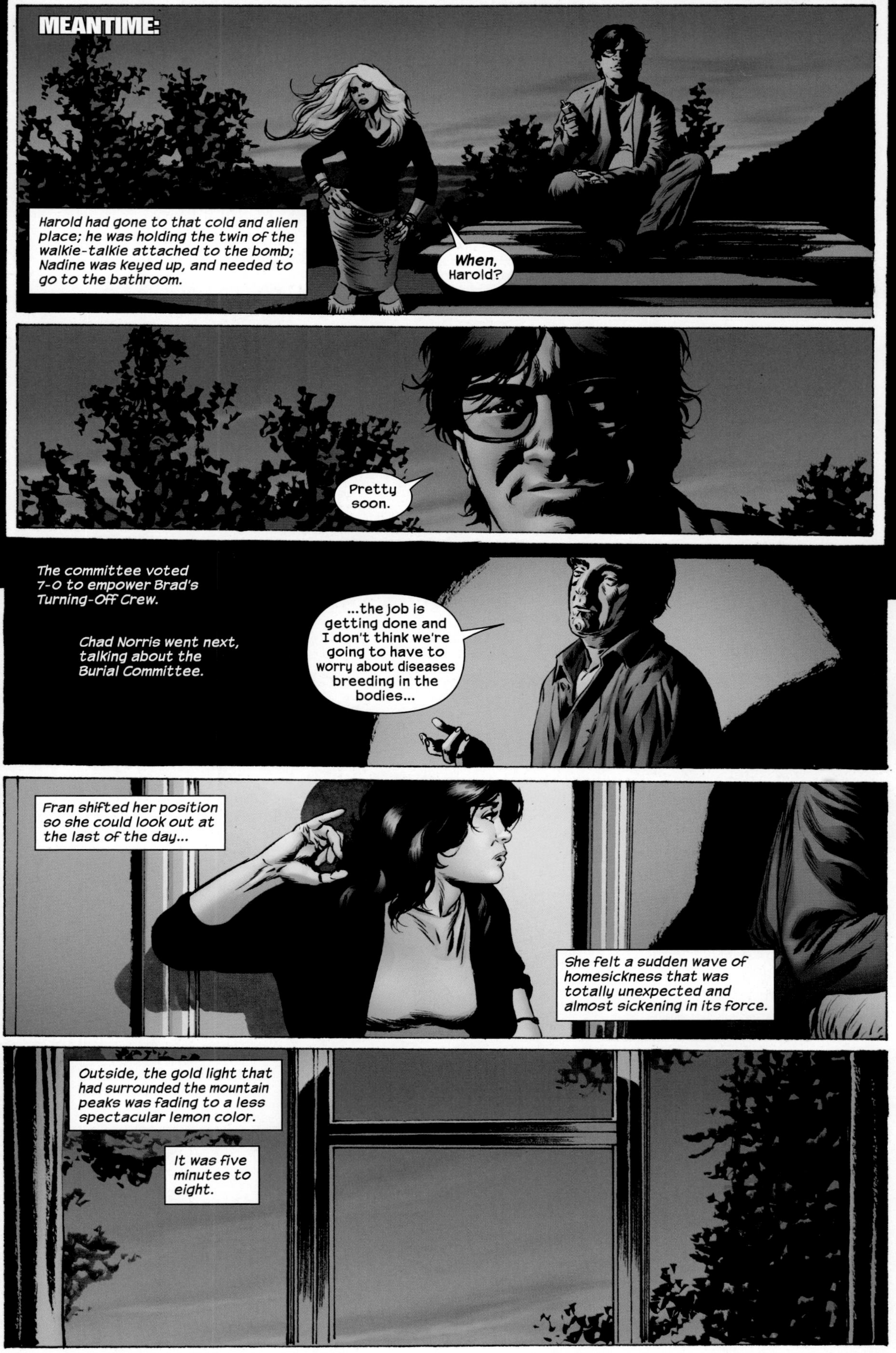
MEANTIME:
Harold had gone to that cold and alien place; he was holding the twin of the walkie-talkie attached to the bomb; Nadine was keyed up, and needed to go to the bathroom.
When, Harold?
Pretty soon.
The committee voted 7-0 to empower Brad's Turning-Off Crew.
Chad Norris went next, talking about the Burial Committee.
...the job is getting done and I don't think we're going to have to worry about diseases breeding in the bodies...
Fran shifted her position so she could look out at the last of the day...
She felt a sudden wave of homesickness that was totally unexpected and almost sickening in its force.
Outside, the gold light that had surrounded the mountain peaks was fading to a less spectacular lemon color.
It was five minutes to eight.

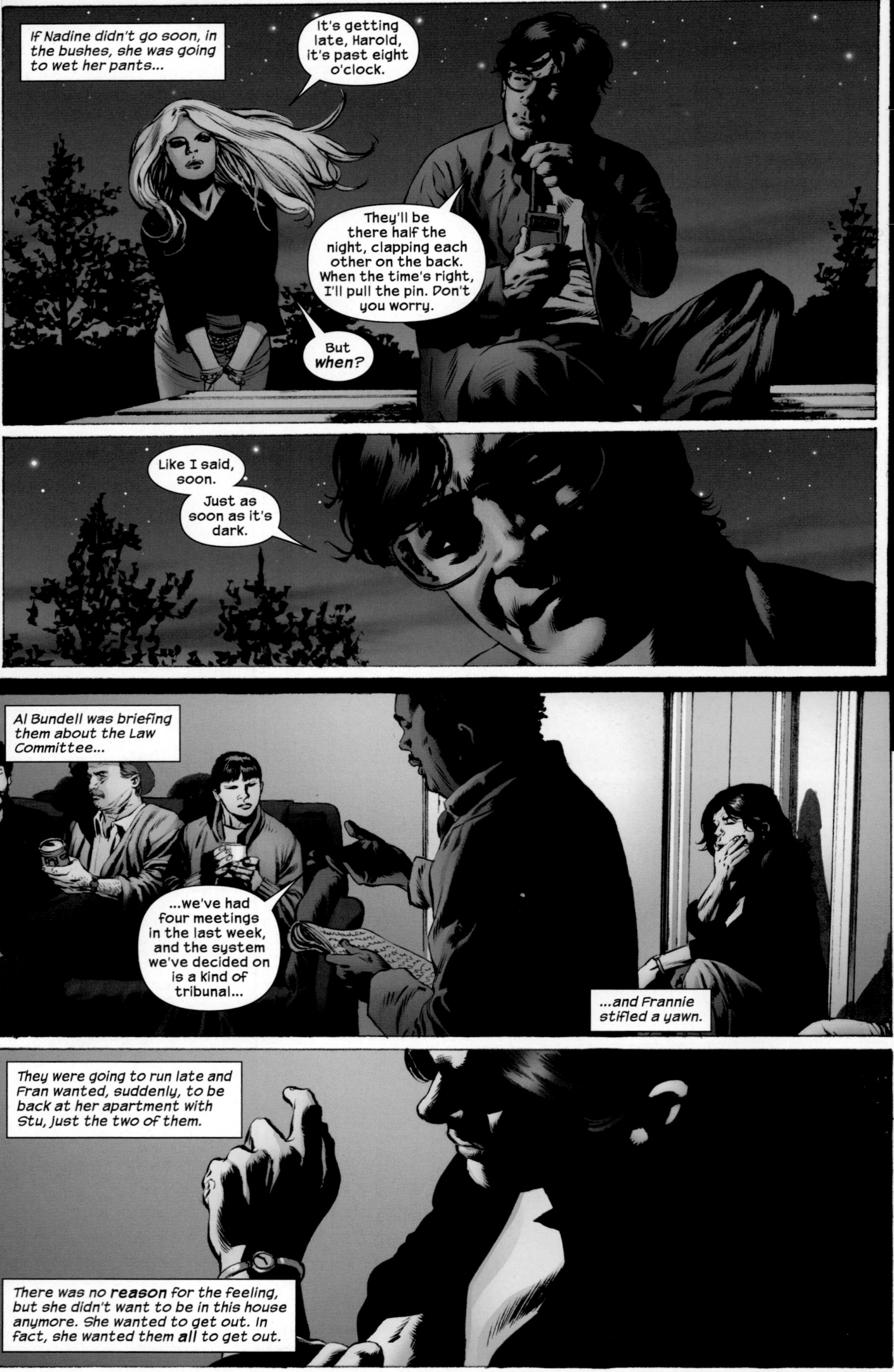
If Nadine didn't go soon, in the bushes, she was going to wet her pants...
It's getting late, Harold, it's past eight o'clock.
They'll be there half the night, clapping each other on the back. When the time's right, I'll pull the pin. Don't you worry.
But *when?*
Like I said, soon.
Just as soon as it's dark.
Al Bundell was briefing them about the Law Committee...
...we've had four meetings in the last week, and the system we've decided on is a kind of tribunal...
...and Frannie stifled a yawn.
They were going to run late and Fran wanted, suddenly, to be back at her apartment with Stu, just the two of them.
There was no **reason** for the feeling, but she didn't want to be in this house anymore. She wanted to get out. In fact, she wanted them **all** to get out.

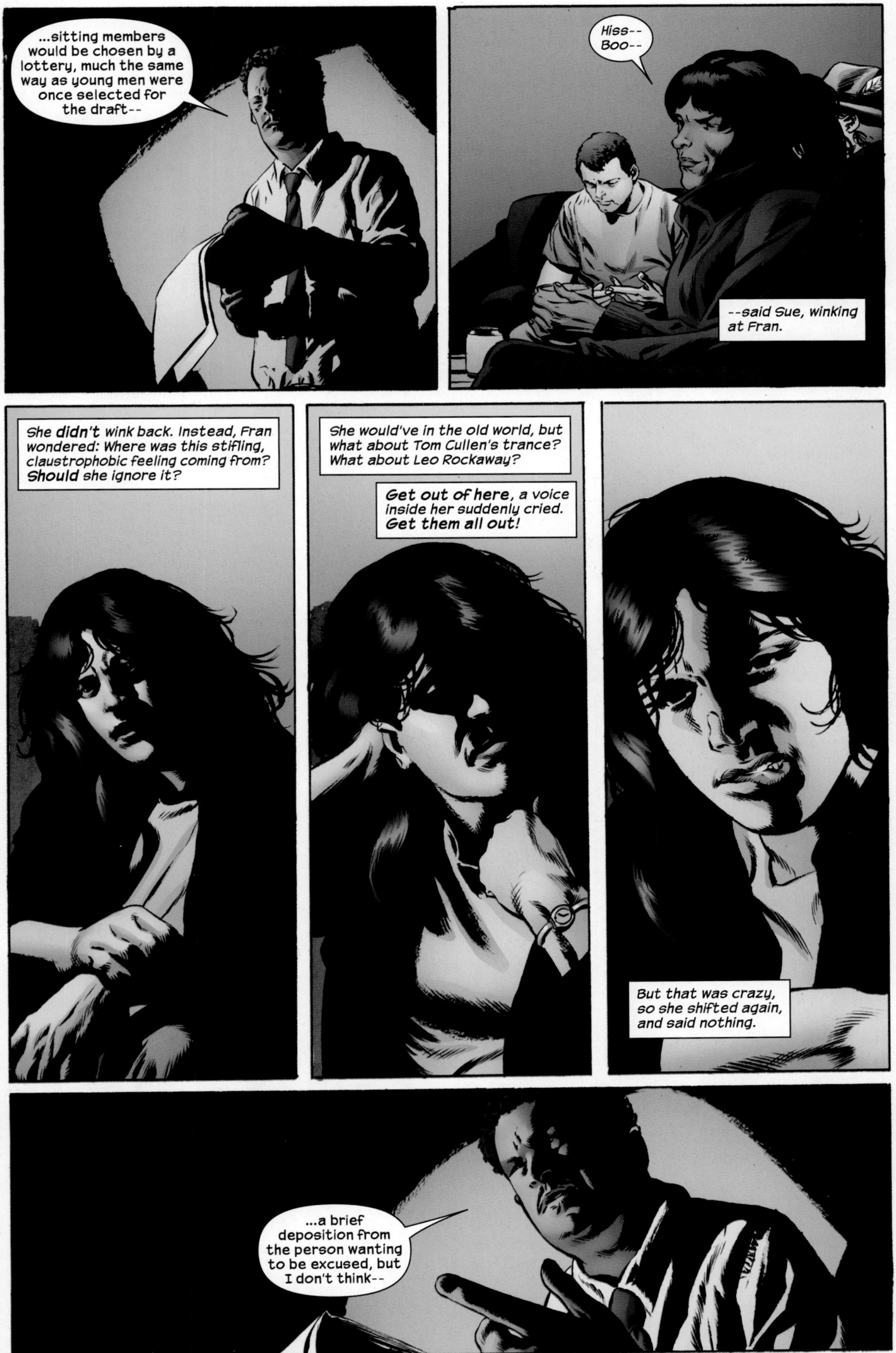
...sitting members would be chosen by a lottery, much the same way as young men were once selected for the draft--
Hiss-- Boo--
--said Sue, winking at Fran.
She didn't wink back. Instead, Fran wondered: Where was this stifling, claustrophobic feeling coming from? Should she ignore it?
She would've in the old world, but what about Tom Cullen's trance? What about Leo Rockaway?
Get out of here, a voice inside her suddenly cried. Get them all out!
But that was crazy, so she shifted again, and said nothing.
...a brief deposition from the person wanting to be excused, but I don't think--

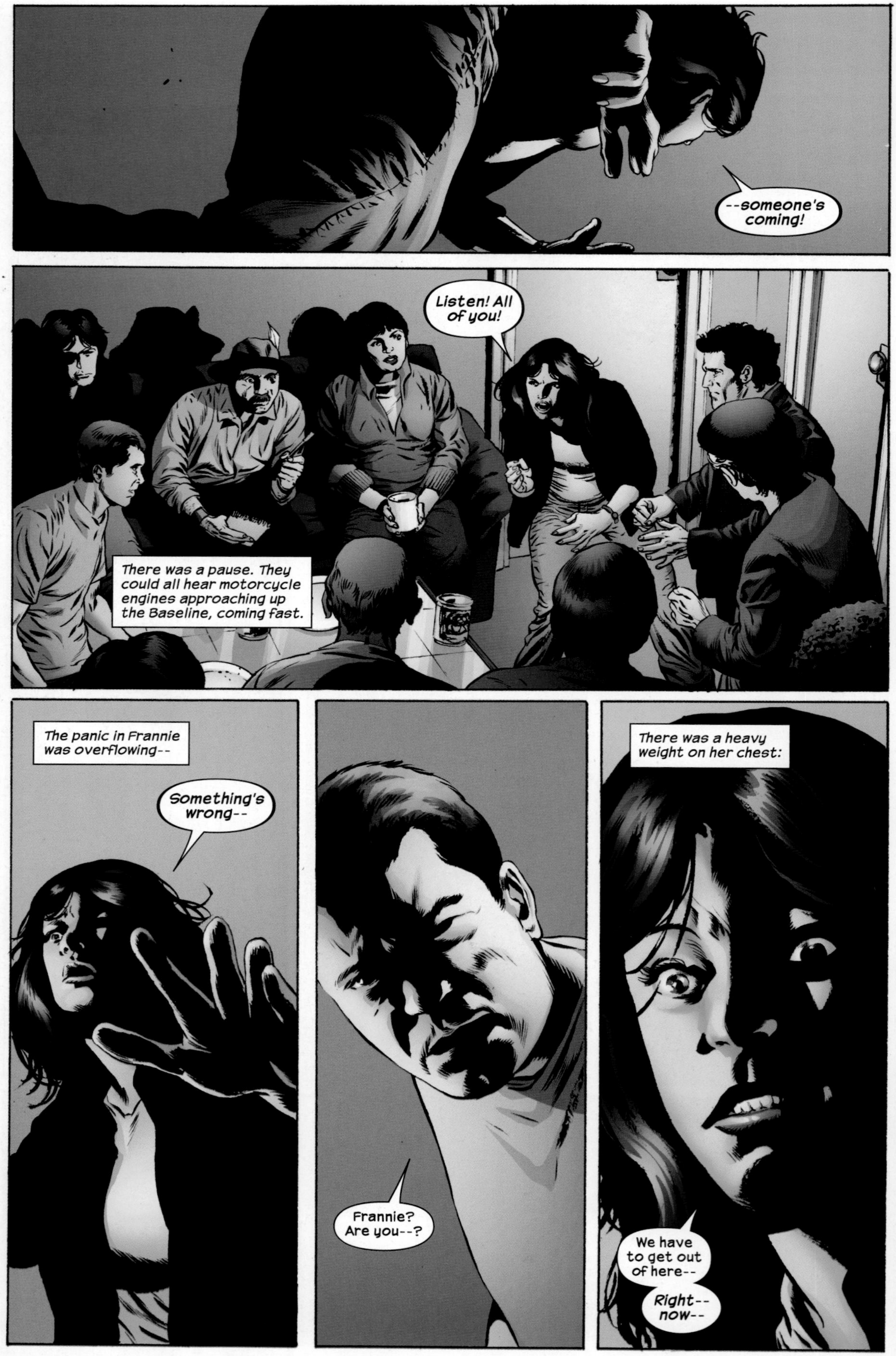
--someone's coming!
Listen! All of you!
There was a pause. They could all hear motorcycle engines approaching up the Baseline, coming fast.
The panic in Frannie was overflowing--
Something's wrong--
Frannie? Are you--?
There was a heavy weight on her chest:
We have to get out of here--
Right-- now--

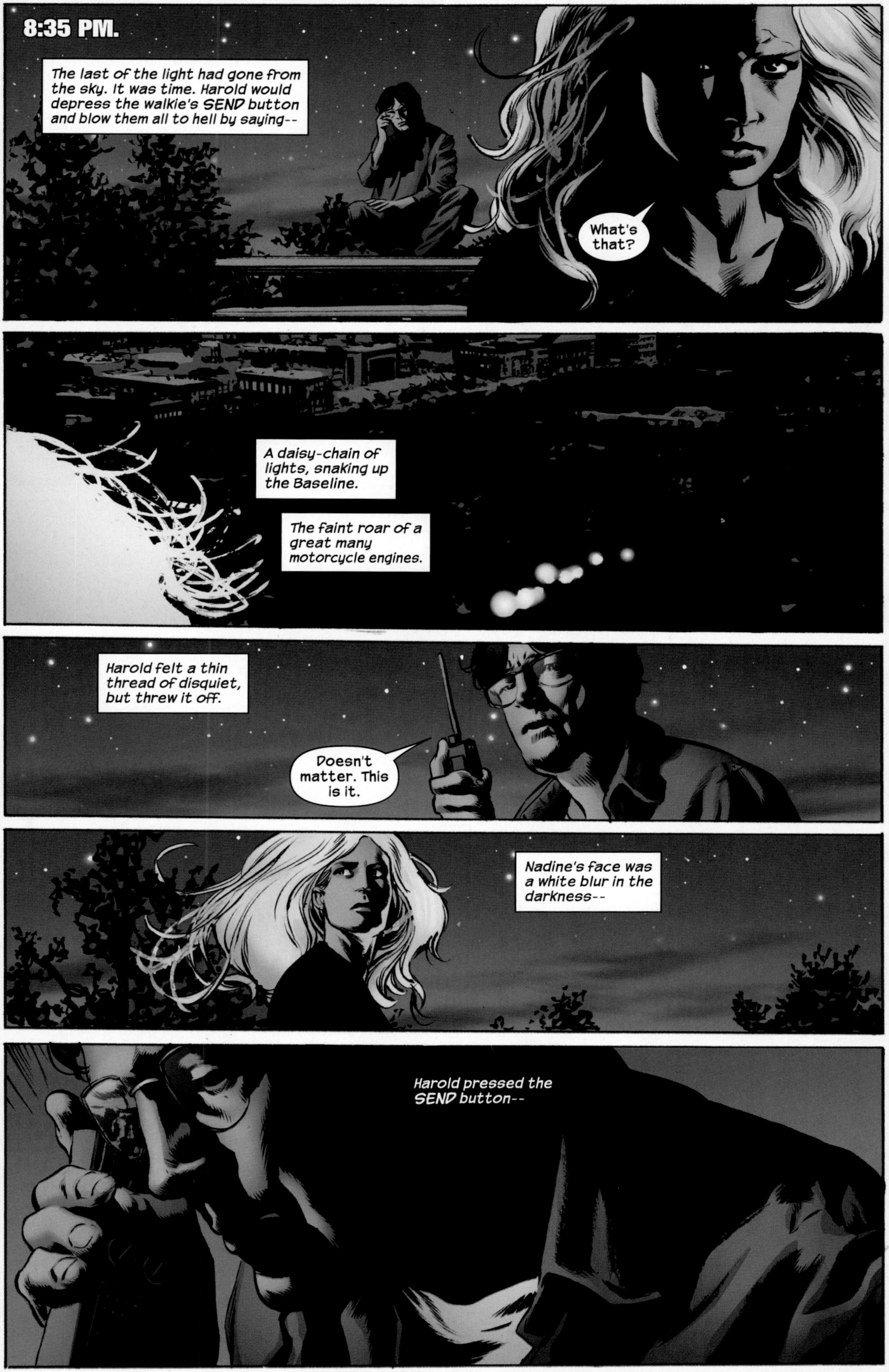
8:35 PM.
The last of the light had gone from the sky. It was time. Harold would depress the walkie's SEND button and blow them all to hell by saying--
What's that?
A daisy-chain of lights, snaking up the Baseline.
The faint roar of a great many motorcycle engines.
Harold felt a thin thread of disquiet, but threw it off.
Doesn't matter. This is it.
Nadine's face was a white blur in the darkness--
Harold pressed the SEND button--

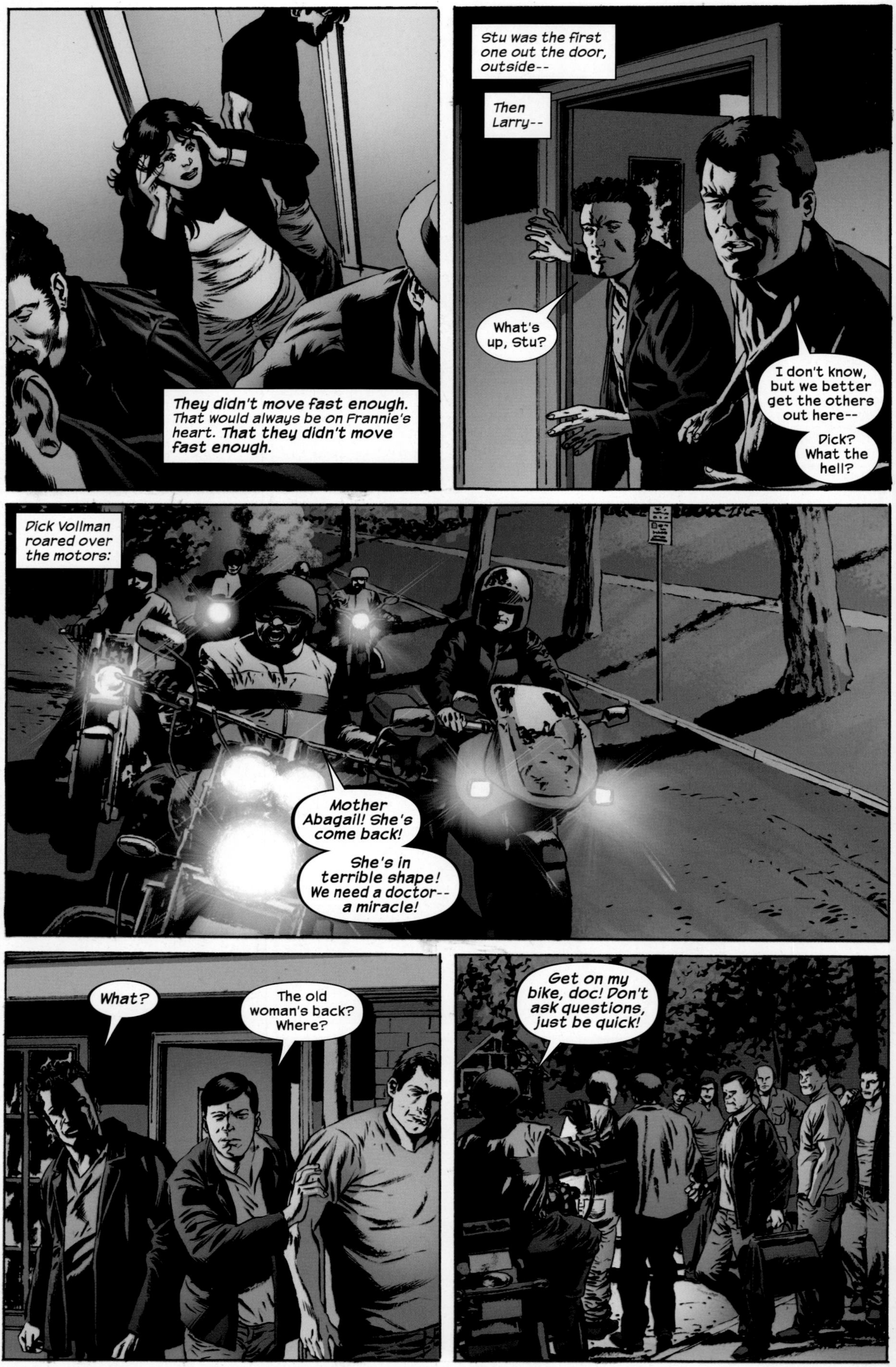
They didn't move fast enough. That would always be on Frannie's heart. That they didn't move fast enough.
Stu was the first one out the door, outside--
Then Larry--
What's up, Stu?
I don't know, but we better get the others out here--
Dick? What the hell?
Dick Vollman roared over the motors:
Mother Abagail! She's come back!
She's in terrible shape! We need a doctor-- a miracle!
What?
The old woman's back? Where?
Get on my bike, doc! Don't ask questions, just be quick!

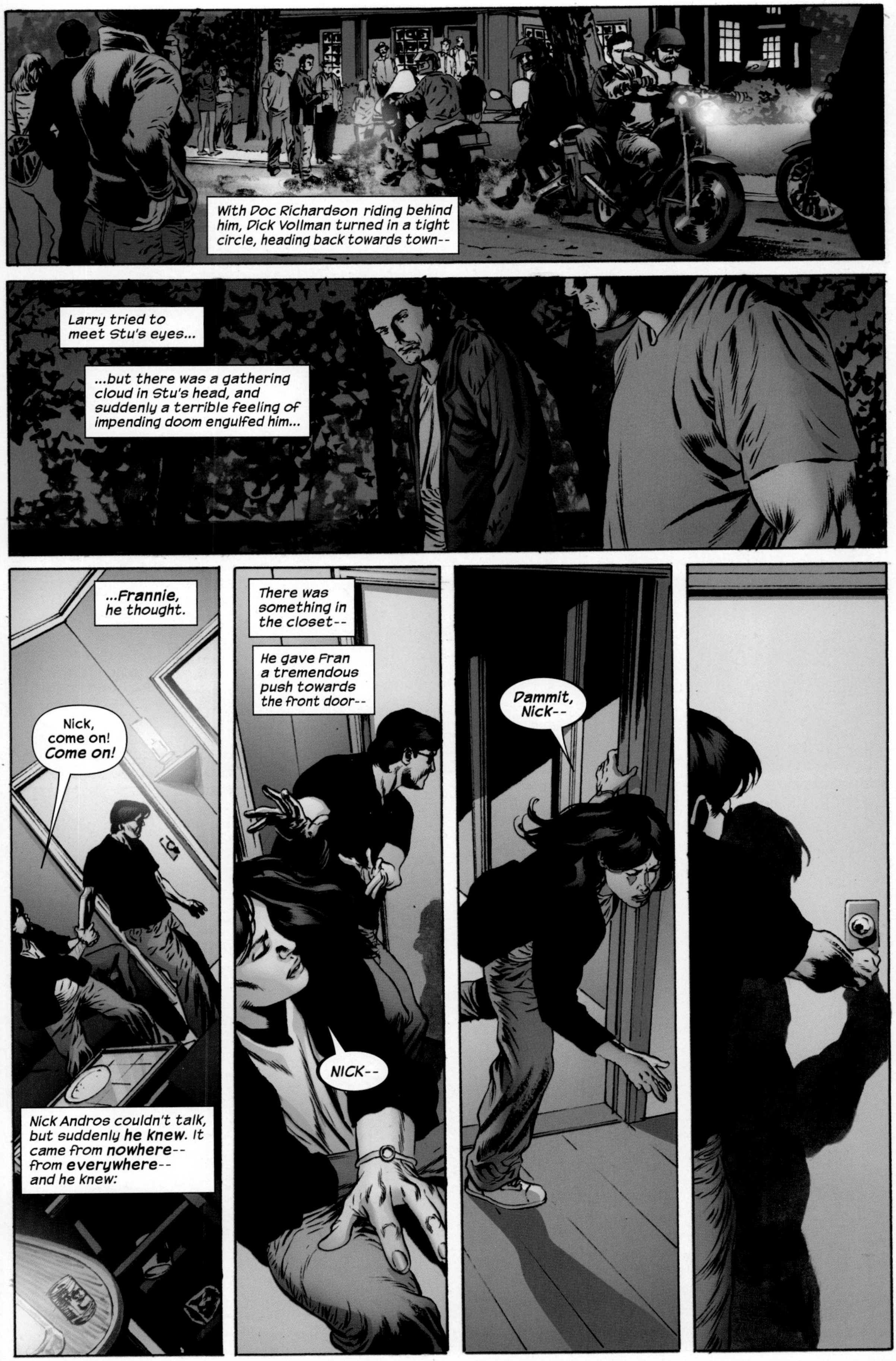
With Doc Richardson riding behind him, Dick Vollman turned in a tight circle, heading back towards town--
Larry tried to meet Stu's eyes...
...but there was a gathering cloud in Stu's head, and suddenly a terrible feeling of impending doom engulfed him...
...Frannie, he thought.
Nick, come on! Come on!
Nick Andros couldn't talk, but suddenly he knew. It came from nowhere-- from everywhere-- and he knew:
There was something in the closet--
He gave Fran a tremendous push towards the front door--
NICK--
Dammit, Nick--

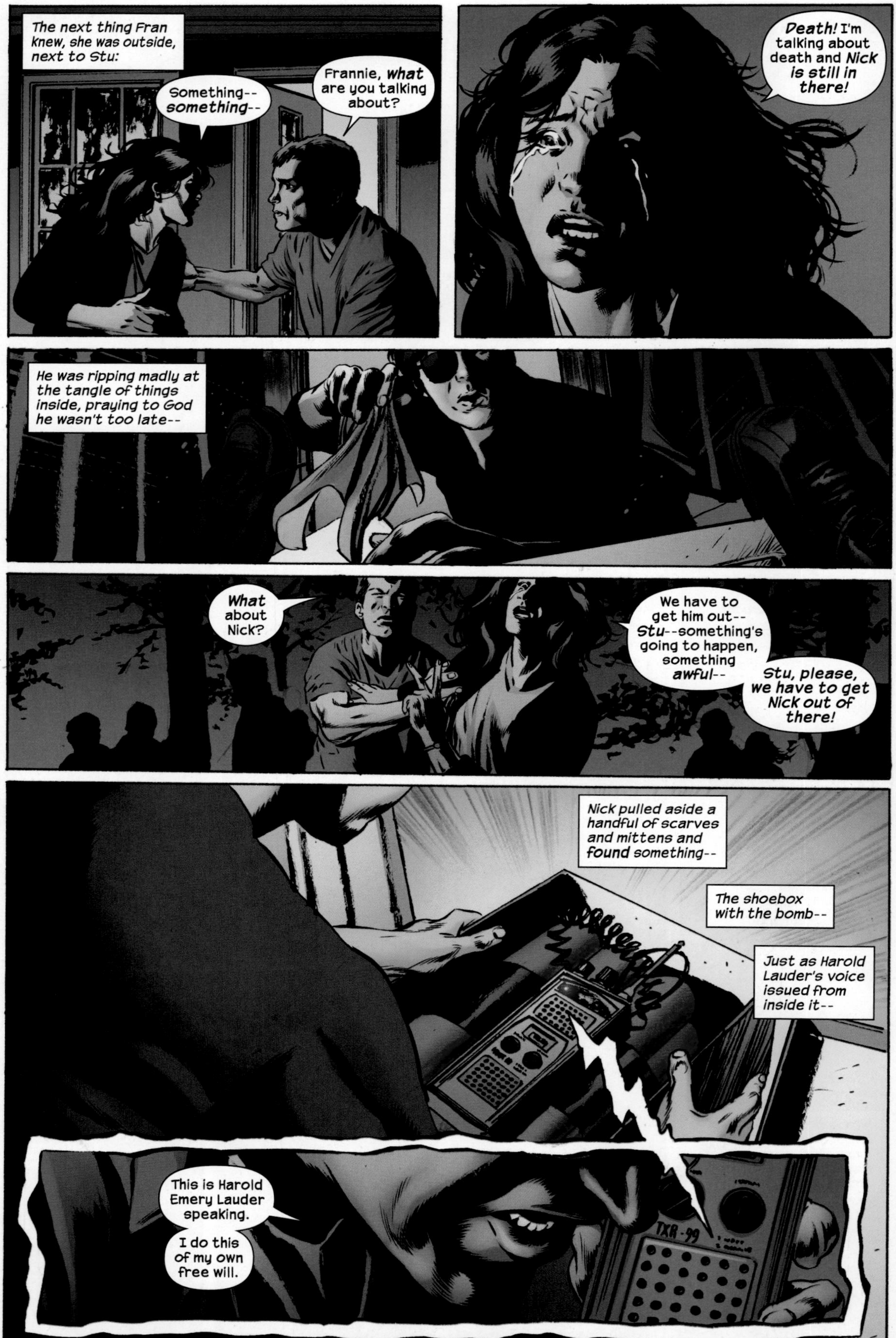

The next thing Fran knew, she was outside, next to Stu:
Something-- something--
Frannie, what are you talking about?
Death! I'm talking about death and Nick is still in there!
He was ripping madly at the tangle of things inside, praying to God he wasn't too late--
What about Nick?
We have to get him out-- Stu--something's going to happen, something awful--
Stu, please, we have to get Nick out of there!
Nick pulled aside a handful of scarves and mittens and found something--
The shoebox with the bomb--
Just as Harold Lauder's voice issued from inside it--
This is Harold Emery Lauder speaking.
I do this of my own free will.
TXR-99

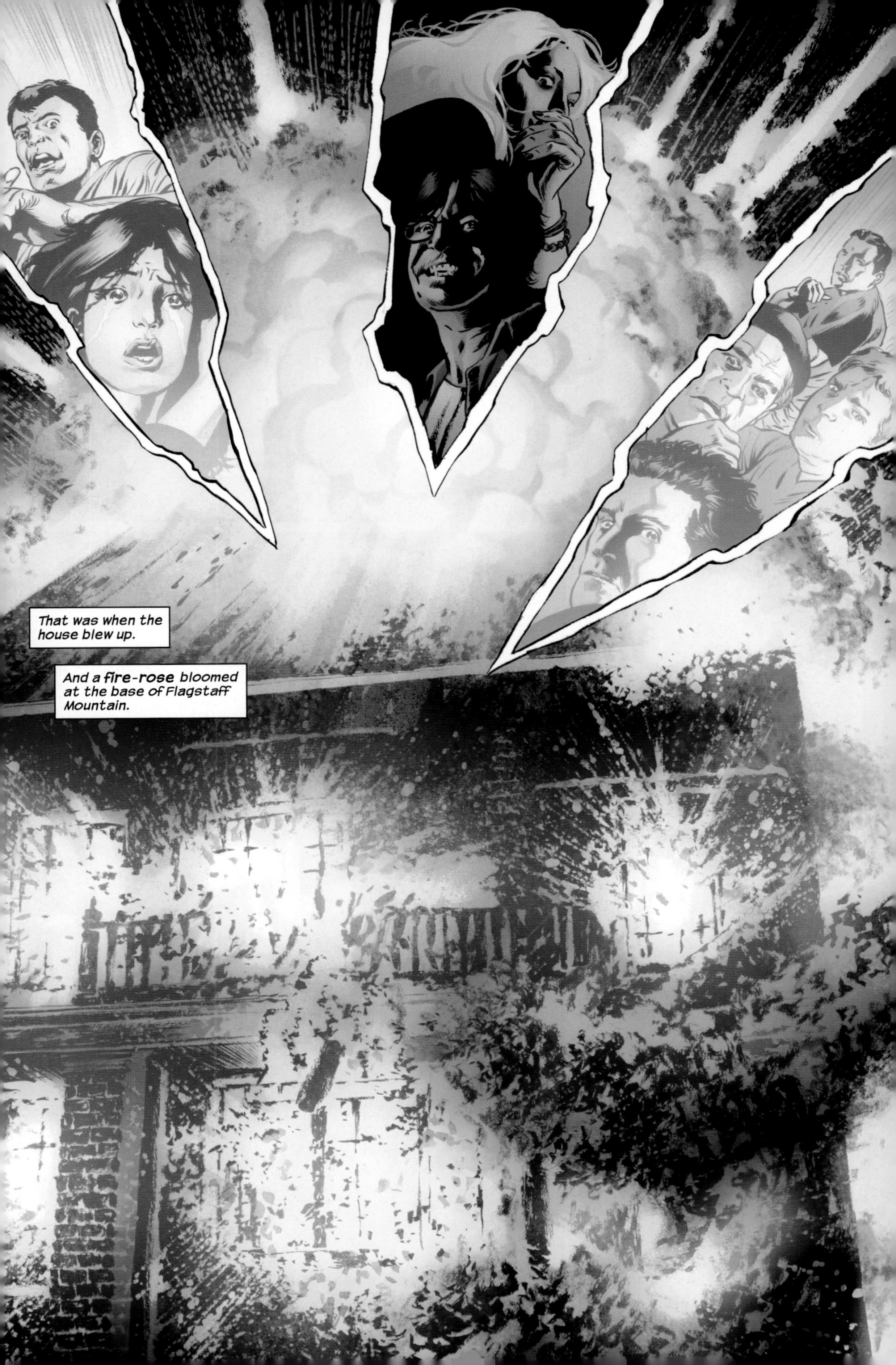
That was when the house blew up.
And a fire-rose bloomed at the base of Flagstaff Mountain.

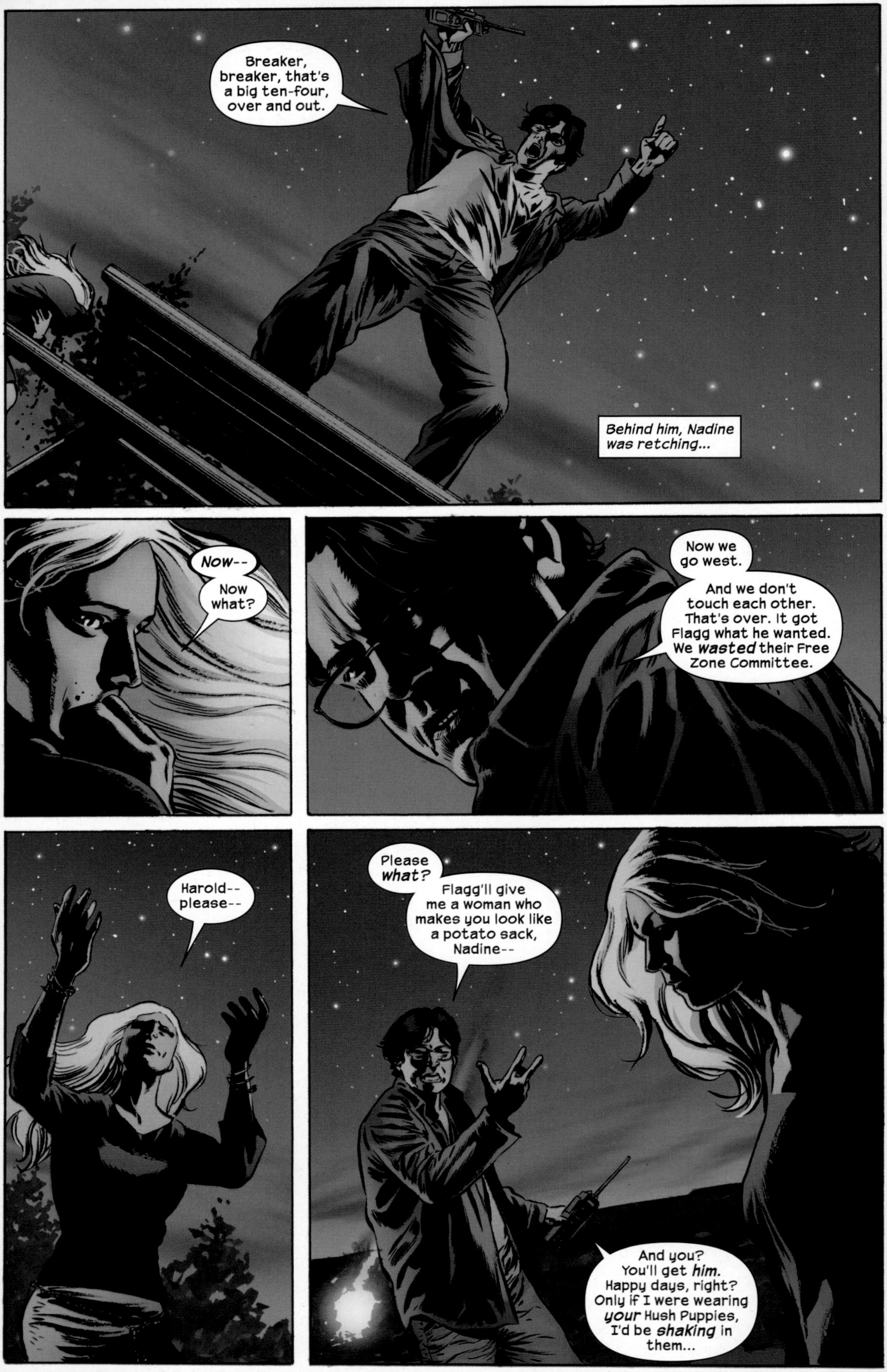

Breaker, breaker, that's a big ten-four, over and out.
Behind him, Nadine was retching...
Now--
Now what?
Now we go west.
And we don't touch each other. That's over. It got Flagg what he wanted. We wasted their Free Zone Committee.
Harold-- please--
Please what?
Flagg'll give me a woman who makes you look like a potato sack, Nadine--
And you? You'll get him. Happy days, right? Only if I were wearing your Hush Puppies, I'd be shaking in them...

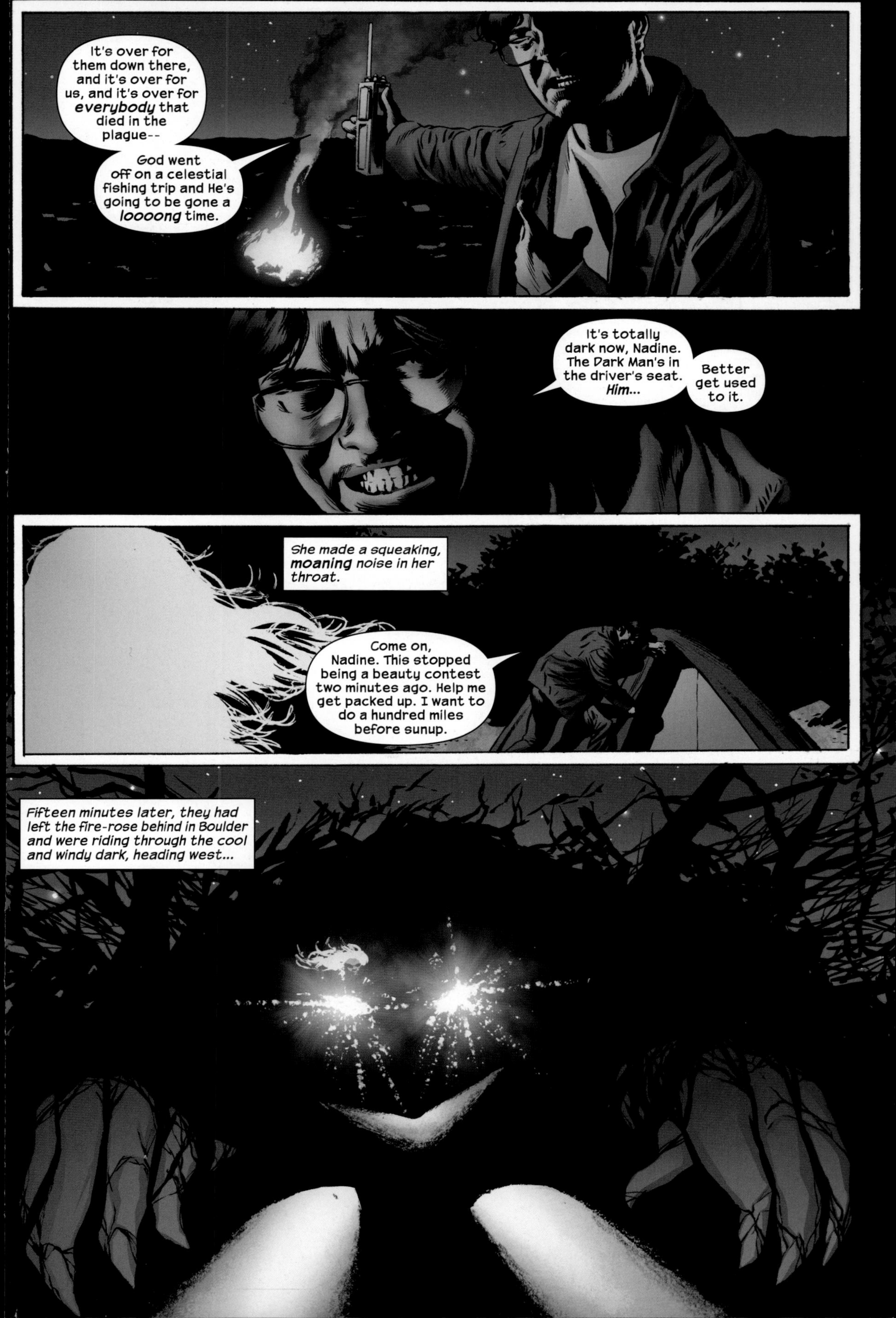
It's over for them down there, and it's over for us, and it's over for *everybody* that died in the plague--
God went off on a celestial fishing trip and He's going to be gone a *loooong* time.
It's totally dark now, Nadine. The Dark Man's in the driver's seat. *Him*...
Better get used to it.
She made a squeaking, ***moaning*** *noise in her throat.*
Come on, Nadine. This stopped being a beauty contest two minutes ago. Help me get packed up. I want to do a hundred miles before sunup.
Fifteen minutes later, they had left the fire-rose behind in Boulder and were riding through the cool and windy dark, heading west...

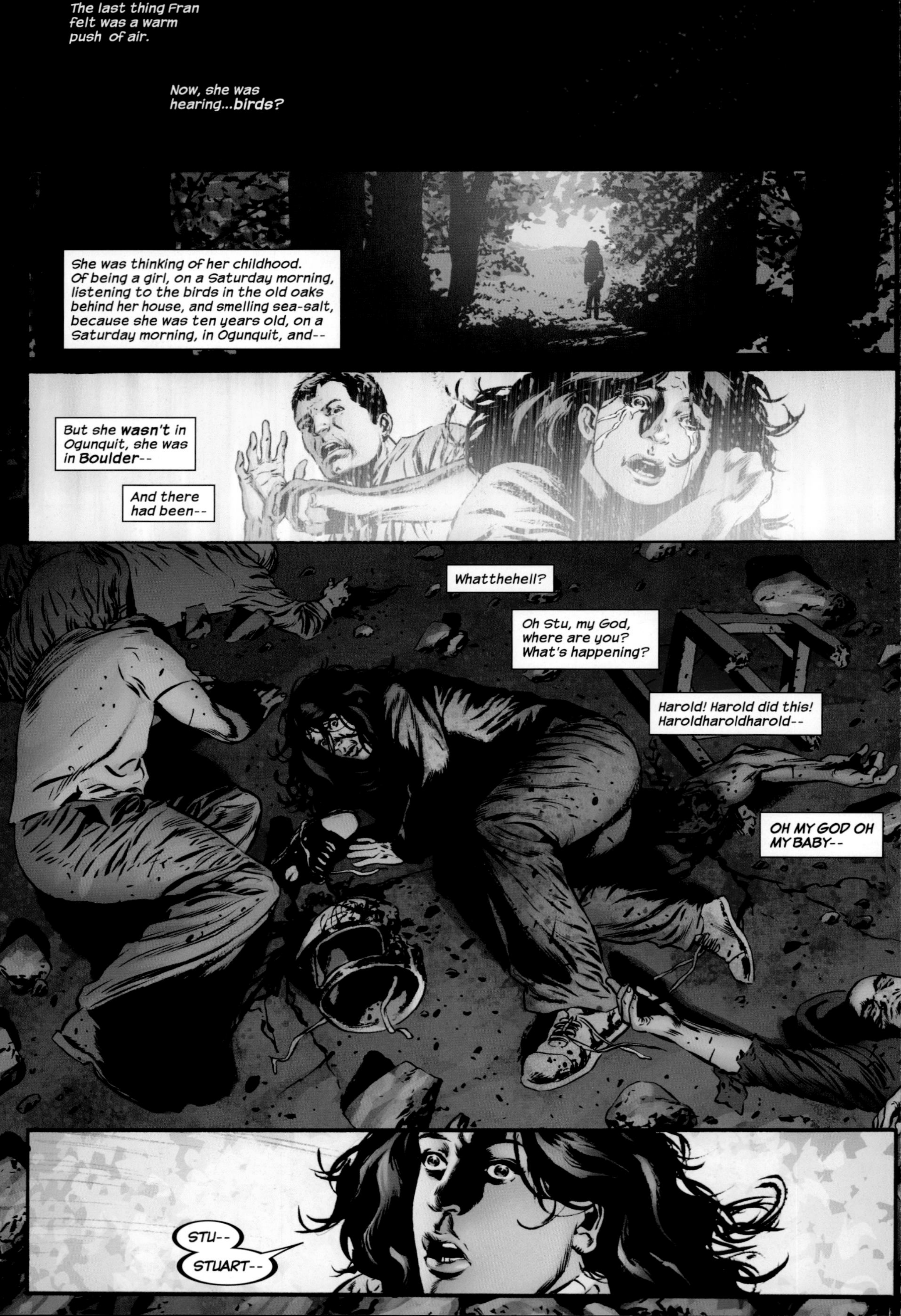
The last thing Fran felt was a warm push of air.
Now, she was hearing...birds?
She was thinking of her childhood. Of being a girl, on a Saturday morning, listening to the birds in the old oaks behind her house, and smelling sea-salt, because she was ten years old, on a Saturday morning, in Ogunquit, and--
But she wasn't in Ogunquit, she was in Boulder--
And there had been--
Whatthehell?
Oh Stu, my God, where are you? What's happening?
Harold! Harold did this! Haroldharoldharold--
OH MY GOD OH MY BABY--
STU--
STUART--

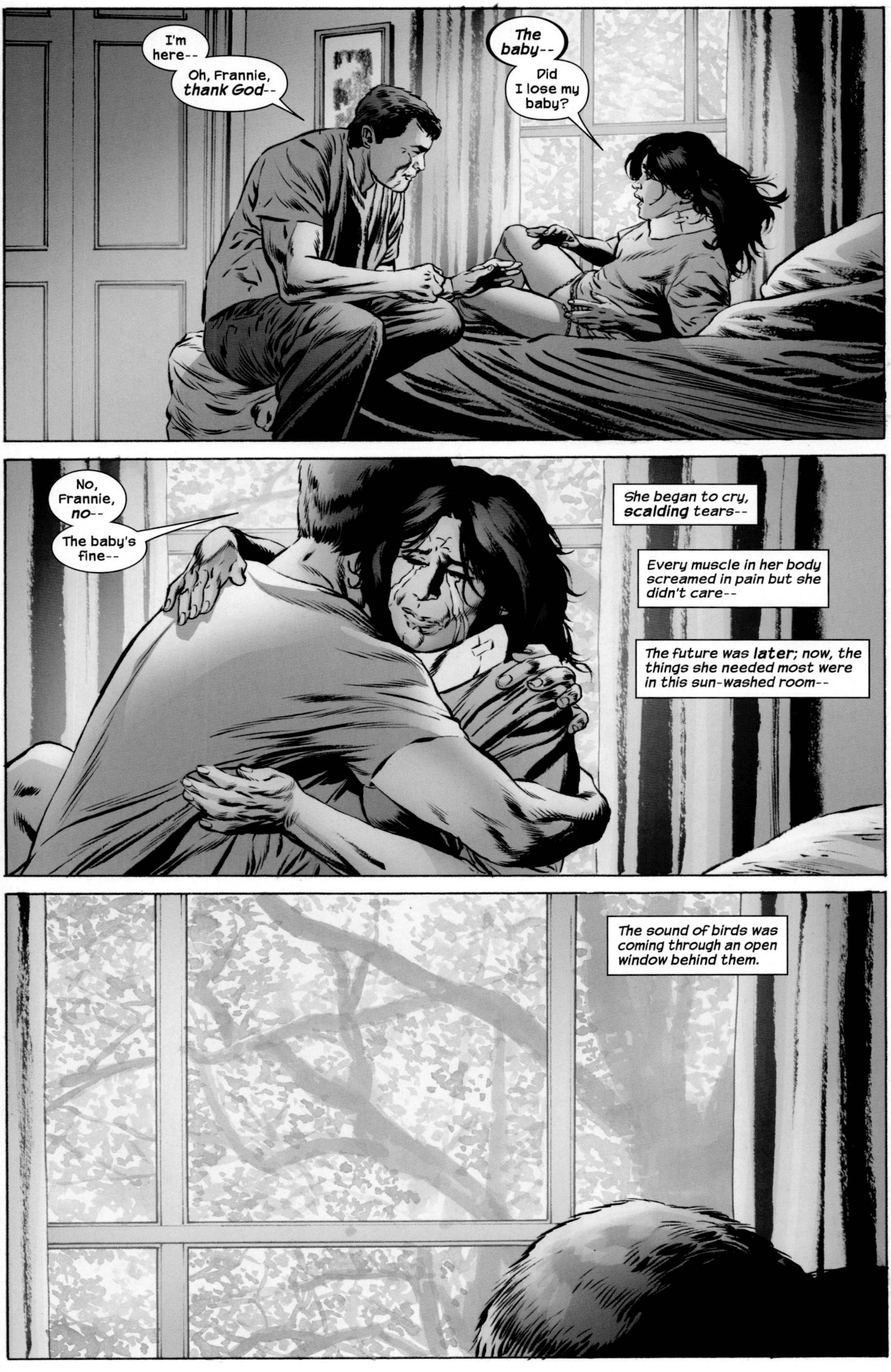
I'm here--
Oh, Frannie, thank God--
The baby--
Did I lose my baby?
No, Frannie, no--
The baby's fine--
She began to cry, scalding tears--
Every muscle in her body screamed in pain but she didn't care--
The future was later; now, the things she needed most were in this sun-washed room--
The sound of birds was coming through an open window behind them.

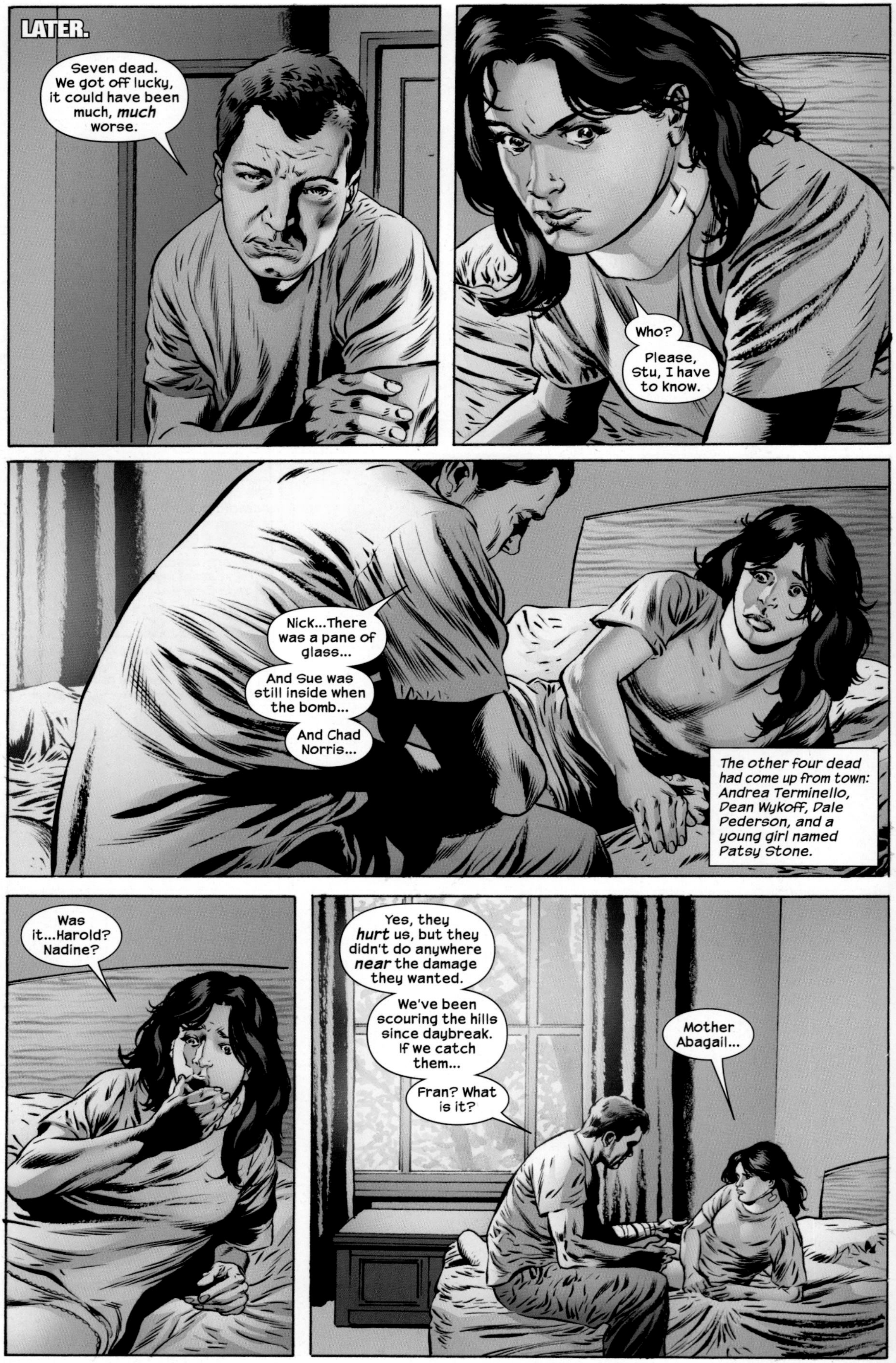
LATER.
Seven dead. We got off lucky, it could have been much, *much* worse.
Who?
Please, Stu, I have to know.
Nick...There was a pane of glass...
And Sue was still inside when the bomb...
And Chad Norris...
The other four dead had come up from town: Andrea Terminello, Dean Wykoff, Dale Pederson, and a young girl named Patsy Stone.
Was it...Harold? Nadine?
Yes, they *hurt* us, but they didn't do anywhere *near* the damage they wanted.
We've been scouring the hills since daybreak. If we catch them...
Fran? What is it?
Mother Abagail...

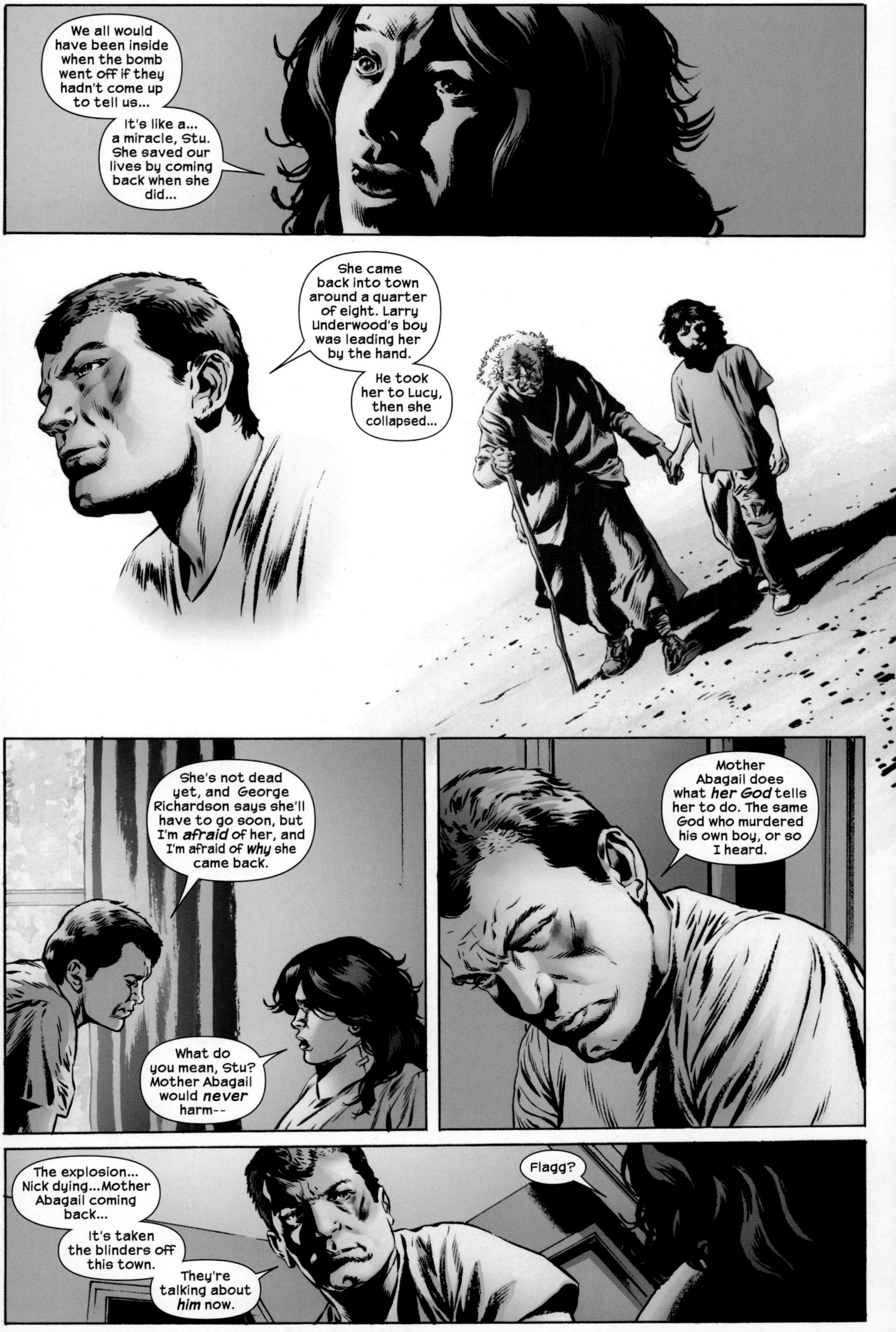
We all would have been inside when the bomb went off if they hadn't come up to tell us...
It's like a... a miracle, Stu. She saved our lives by coming back when she did...
She came back into town around a quarter of eight. Larry Underwood's boy was leading her by the hand.
He took her to Lucy, then she collapsed...
She's not dead yet, and George Richardson says she'll have to go soon, but I'm *afraid* of her, and I'm afraid of *why* she came back.
What do you mean, Stu? Mother Abagail would *never* harm--
Mother Abagail does what *her God* tells her to do. The same God who murdered his own boy, or so I heard.
The explosion... Nick dying...Mother Abagail coming back...
It's taken the blinders off this town.
They're talking about *him* now.
Flagg?

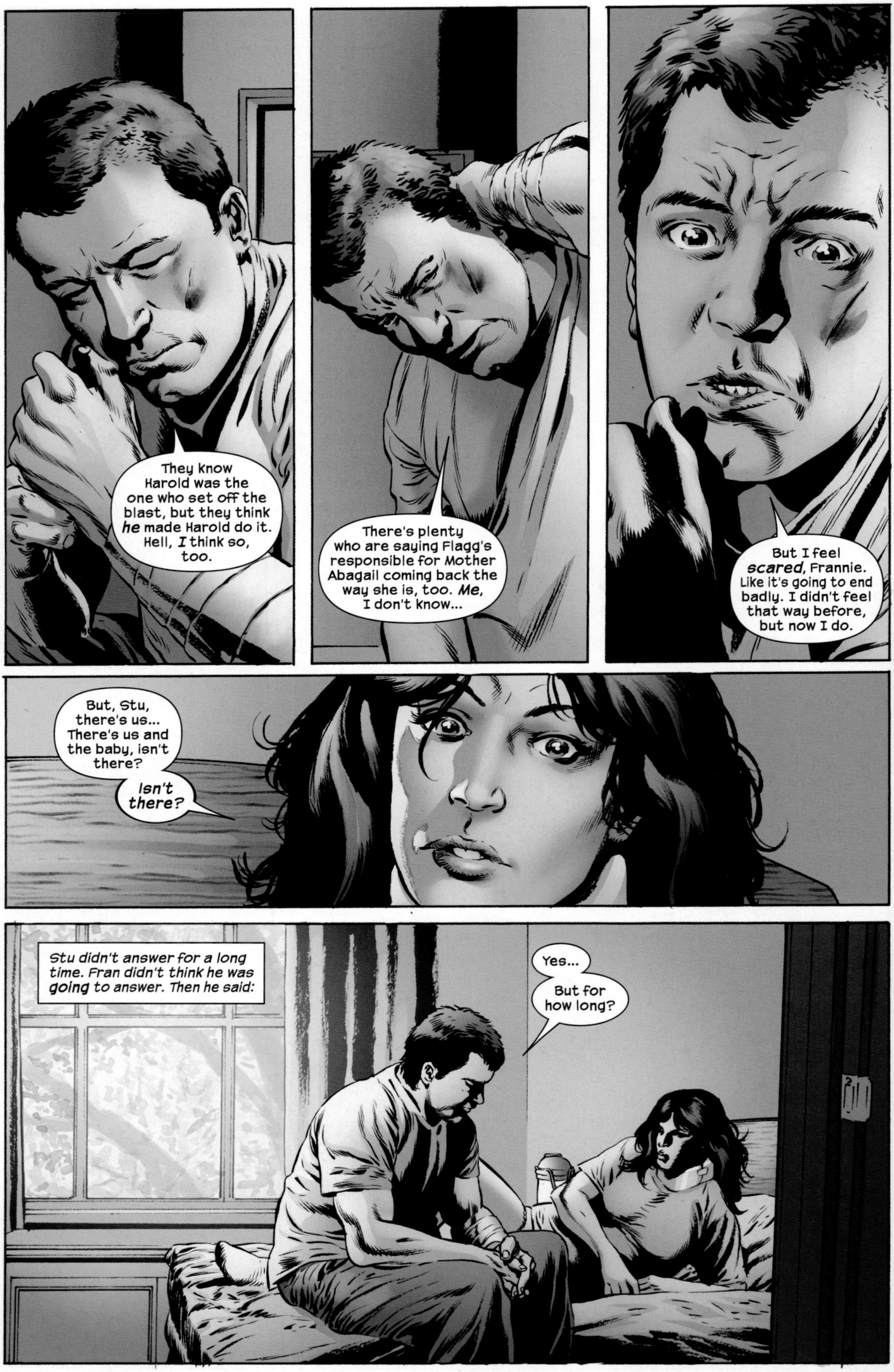

They know Harold was the one who set off the blast, but they think *he* made Harold do it. Hell, *I* think so, too.
There's plenty who are saying Flagg's responsible for Mother Abagail coming back the way she is, too. *Me*, I don't know...
But I feel *scared*, Frannie. Like it's going to end badly. I didn't feel that way before, but now I do.
But, Stu, there's us... There's us and the baby, isn't there?
Isn't there?
*Stu didn't answer for a long time. Fran didn't think he was **going** to answer. Then he said:*
Yes...
But for how long?

chapter FIVE

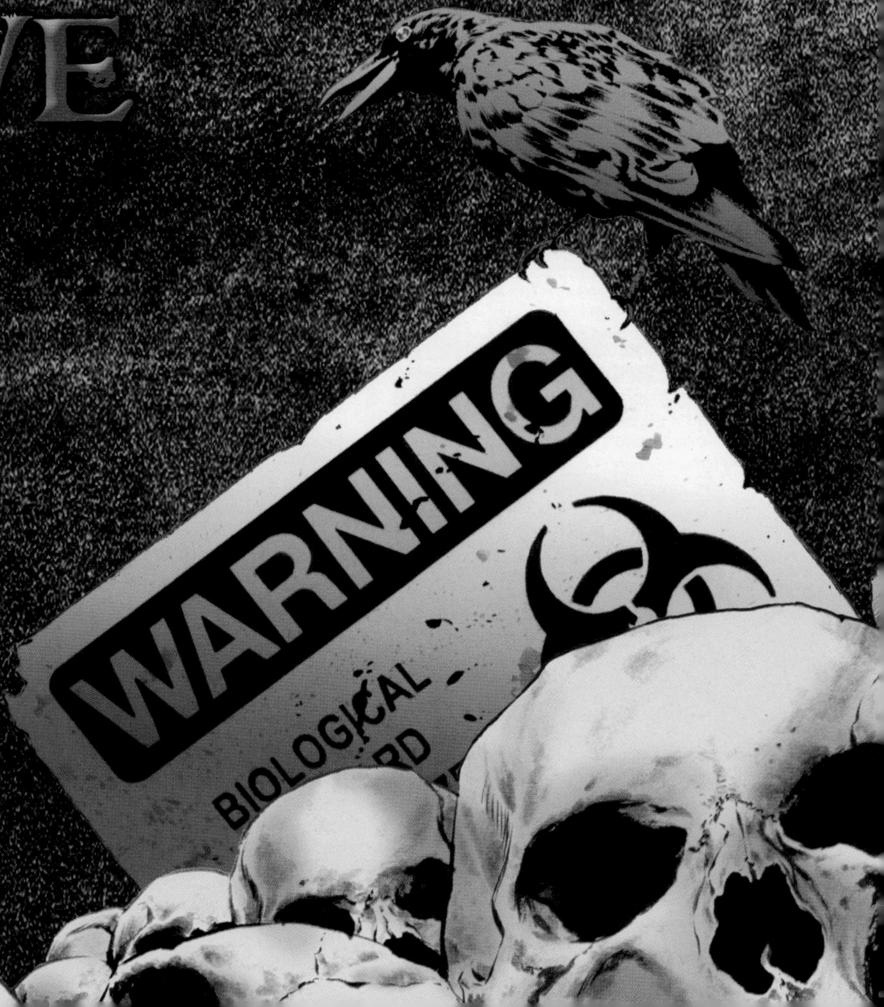
WARNING
BIOLOGICAL

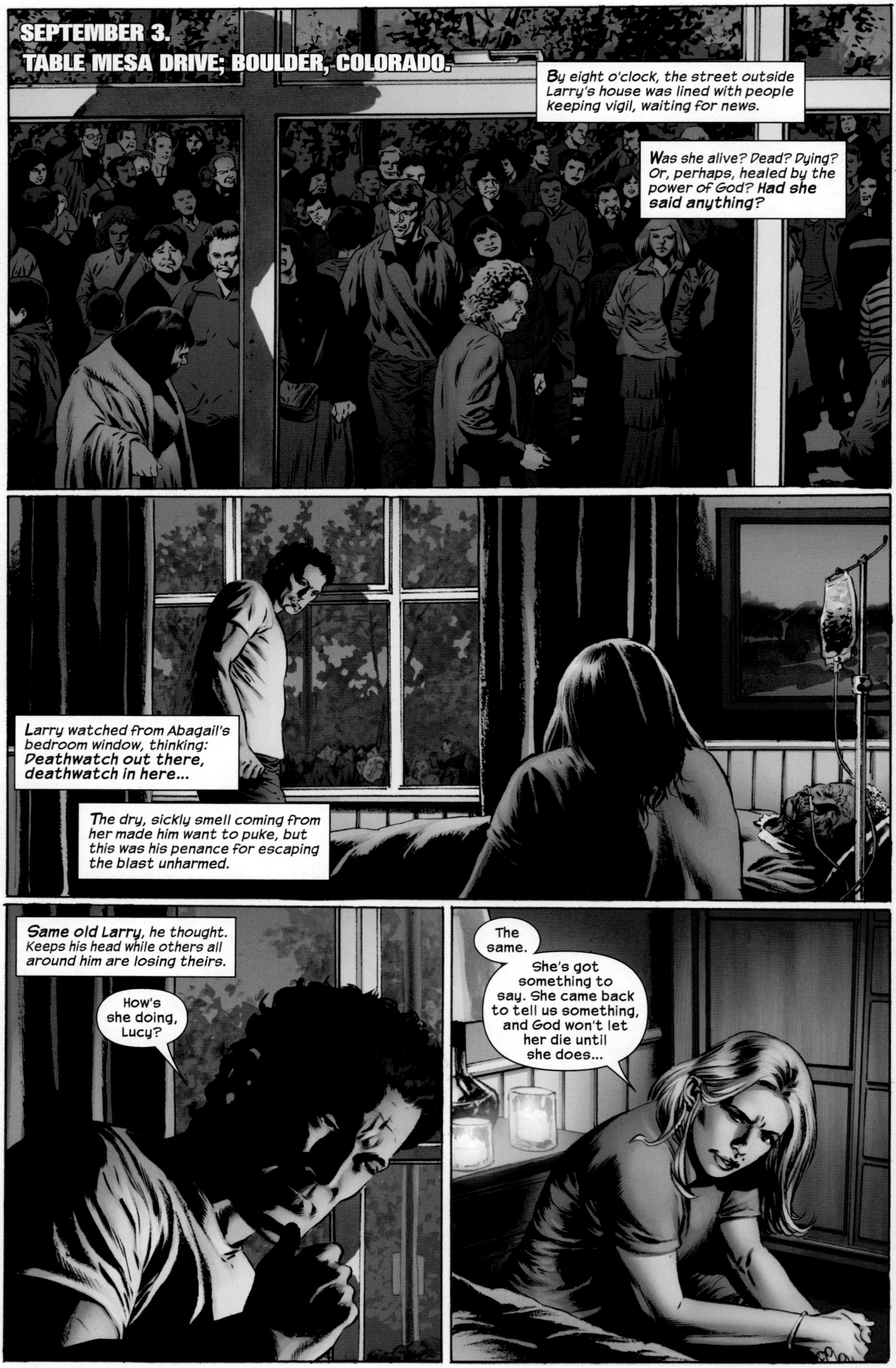
SEPTEMBER 3.
TABLE MESA DRIVE; BOULDER, COLORADO.
By eight o'clock, the street outside Larry's house was lined with people keeping vigil, waiting for news.
Was she alive? Dead? Dying? Or, perhaps, healed by the power of God? Had she said anything?
Larry watched from Abagail's bedroom window, thinking: Deathwatch out there, deathwatch in here...
The dry, sickly smell coming from her made him want to puke, but this was his penance for escaping the blast unharmed.
Same old Larry, he thought. Keeps his head while others all around him are losing theirs.
How's she doing, Lucy?
The same.
She's got something to say. She came back to tell us something, and God won't let her die until she does...

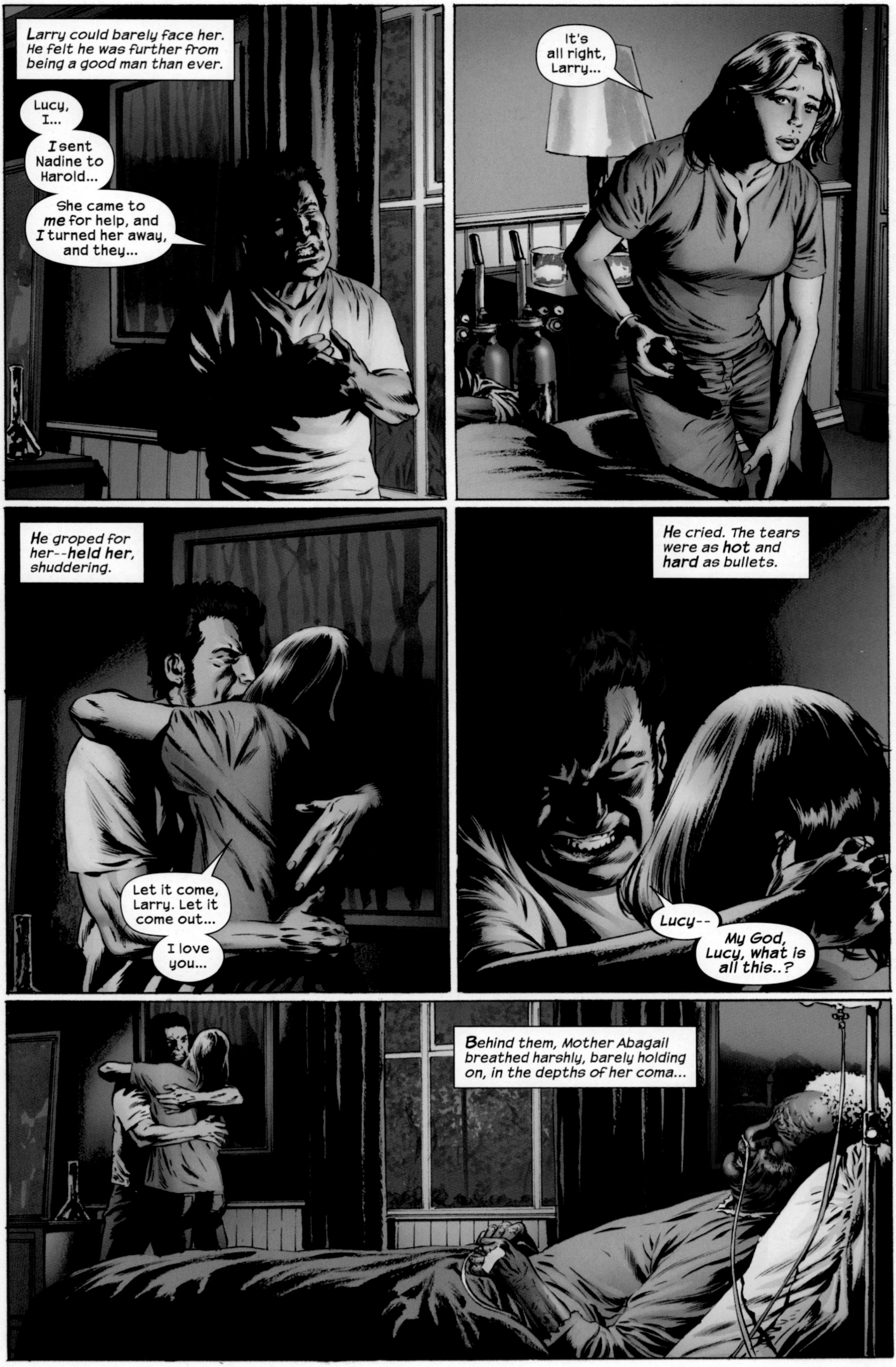
Larry could barely face her. He felt he was further from being a good man than ever.
Lucy, I...
I sent Nadine to Harold...
She came to me for help, and I turned her away, and they...
It's all right, Larry...
He groped for her--held her, shuddering.
Let it come, Larry. Let it come out...
I love you...
He cried. The tears were as hot and hard as bullets.
Lucy--
My God, Lucy, what is all this..?
Behind them, Mother Abagail breathed harshly, barely holding on, in the depths of her coma...

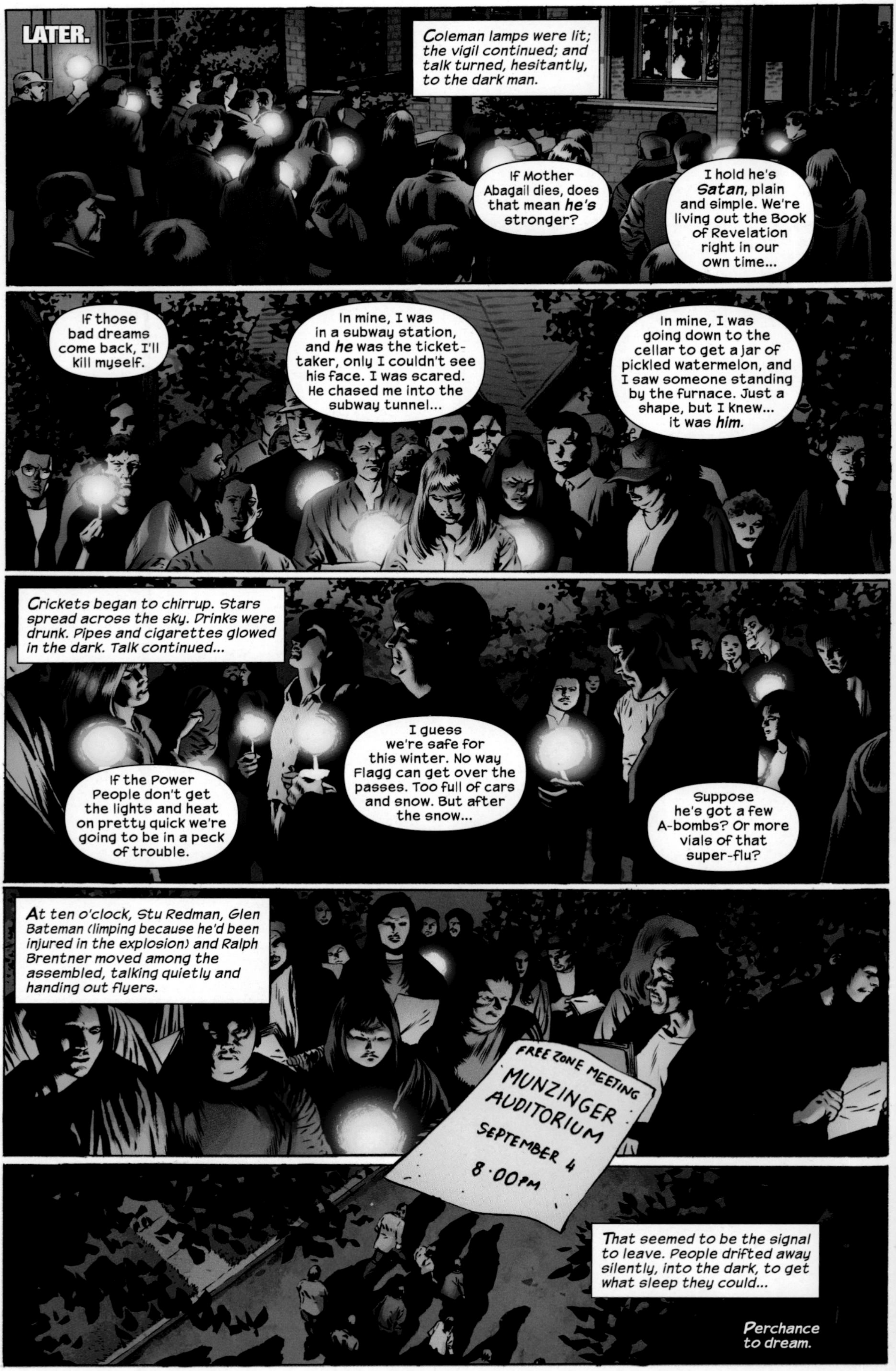
LATER.
Coleman lamps were lit; the vigil continued; and talk turned, hesitantly, to the dark man.
If Mother Abagail dies, does that mean he's stronger?
I hold he's Satan, plain and simple. We're living out the Book of Revelation right in our own time...
If those bad dreams come back, I'll kill myself.
In mine, I was in a subway station, and he was the ticket-taker, only I couldn't see his face. I was scared. He chased me into the subway tunnel...
In mine, I was going down to the cellar to get a jar of pickled watermelon, and I saw someone standing by the furnace. Just a shape, but I knew... it was him.
Crickets began to chirrup. Stars spread across the sky. Drinks were drunk. Pipes and cigarettes glowed in the dark. Talk continued...
If the Power People don't get the lights and heat on pretty quick we're going to be in a peck of trouble.
I guess we're safe for this winter. No way Flagg can get over the passes. Too full of cars and snow. But after the snow...
Suppose he's got a few A-bombs? Or more vials of that super-flu?
At ten o'clock, Stu Redman, Glen Bateman (limping because he'd been injured in the explosion) and Ralph Brentner moved among the assembled, talking quietly and handing out flyers.
FREE ZONE MEETING
MUNZINGER AUDITORIUM
SEPTEMBER 4
8:00PM
That seemed to be the signal to leave. People drifted away silently, into the dark, to get what sleep they could...
Perchance to dream.

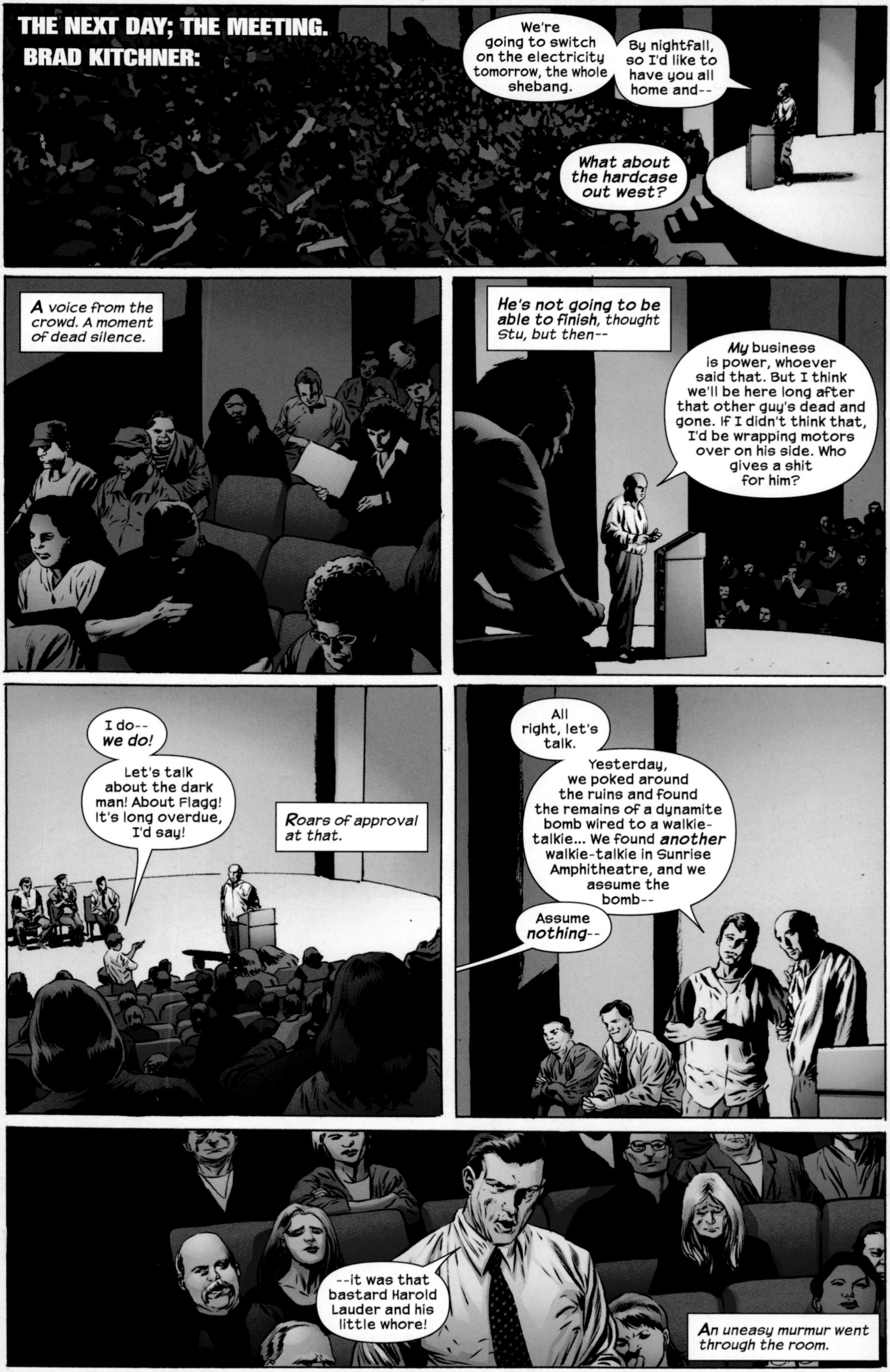
THE NEXT DAY; THE MEETING.
BRAD KITCHNER:
We're going to switch on the electricity tomorrow, the whole shebang.
By nightfall, so I'd like to have you all home and--
What about the hardcase out west?
A voice from the crowd. A moment of dead silence.
He's not going to be able to finish, thought Stu, but then--
My business is power, whoever said that. But I think we'll be here long after that other guy's dead and gone. If I didn't think that, I'd be wrapping motors over on his side. Who gives a shit for him?
I do-- we do!
Let's talk about the dark man! About Flagg! It's long overdue, I'd say!
Roars of approval at that.
All right, let's talk.
Yesterday, we poked around the ruins and found the remains of a dynamite bomb wired to a walkie-talkie... We found another walkie-talkie in Sunrise Amphitheatre, and we assume the bomb--
Assume nothing--
--it was that bastard Harold Lauder and his little whore!
An uneasy murmur went through the room.

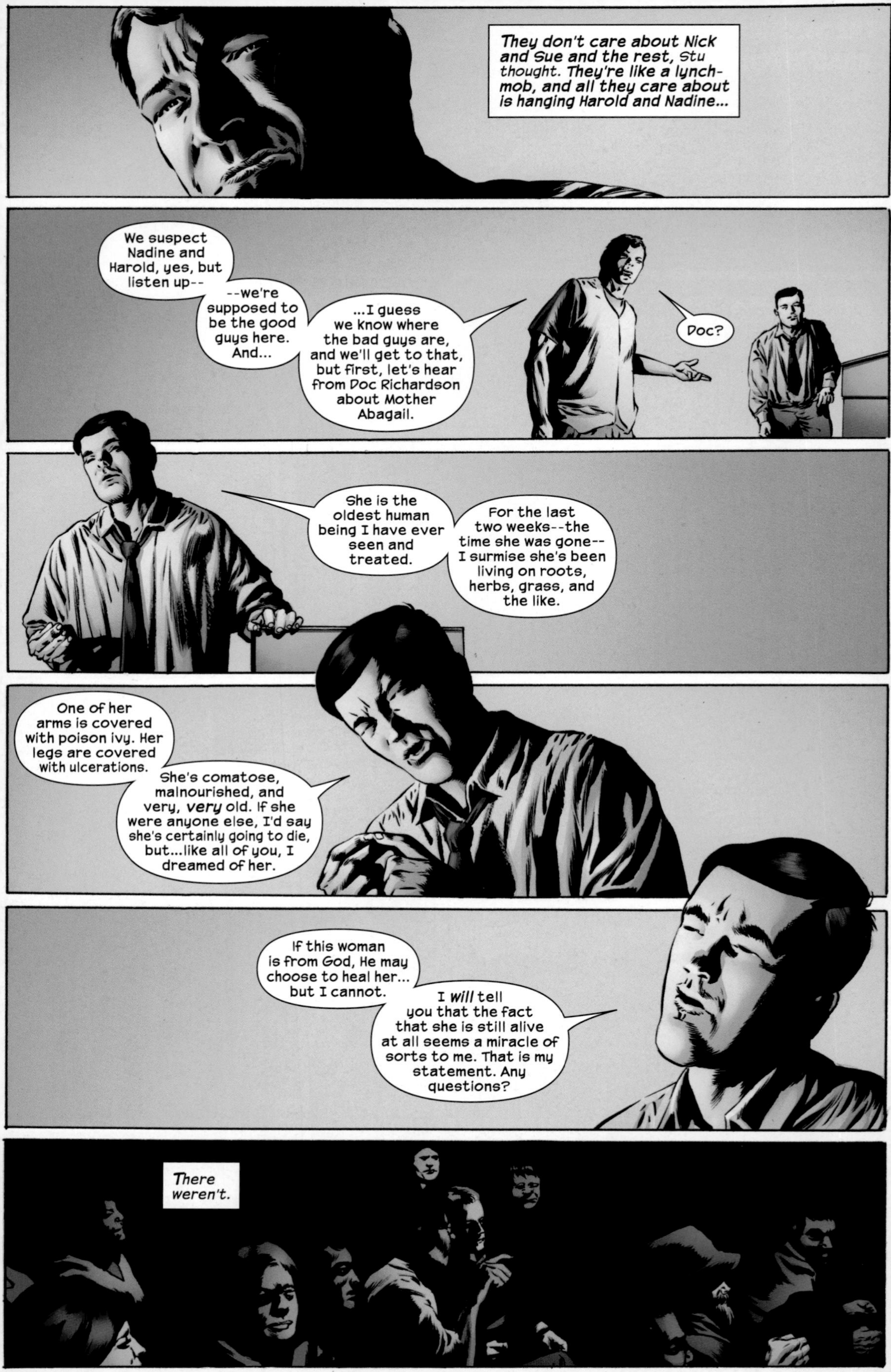
They don't care about Nick and Sue and the rest, Stu thought. They're like a lynch-mob, and all they care about is hanging Harold and Nadine...
We suspect Nadine and Harold, yes, but listen up--
--we're supposed to be the good guys here. And...
...I guess we know where the bad guys are, and we'll get to that, but first, let's hear from Doc Richardson about Mother Abagail.
Doc?
She is the oldest human being I have ever seen and treated.
For the last two weeks--the time she was gone--I surmise she's been living on roots, herbs, grass, and the like.
One of her arms is covered with poison ivy. Her legs are covered with ulcerations.
She's comatose, malnourished, and very, *very* old. If she were anyone else, I'd say she's certainly going to die, but...like all of you, I dreamed of her.
If this woman is from God, He may choose to heal her... but I cannot.
I *will* tell you that the fact that she is still alive at all seems a miracle of sorts to me. That is my statement. Any questions?
There weren't.

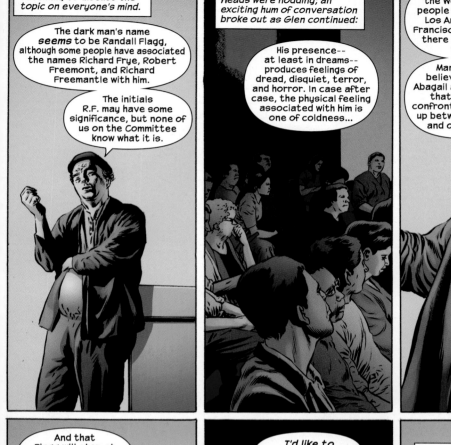

Next, Stu introduced Glen Bateman, to discuss the topic on everyone's mind.

The dark man's name *seems* to be Randall Flagg, although some people have associated the names Richard Frye, Robert Freemont, and Richard Freemantle with him.

The initials R.F. may have some significance, but none of us on the Committee know what it is.

Heads were nodding; an exciting hum of conversation broke out as Glen continued:

His presence-- at least in dreams-- produces feelings of dread, disquiet, terror, and horror. In case after case, the physical feeling associated with him is one of coldness...

This Flagg is in the West, crucifying people in Las Vegas, or Los Angeles, or San Francisco, or Portland-- there are conflicting reports.

Many people believe--Mother Abagail among them-- that there is a confrontation shaping up between this man and ourselves...

And that Flagg will stop at nothing to bring us down. Including nuclear weapons and, perhaps...plague.

I'd like to catch hold of that dirty bastard!

I'd give him a dose of the everloving plague!

Glen grinned at the tension-relieving laughter that burst from the crowd. He'd given Rich Moffat his cue line a half-hour before the meeting started and Rich delivered it beautifully.

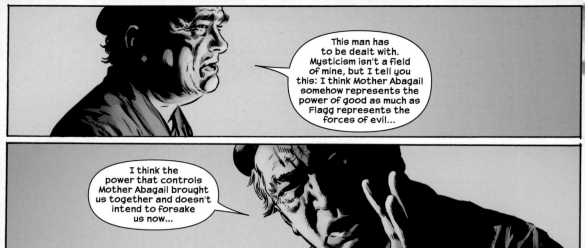

This man has to be dealt with. Mysticism isn't a field of mine, but I tell you this: I think Mother Abagail somehow represents the power of good as much as Flagg represents the forces of evil...

I think the power that controls Mother Abagail brought us together and doesn't intend to forsake us now...

Maybe we need to talk it over and let some air into our nightmares...

Maybe we need to begin by deciding what we're going to do about him...

But he won't just walk into the Zone next spring and take over, not if you people are standing watch...

Glen's last sentence was lost in a crash of applause.

The assembled were more mad than scared, and ready (it seemed) for a challenge...

Also...they were ready to talk.

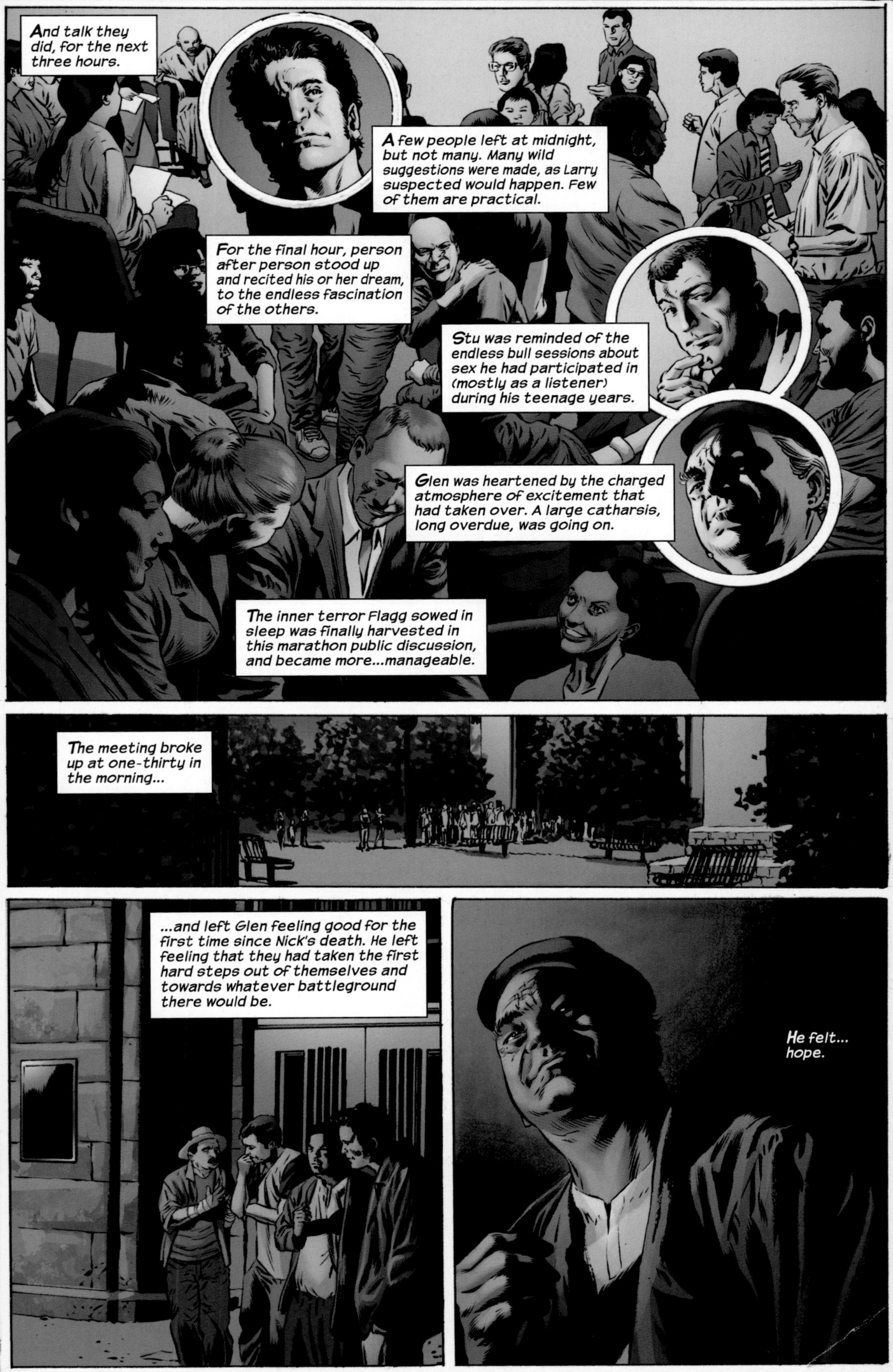
And talk they did, for the next three hours.
A few people left at midnight, but not many. Many wild suggestions were made, as Larry suspected would happen. Few of them are practical.
For the final hour, person after person stood up and recited his or her dream, to the endless fascination of the others.
Stu was reminded of the endless bull sessions about sex he had participated in (mostly as a listener) during his teenage years.
Glen was heartened by the charged atmosphere of excitement that had taken over. A large catharsis, long overdue, was going on.
The inner terror Flagg sowed in sleep was finally harvested in this marathon public discussion, and became more...manageable.
The meeting broke up at one-thirty in the morning...
...and left Glen feeling good for the first time since Nick's death. He left feeling that they had taken the first hard steps out of themselves and towards whatever battleground there would be.
He felt... hope.

SEPTEMBER 5.

The power went on, just as Brad had promised.

The air raid siren atop the county courthouse went on with a huge, braying whoop...

There was an electrical fire on Willow Street, readily put out...

A manhole cover exploded into the air at Broadway and Walnut...

WHOOPWHOOPW

Stu was with Frannie when the lights in her room buzzed into life.

He watched them for a full three minutes. When he looked at Fran again, her eyes were shiny with tears.

What's wrong, Frannie? Is it your pain?

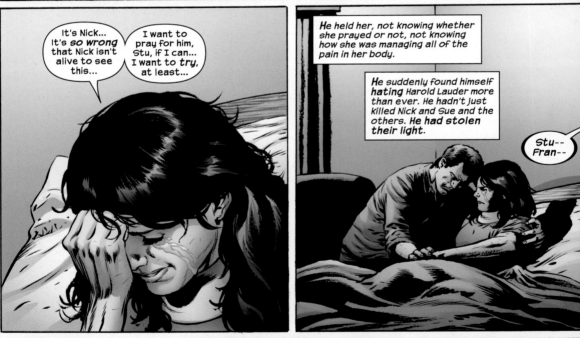

It's Nick... It's *so wrong* that Nick isn't alive to see this...

I want to pray for him, Stu, if I can... I want to *try*, at least...

He held her, not knowing whether she prayed or not, not knowing how she was managing all of the pain in her body.

He suddenly found himself *hating* Harold Lauder more than ever. He hadn't just killed Nick and Sue and the others. He *had* stolen their light.

Stu-- Fran--

It's Mother Abagail. She woke up and wants us. What's left of the committee.

She knew Nick and Sue were dead... *Somehow,* she knew...

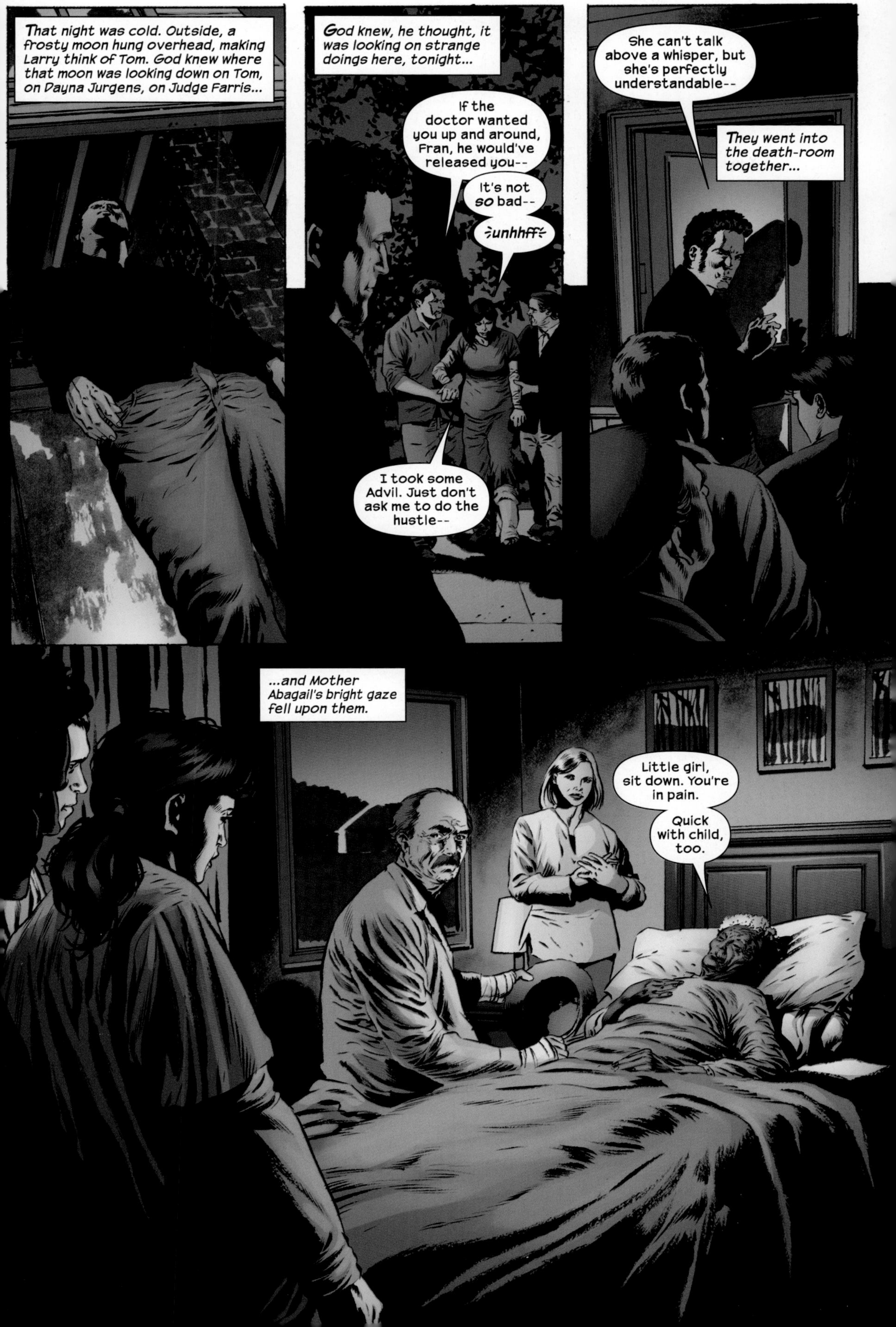
That night was cold. Outside, a frosty moon hung overhead, making Larry think of Tom. God knew where that moon was looking down on Tom, on Dayna Jurgens, on Judge Farris...
God knew, he thought, it was looking on strange doings here, tonight...
If the doctor wanted you up and around, Fran, he would've released you--
It's not so bad--
unhhff
I took some Advil. Just don't ask me to do the hustle--
She can't talk above a whisper, but she's perfectly understandable--
They went into the death-room together...
...and Mother Abagail's bright gaze fell upon them.
Little girl, sit down. You're in pain.
Quick with child, too.

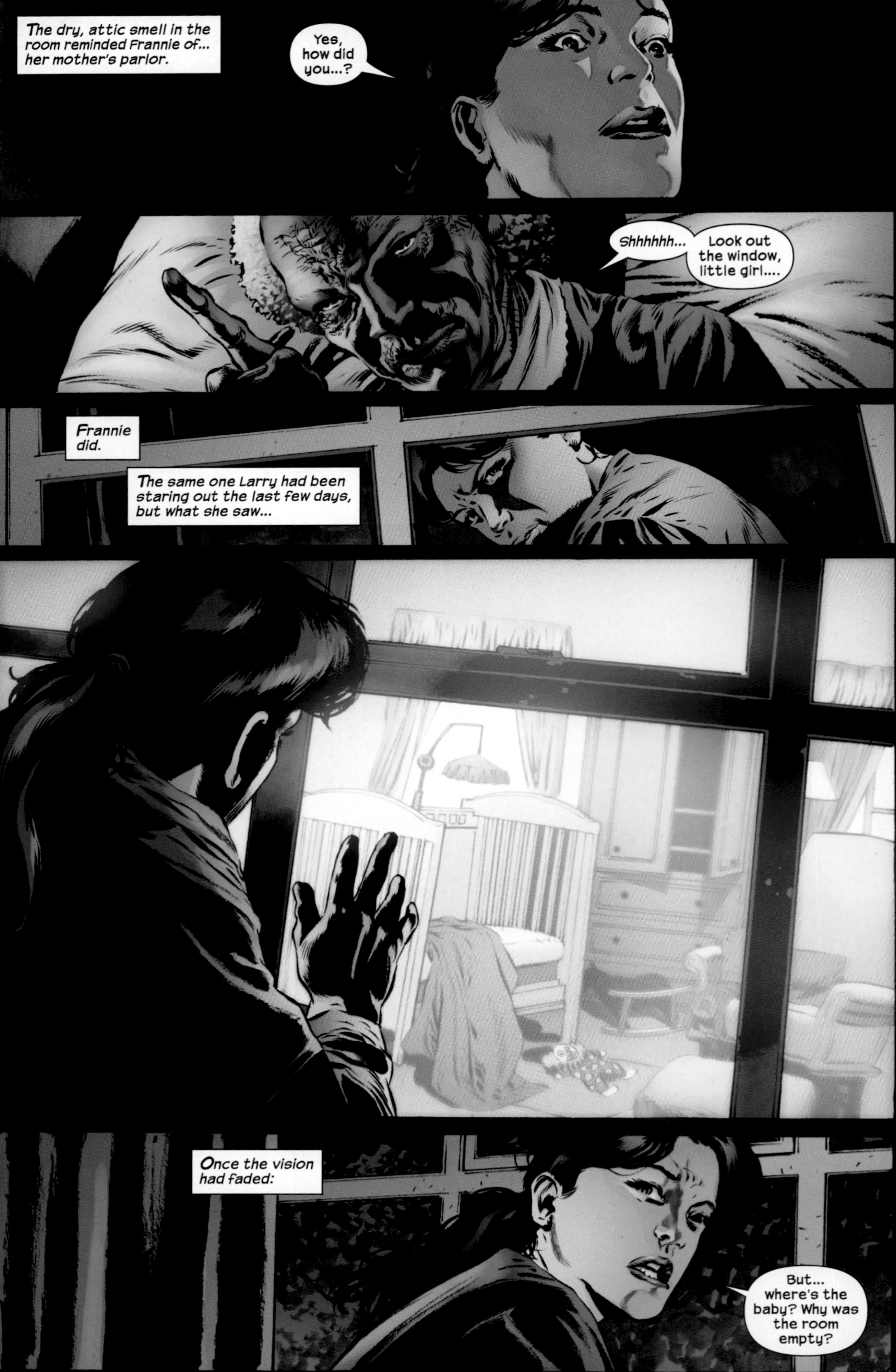
The dry, attic smell in the room reminded Frannie of... her mother's parlor.
Yes, how did you...?
Shhhhhh...
Look out the window, little girl....
Frannie did.
The same one Larry had been staring out the last few days, but what she saw...
Once the vision had faded:
But... where's the baby? Why was the room empty?

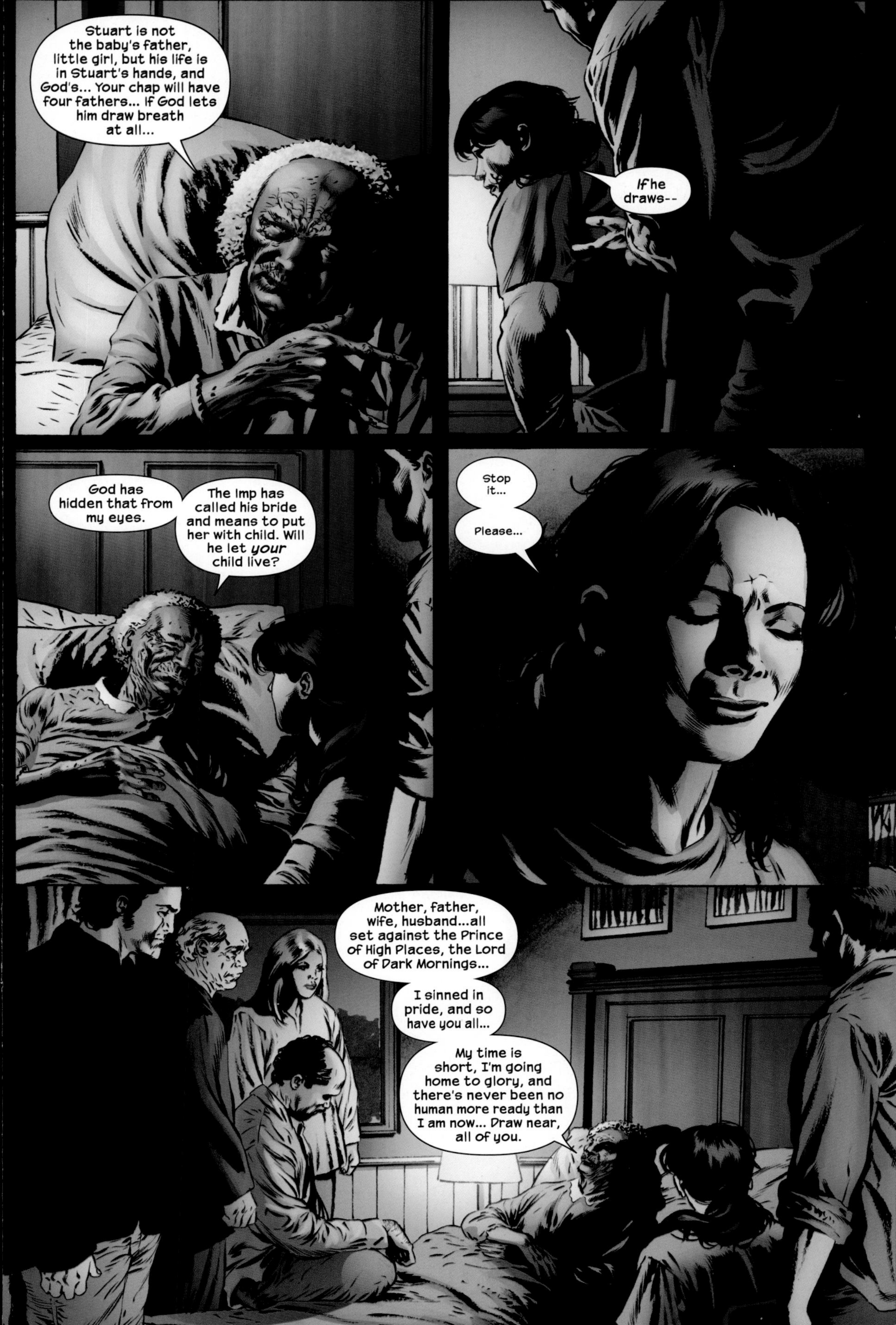
Stuart is not the baby's father, little girl, but his life is in Stuart's hands, and God's... Your chap will have four fathers... If God lets him draw breath at all...
If he draws--
God has hidden that from my eyes.
The Imp has called his bride and means to put her with child. Will he let *your* child live?
Stop it...
Please...
Mother, father, wife, husband...all set against the Prince of High Places, the Lord of Dark Mornings...
I sinned in pride, and so have you all...
My time is short, I'm going home to glory, and there's never been no human more ready than I am now... Draw near, all of you.

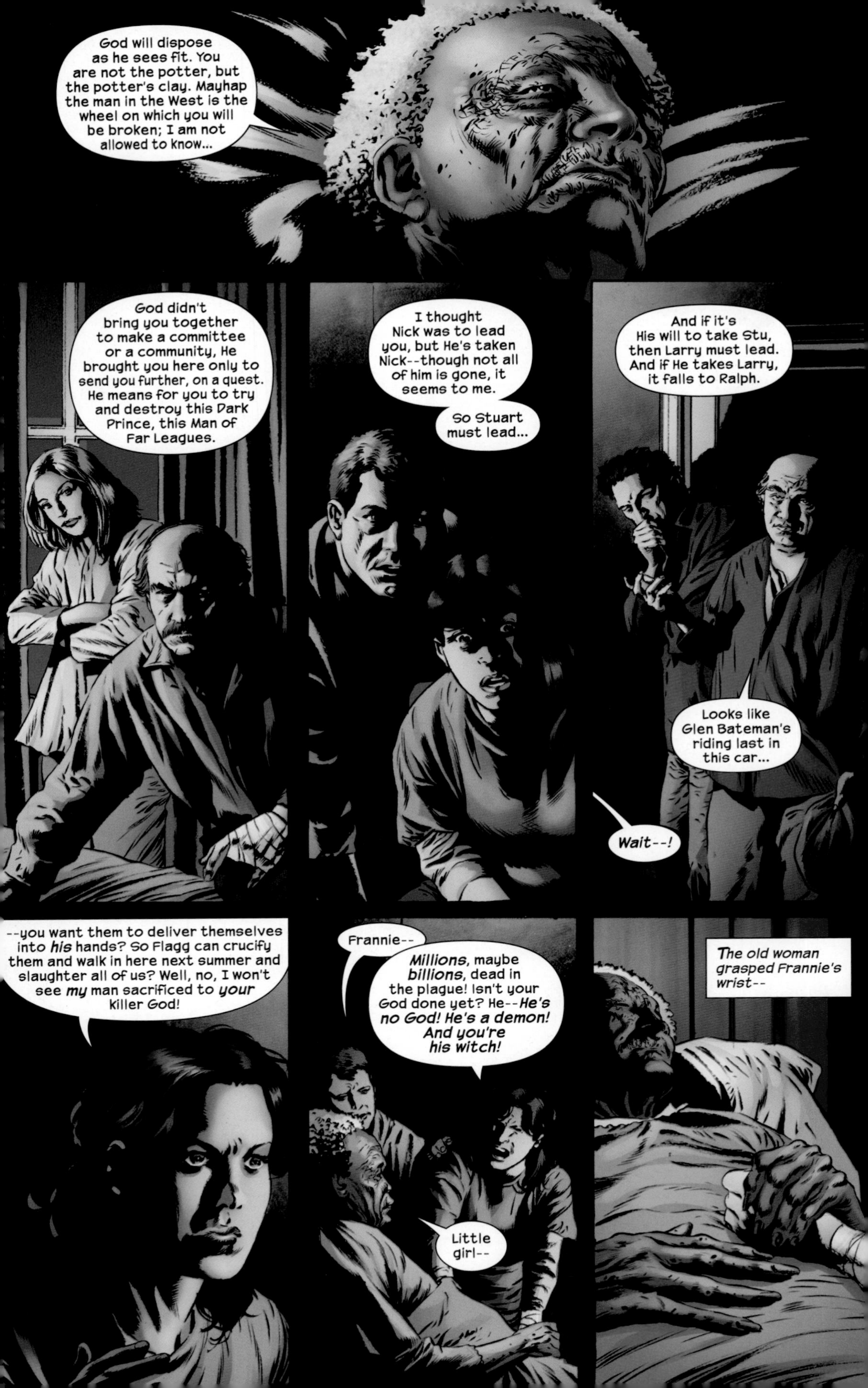
God will dispose as he sees fit. You are not the potter, but the potter's clay. Mayhap the man in the West is the wheel on which you will be broken; I am not allowed to know...
God didn't bring you together to make a committee or a community, He brought you here only to send you further, on a quest. He means for you to try and destroy this Dark Prince, this Man of Far Leagues.
I thought Nick was to lead you, but He's taken Nick--though not all of him is gone, it seems to me.
So Stuart must lead...
And if it's His will to take Stu, then Larry must lead. And if He takes Larry, it falls to Ralph.
Looks like Glen Bateman's riding last in this car...
Wait--!
--you want them to deliver themselves into *his* hands? So Flagg can crucify them and walk in here next summer and slaughter all of us? Well, no, I won't see *my* man sacrificed to *your* killer God!
Frannie--
Millions, maybe *billions*, dead in the plague! Isn't your God done yet? He--*He's no God! He's a demon! And you're his witch!*
Little girl--
The old woman grasped Frannie's wrist--

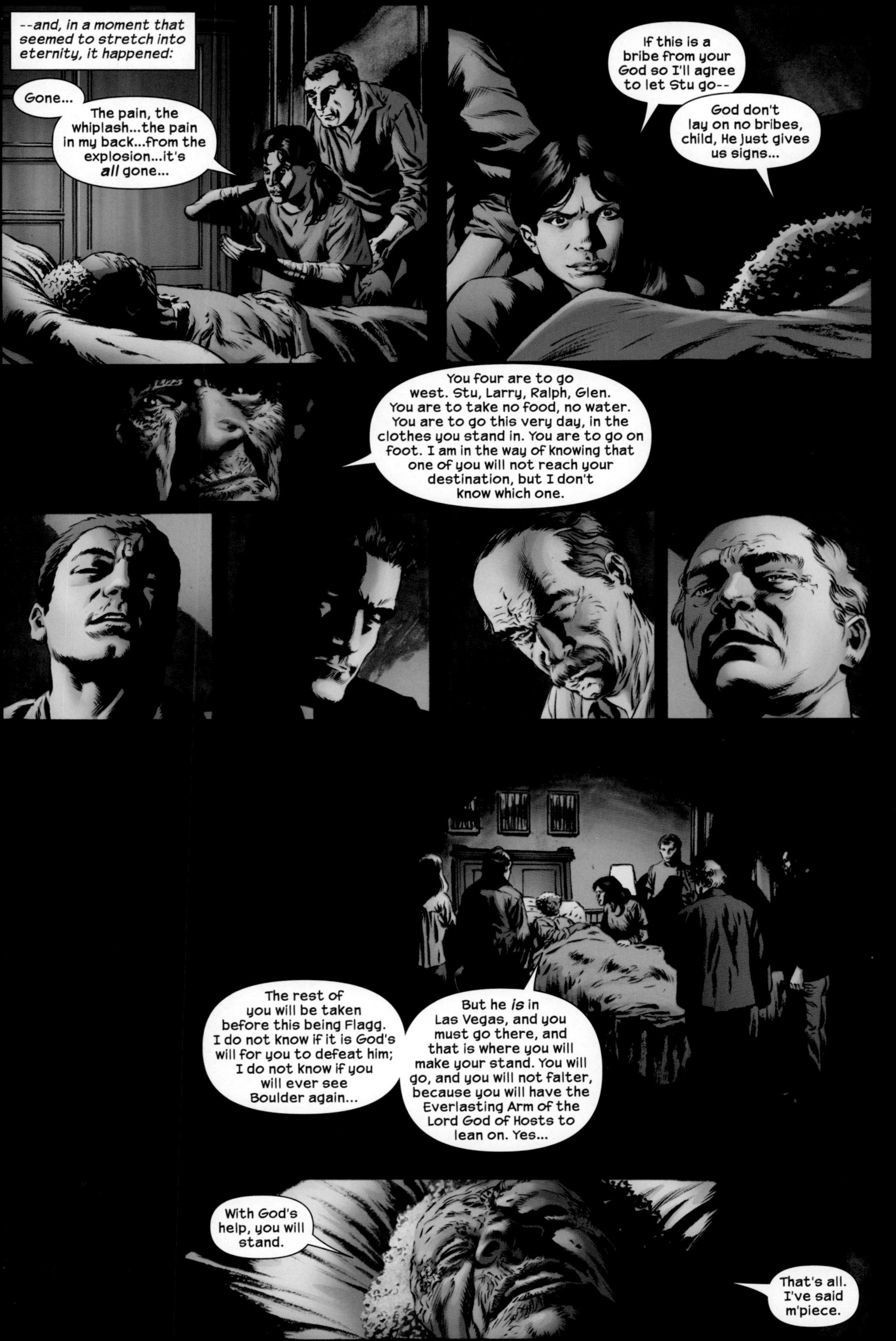

--and, in a moment that seemed to stretch into eternity, it happened:
Gone...
The pain, the whiplash...the pain in my back...from the explosion...it's *all* gone...
If this is a bribe from your God so I'll agree to let Stu go--
God don't lay on no bribes, child, He just gives us signs...
You four are to go west. Stu, Larry, Ralph, Glen. You are to take no food, no water. You are to go this very day, in the clothes you stand in. You are to go on foot. I am in the way of knowing that one of you will not reach your destination, but I don't know which one.
The rest of you will be taken before this being Flagg. I do not know if it is God's will for you to defeat him; I do not know if you will ever see Boulder again...
But he *is* in Las Vegas, and you must go there, and that is where you will make your stand. You will go, and you will not falter, because you will have the Everlasting Arm of the Lord God of Hosts to lean on. Yes...
With God's help, you will stand.
That's all. I've said m'piece.

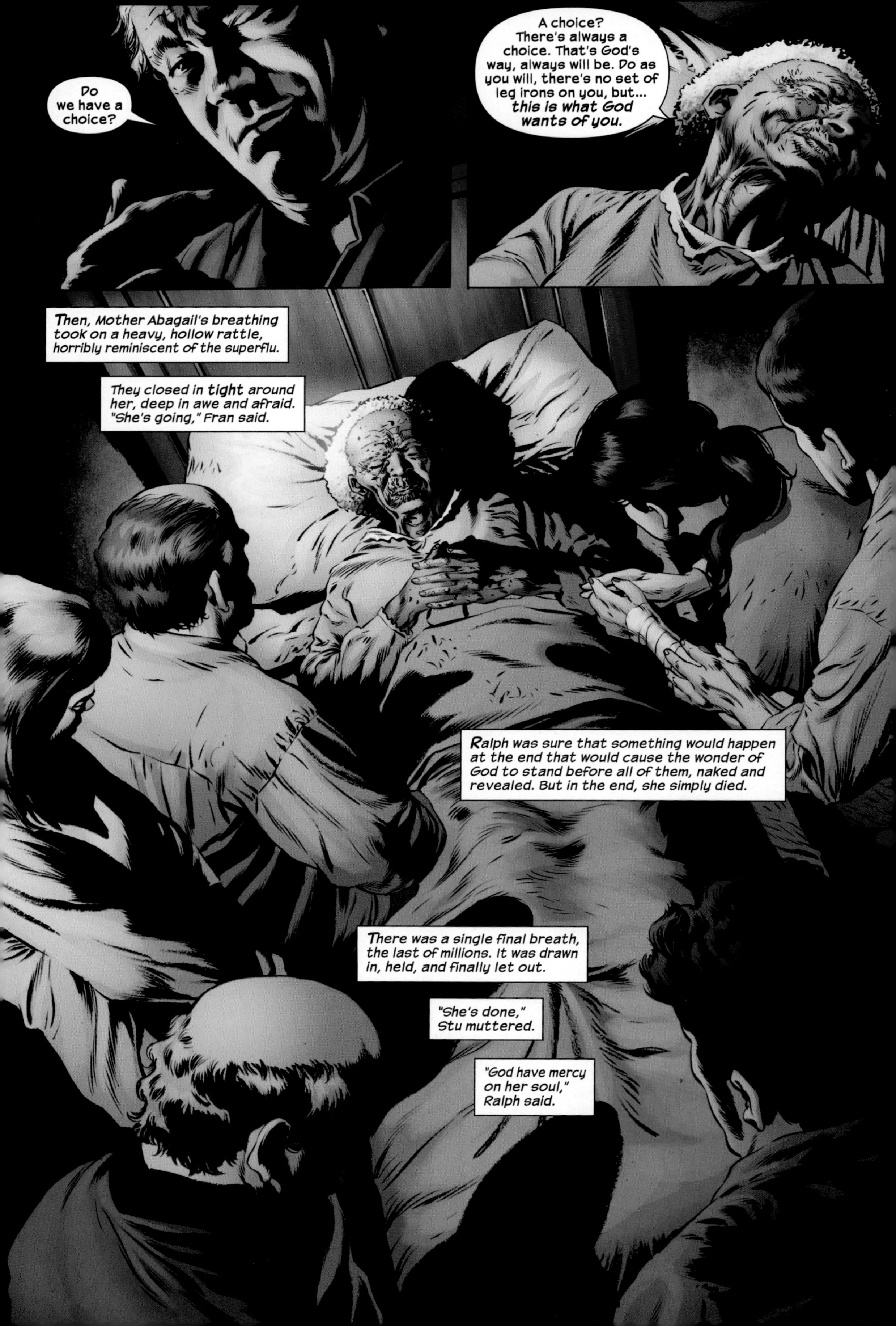
Do we have a choice?
A choice? There's always a choice. That's God's way, always will be. Do as you will, there's no set of leg irons on you, but... this is what God wants of you.
Then, Mother Abagail's breathing took on a heavy, hollow rattle, horribly reminiscent of the superflu.
They closed in tight around her, deep in awe and afraid. "She's going," Fran said.
Ralph was sure that something would happen at the end that would cause the wonder of God to stand before all of them, naked and revealed. But in the end, she simply died.
There was a single final breath, the last of millions. It was drawn in, held, and finally let out.
"She's done," Stu muttered.
"God have mercy on her soul," Ralph said.

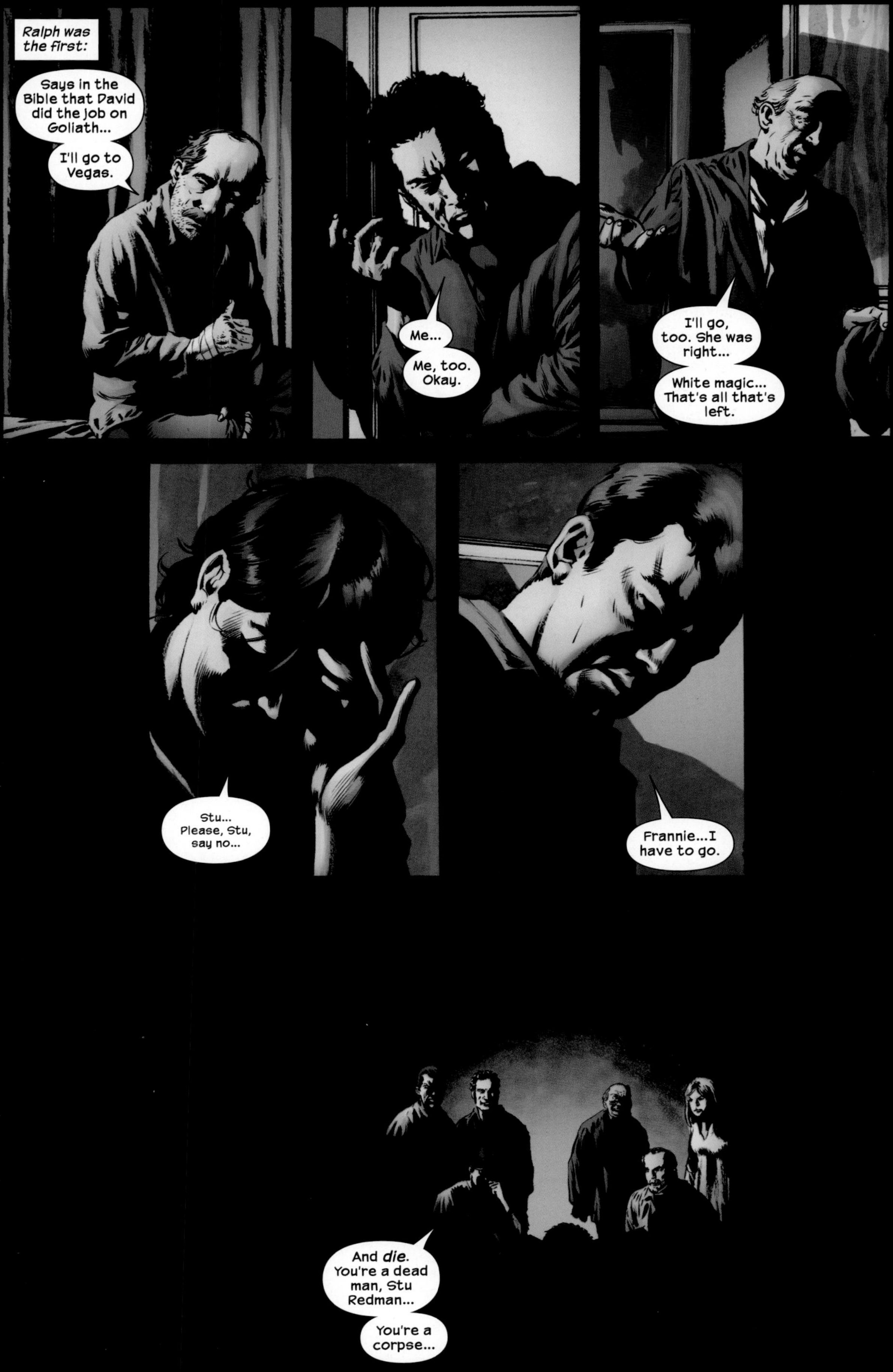

Ralph was the first:
Says in the Bible that David did the job on Goliath...
I'll go to Vegas.
Me...
Me, too. Okay.
I'll go, too. She was right...
White magic... That's all that's left.
Stu... Please, Stu, say no...
Frannie...I have to go.
And *die*. You're a dead man, Stu Redman...
You're a corpse...

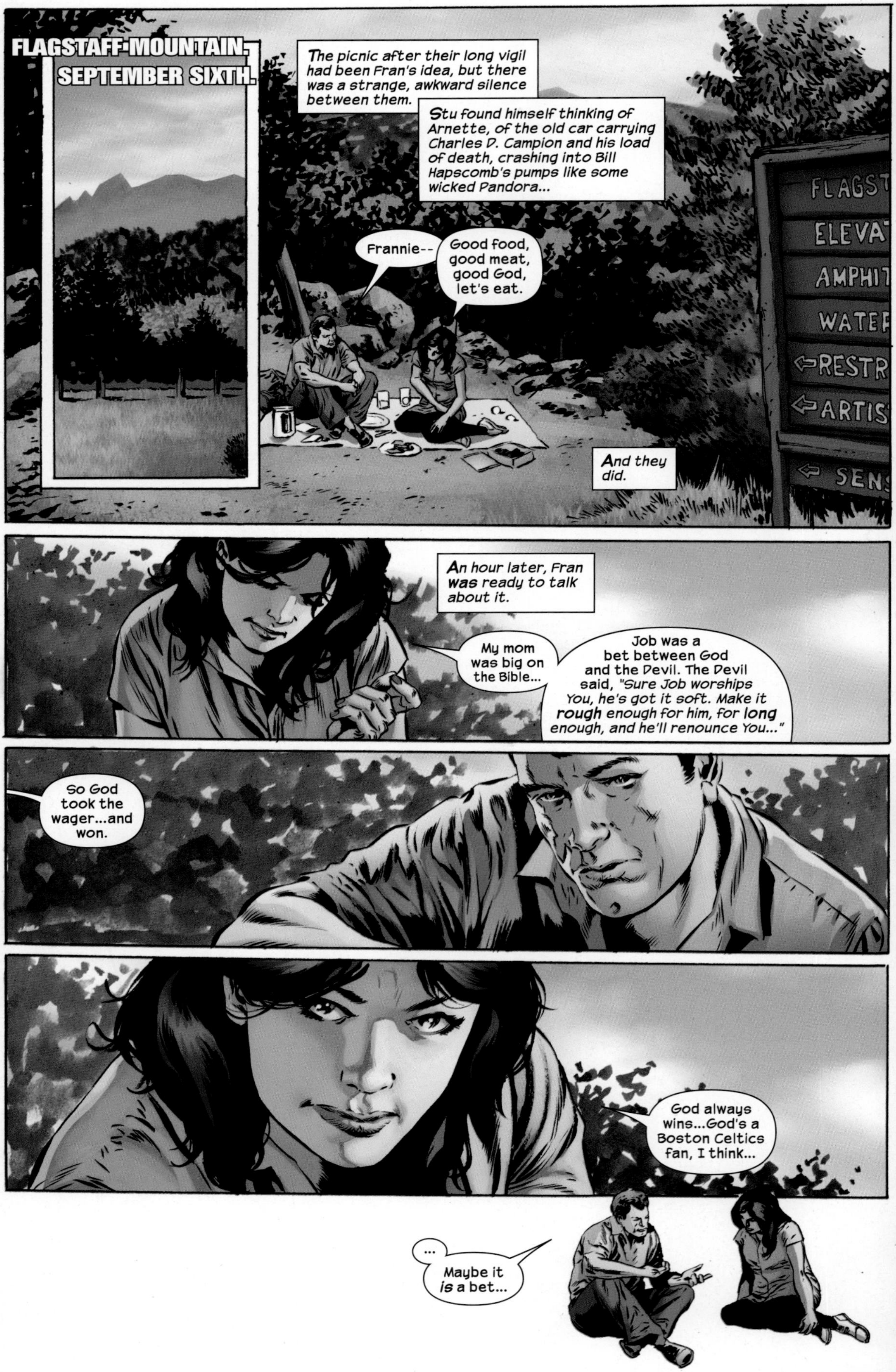
FLAGSTAFF MOUNTAIN. SEPTEMBER SIXTH.
The picnic after their long vigil had been Fran's idea, but there was a strange, awkward silence between them.
Stu found himself thinking of Arnette, of the old car carrying Charles D. Campion and his load of death, crashing into Bill Hapscomb's pumps like some wicked Pandora...
Frannie--
Good food, good meat, good God, let's eat.
FLAGST
ELEVAT
AMPHIT
WATER
RESTR
ARTIS
SENS
And they did.
An hour later, Fran was ready to talk about it.
My mom was big on the Bible...
Job was a bet between God and the Devil. The Devil said, "Sure Job worships You, he's got it soft. Make it rough enough for him, for long enough, and he'll renounce You..."
So God took the wager...and won.
God always wins...God's a Boston Celtics fan, I think...
...
Maybe it is a bet...

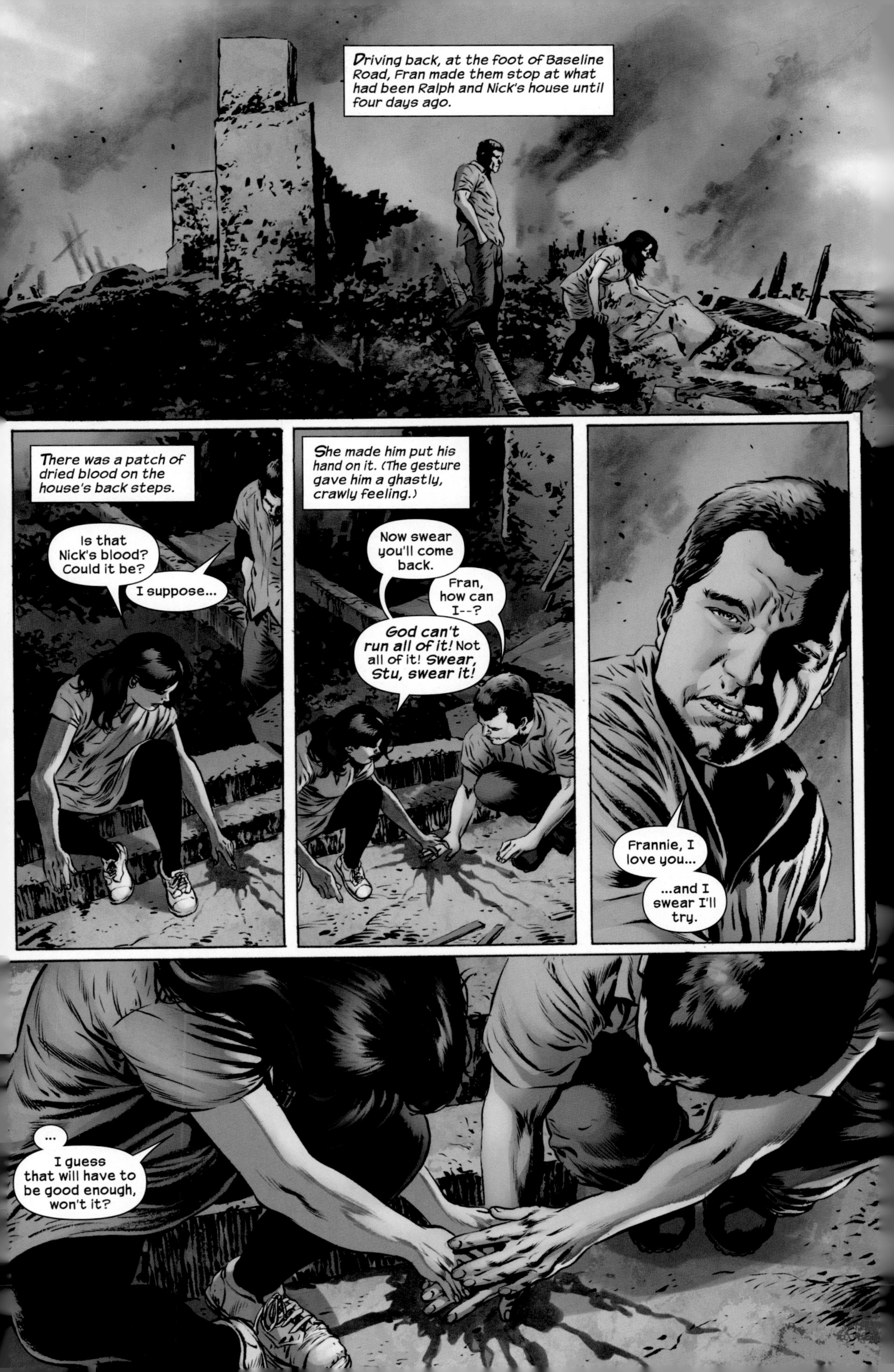
Driving back, at the foot of Baseline Road, Fran made them stop at what had been Ralph and Nick's house until four days ago.
There was a patch of dried blood on the house's back steps.
Is that Nick's blood? Could it be?
I suppose...
She made him put his hand on it. (The gesture gave him a ghastly, crawly feeling.)
Now swear you'll come back.
Fran, how can I--?
God can't run all of it! Not all of it! Swear, Stu, swear it!
Frannie, I love you...
...and I swear I'll try.
...
I guess that will have to be good enough, won't it?

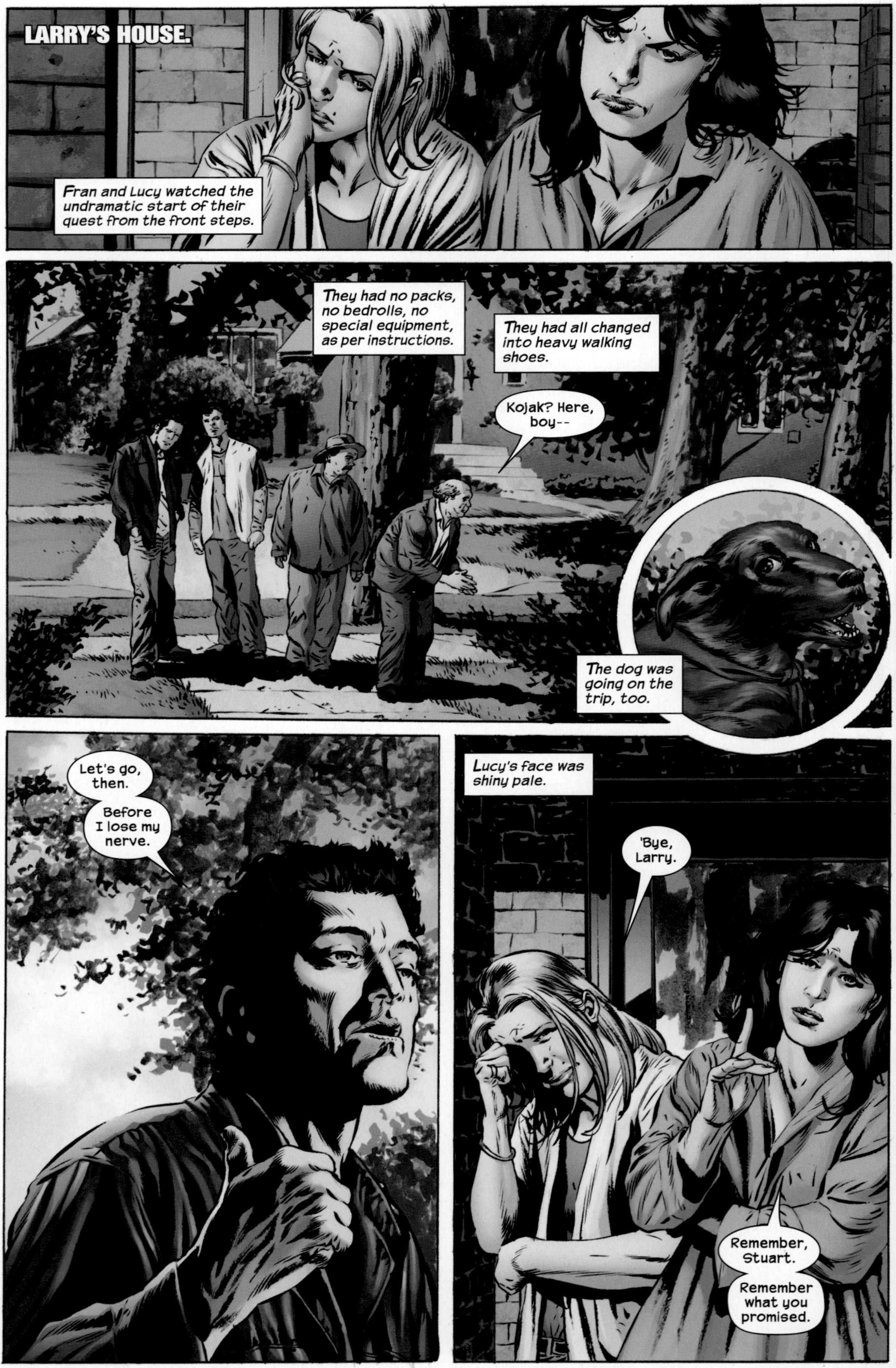
LARRY'S HOUSE.
Fran and Lucy watched the undramatic start of their quest from the front steps.
They had no packs, no bedrolls, no special equipment, as per instructions.
They had all changed into heavy walking shoes.
Kojak? Here, boy--
The dog was going on the trip, too.
Let's go, then.
Before I lose my nerve.
Lucy's face was shiny pale.
'Bye, Larry.
Remember, Stuart.
Remember what you promised.

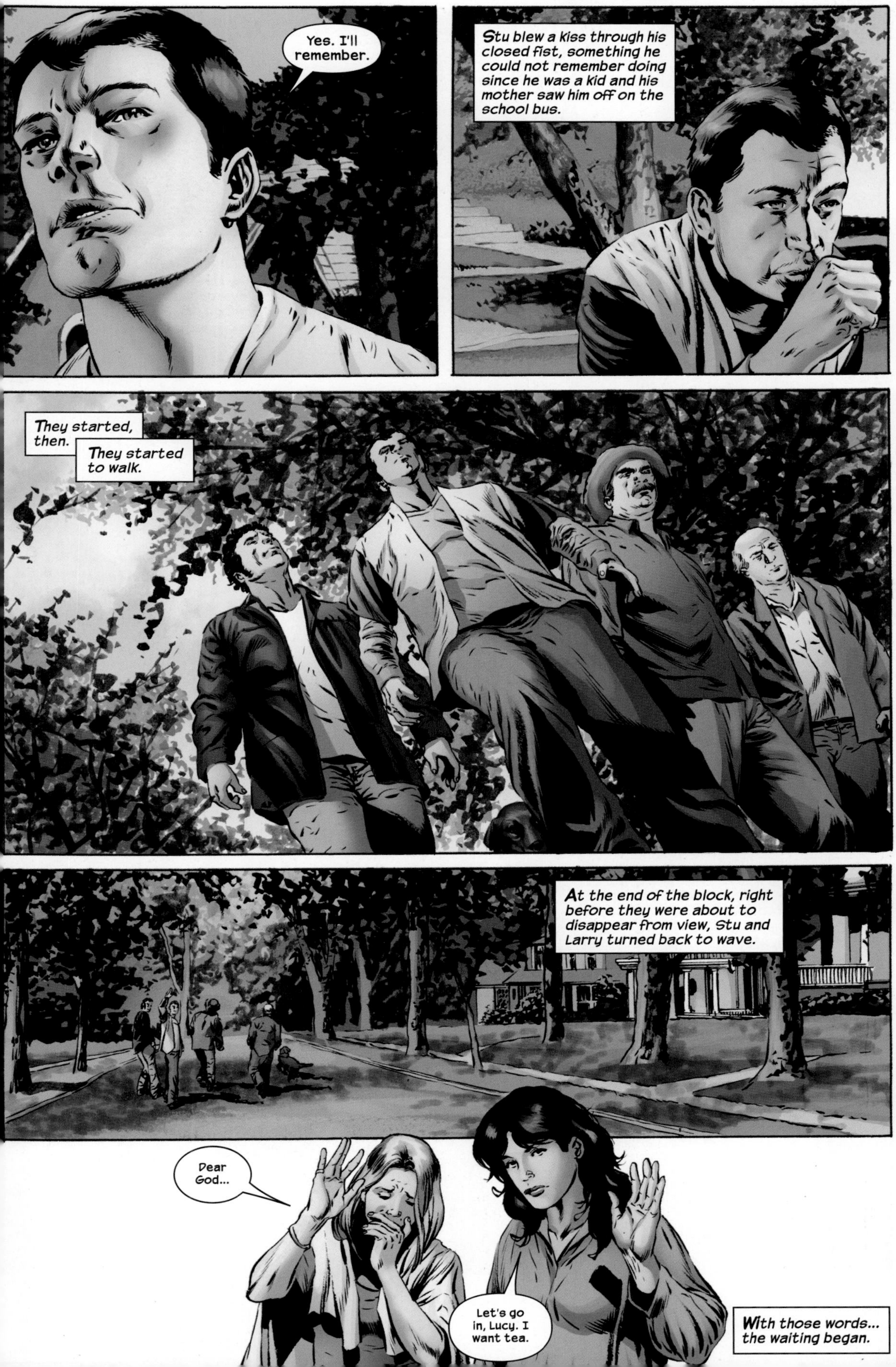
Yes. I'll remember.
Stu blew a kiss through his closed fist, something he could not remember doing since he was a kid and his mother saw him off on the school bus.
They started, then.
They started to walk.
At the end of the block, right before they were about to disappear from view, Stu and Larry turned back to wave.
Dear God...
Let's go in, Lucy. I want tea.
With those words... the waiting began.

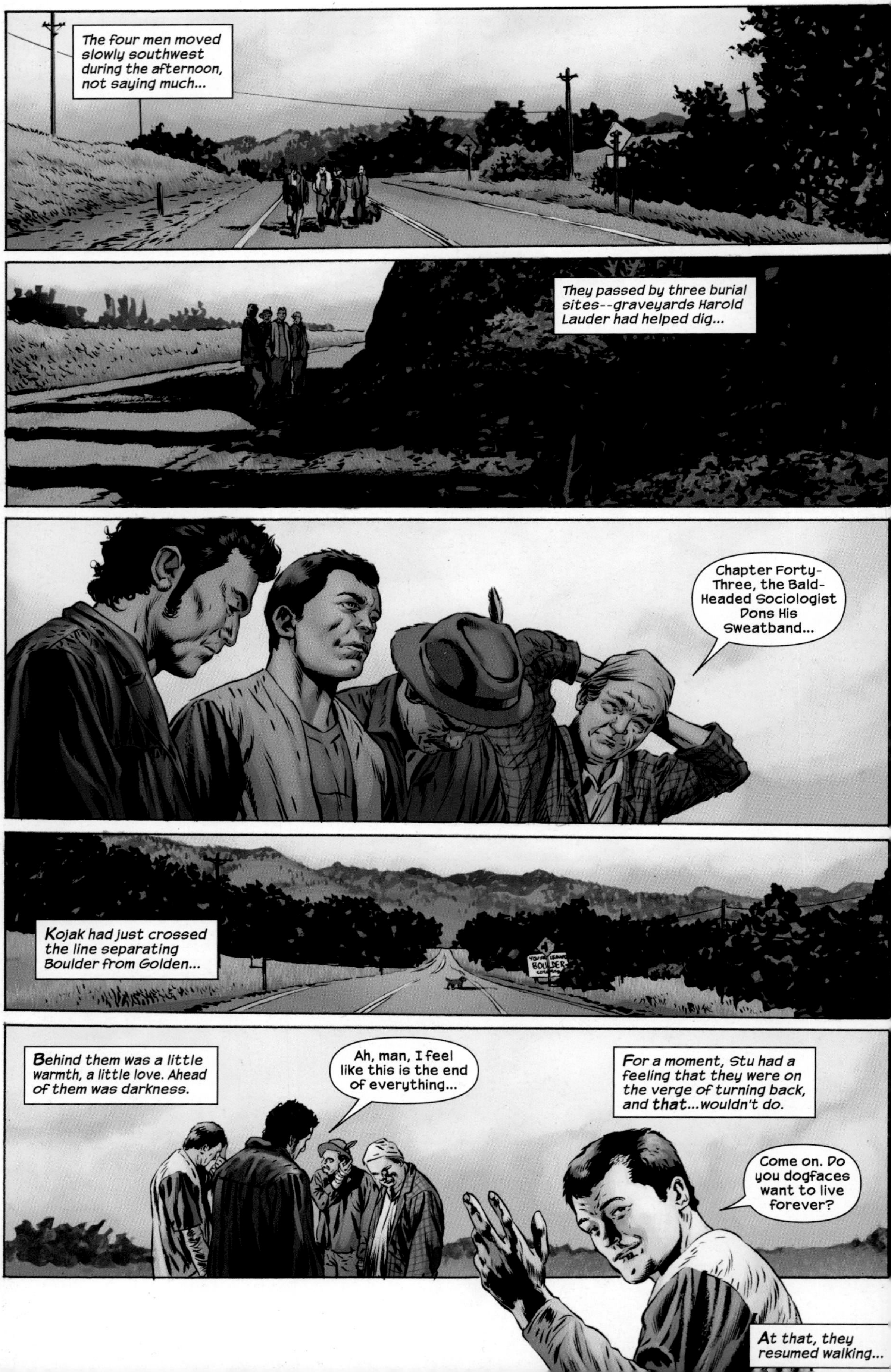
The four men moved slowly southwest during the afternoon, not saying much...
They passed by three burial sites--graveyards Harold Lauder had helped dig...
Chapter Forty-Three, the Bald-Headed Sociologist Dons His Sweatband...
Kojak had just crossed the line separating Boulder from Golden...
Behind them was a little warmth, a little love. Ahead of them was darkness.
Ah, man, I feel like this is the end of everything...
For a moment, Stu had a feeling that they were on the verge of turning back, and that...wouldn't do.
Come on. Do you dogfaces want to live forever?
At that, they resumed walking...

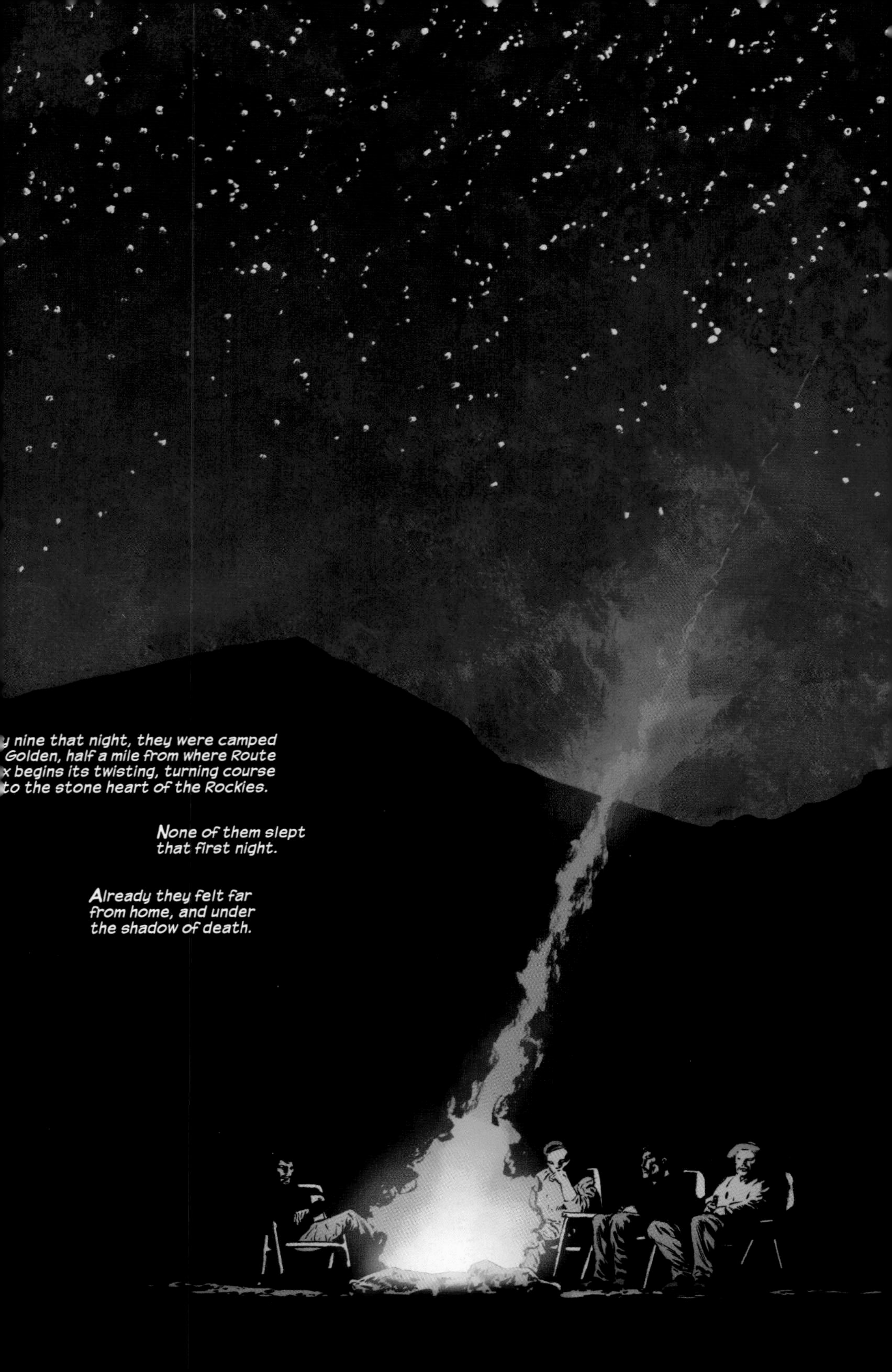
y nine that night, they were camped Golden, half a mile from where Route x begins its twisting, turning course to the stone heart of the Rockies.
None of them slept that first night.
Already they felt far from home, and under the shadow of death.

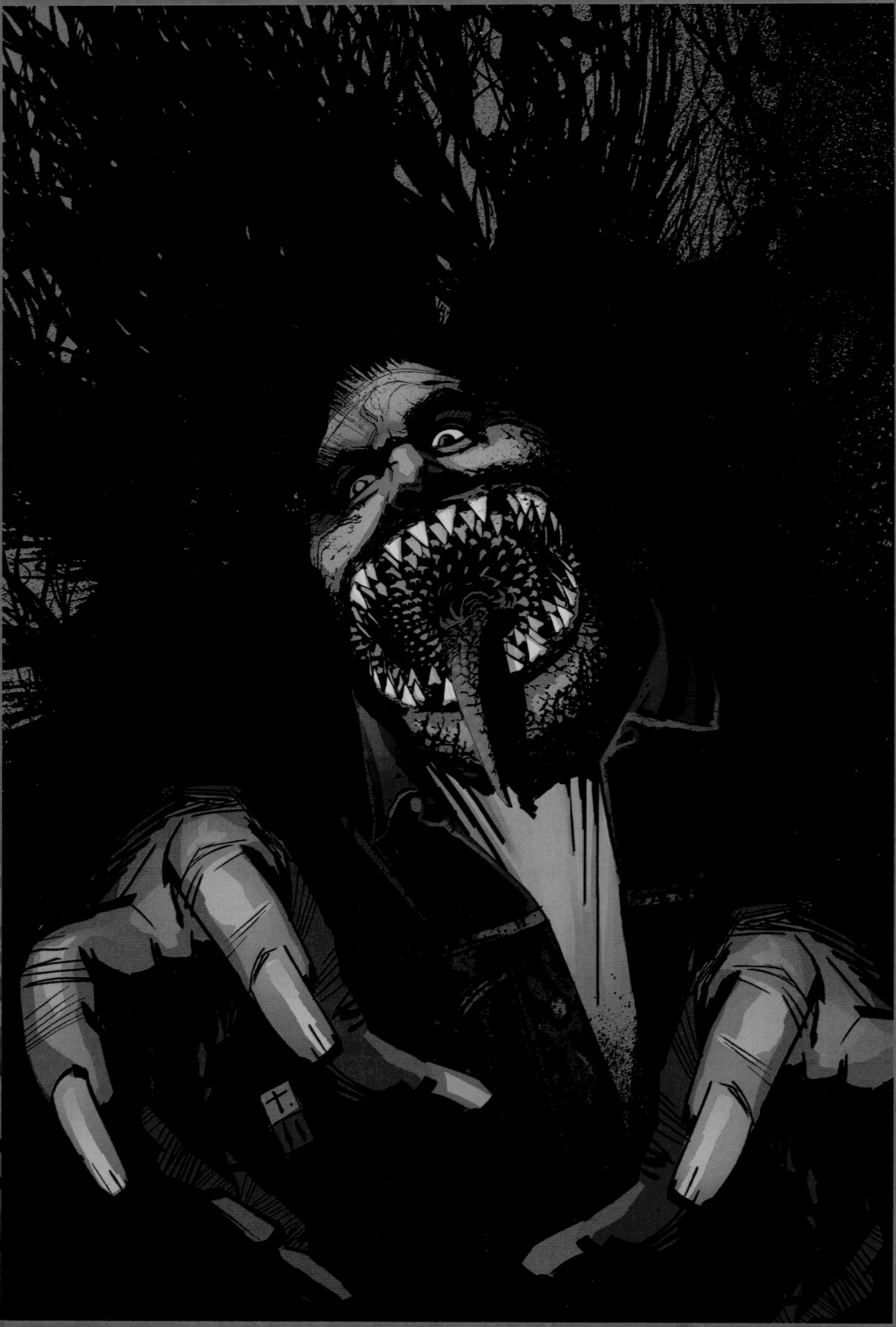

THE STORY STARTS HERE
IN THESE COLLECTIONS

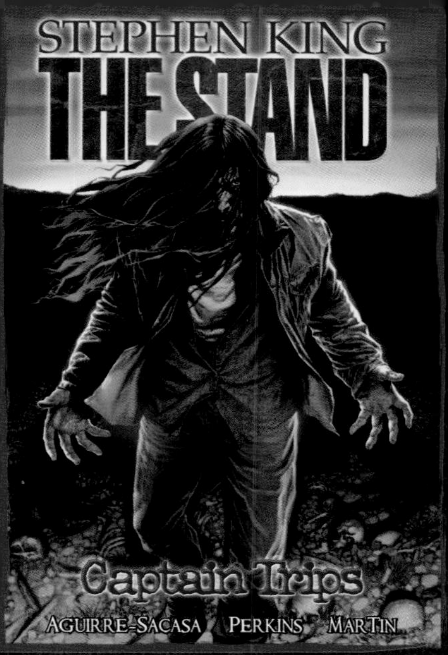
STEPHEN KING
THE STAND
Captain Trips
AGUIRRE-SACASA PERKINS MARTIN

THE STAND:
CAPTAIN TRIPS
ISBN: 978-0-7851-3362-0

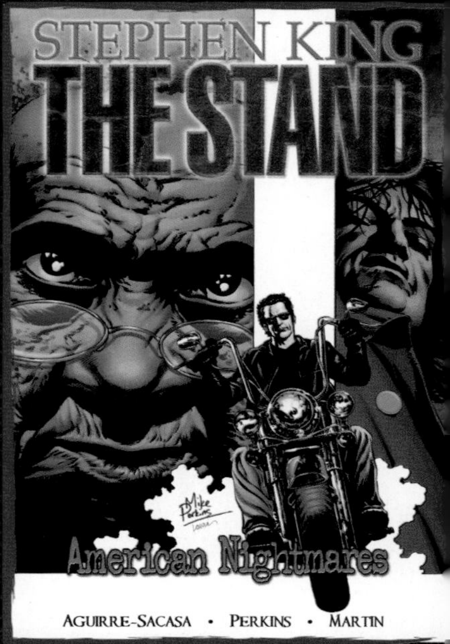
STEPHEN KING
THE STAND
American Nightmares
AGUIRRE-SACASA • PERKINS • MARTIN

THE STAND:
AMERICAN NIGHTMARES
ISBN: 978-0-7851-4274-4

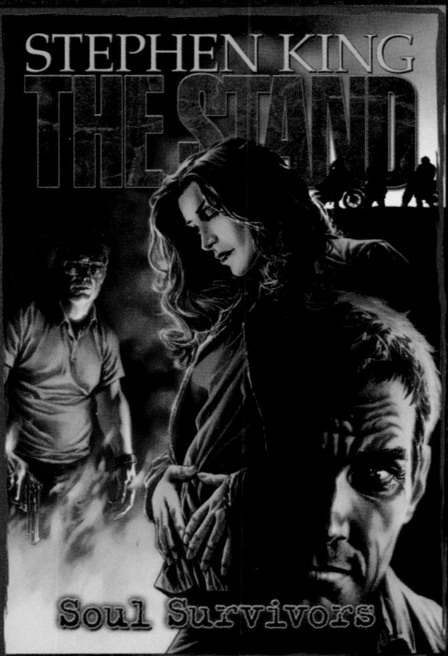
STEPHEN KING
THE STAND
Soul Survivors

THE STAND:
SOUL SURVIVORS
ISBN: 978-0-7851-3622-4

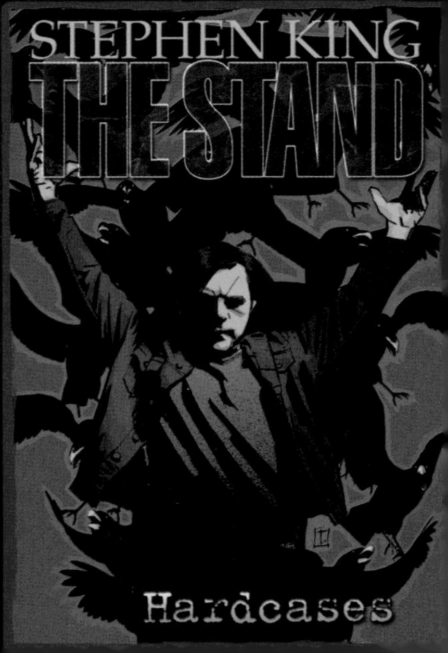
STEPHEN KING
THE STAND
Hardcases

THE STAND:
HARDCASES
ISBN: 978-0-7851-3623-1

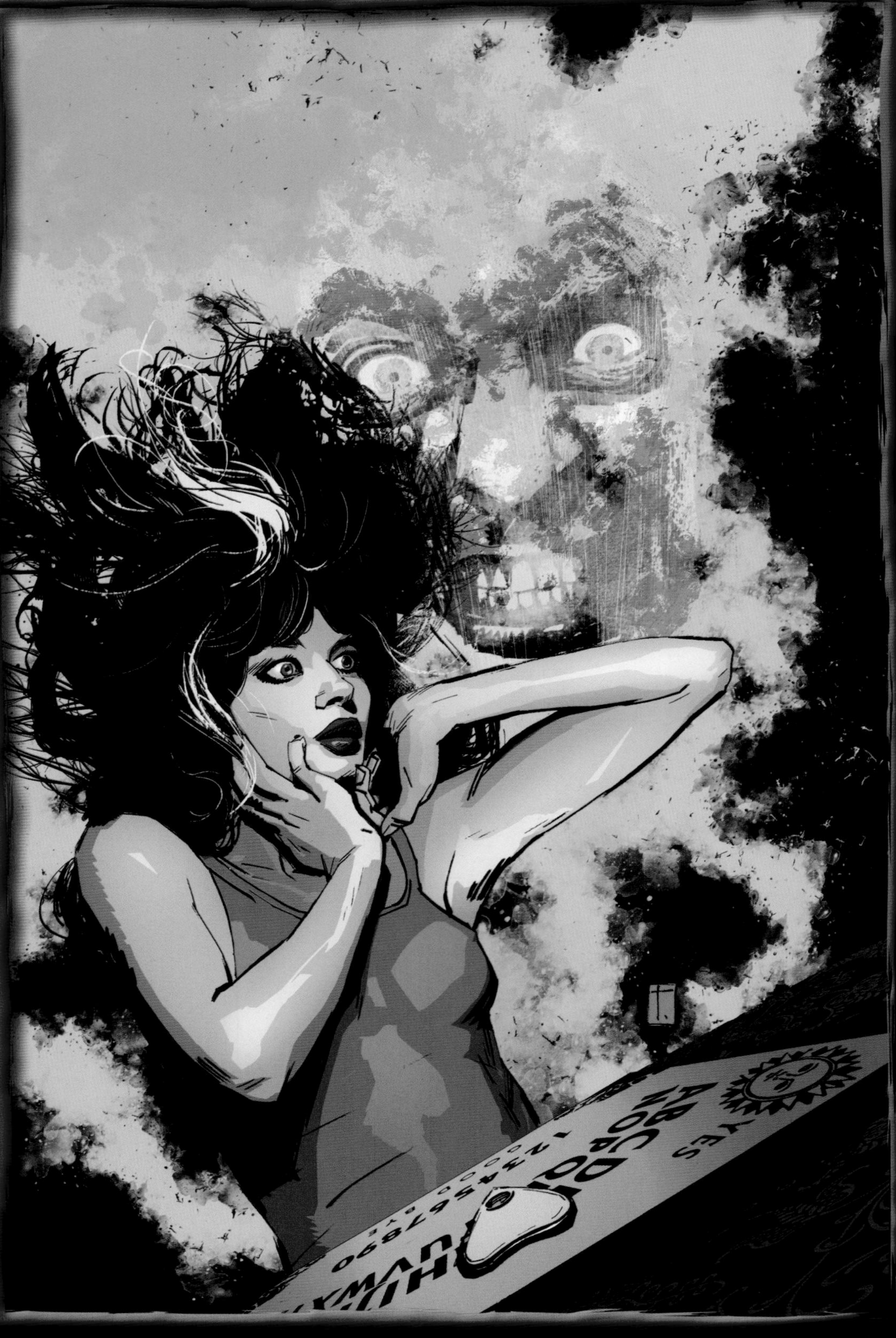
YES
1234567890

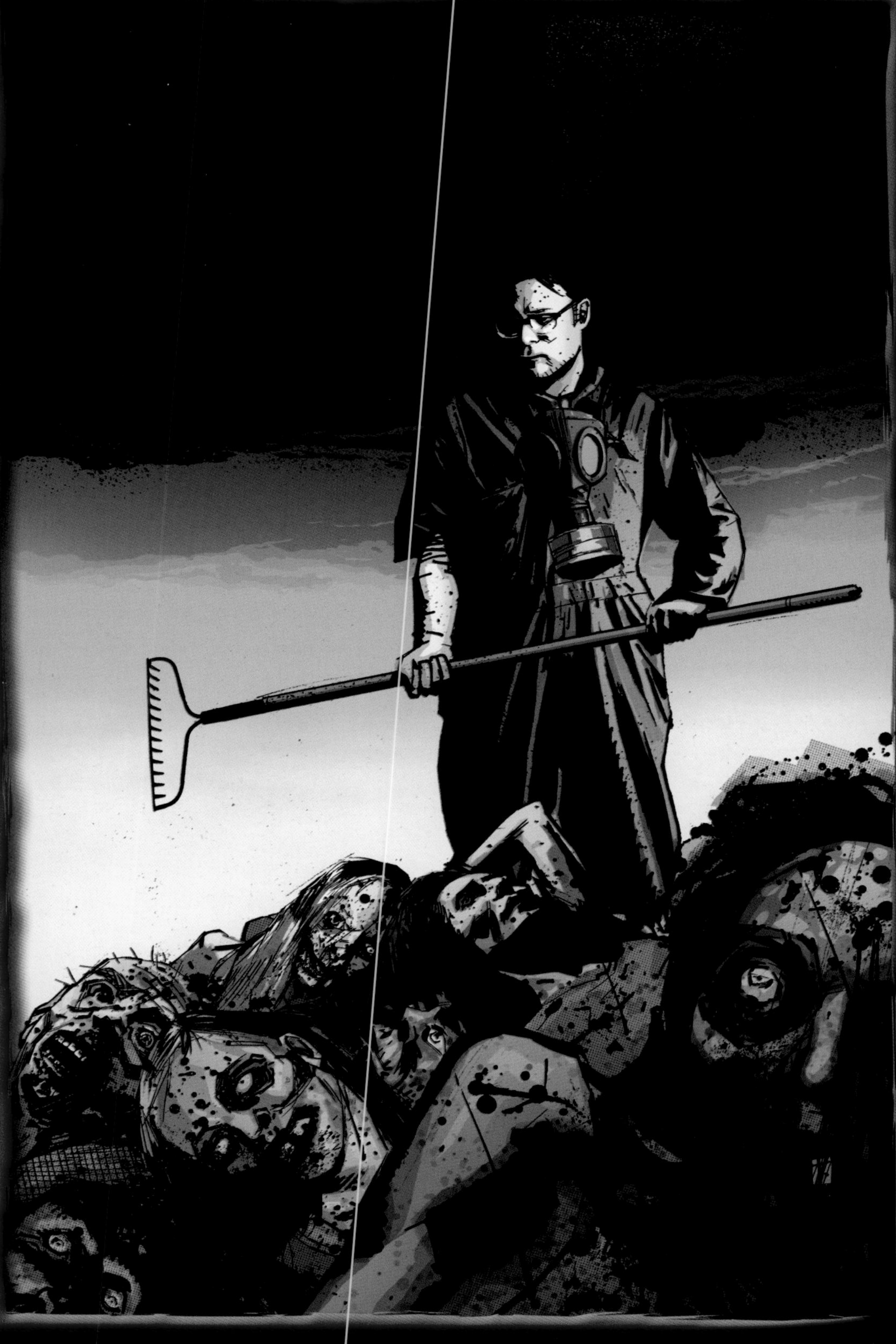

2

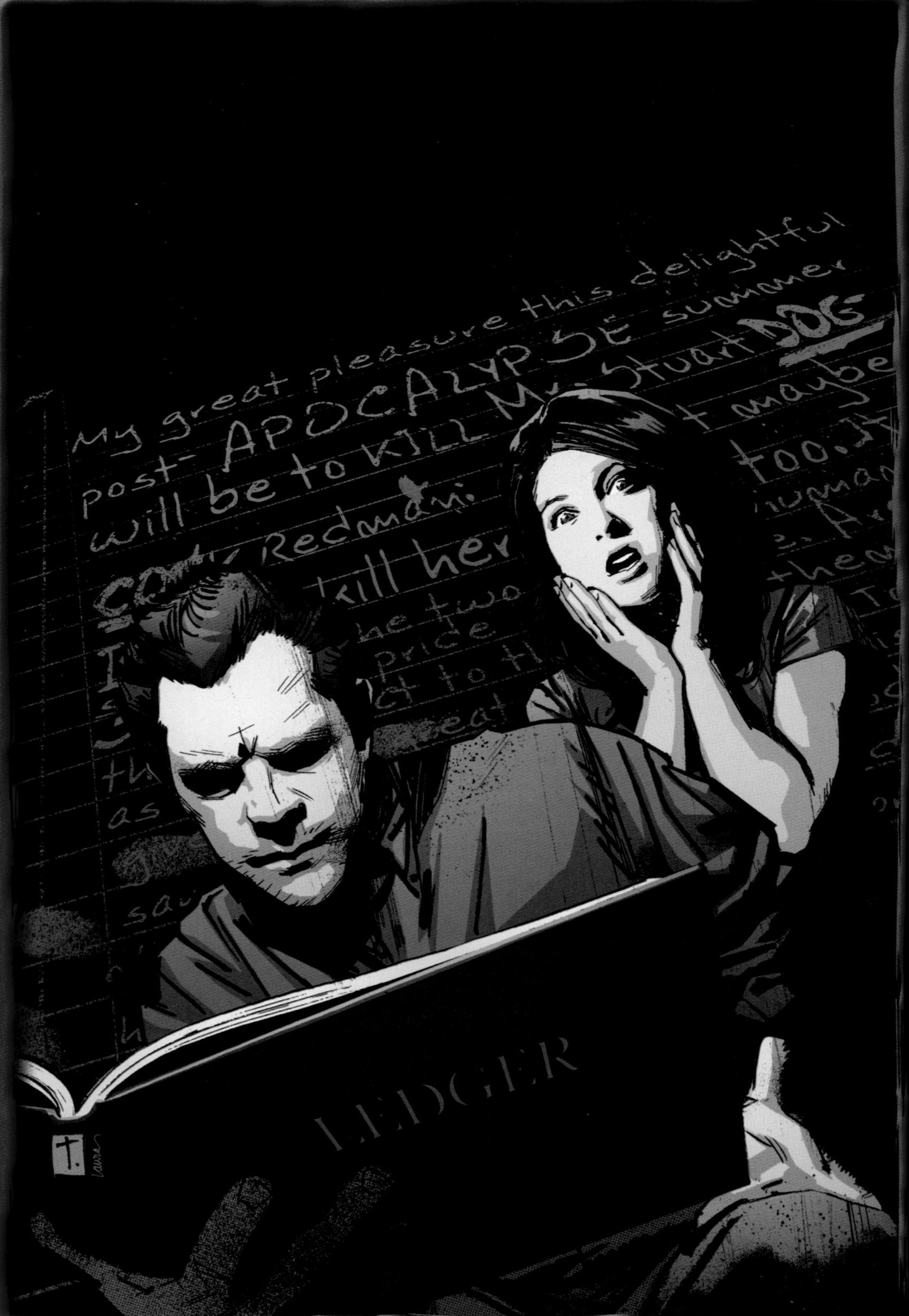
My great pleasure this delightful
post-APOCALYPSE summer
will be to KILL M. Stuart DOG
Redman.
kill her
LEDGER

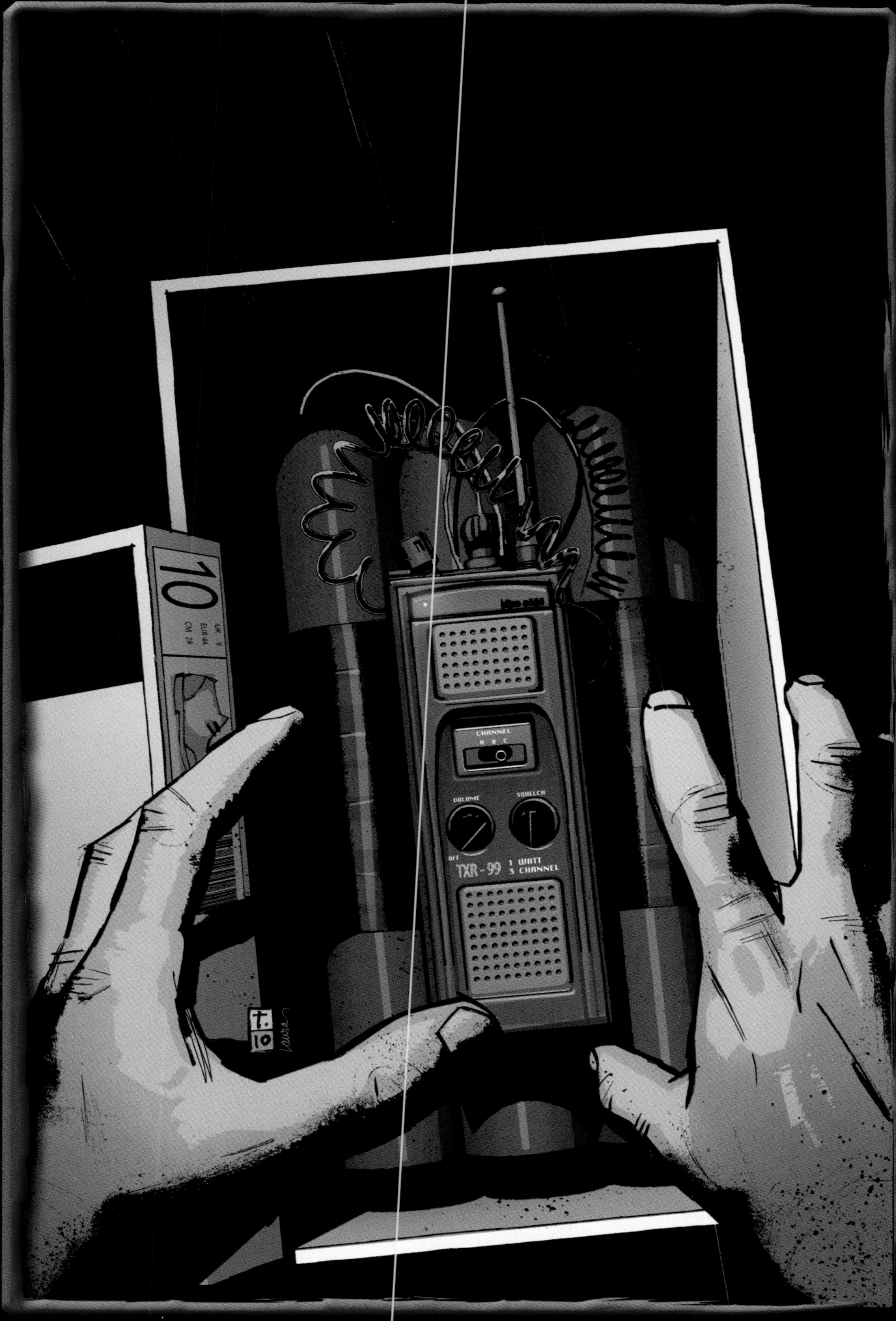
10
UK 9
EUR 44
CM 28
CHANNEL
A B C
VOLUME
SQUELCH
OFF
TXR-99
1 WATT
3 CHANNEL

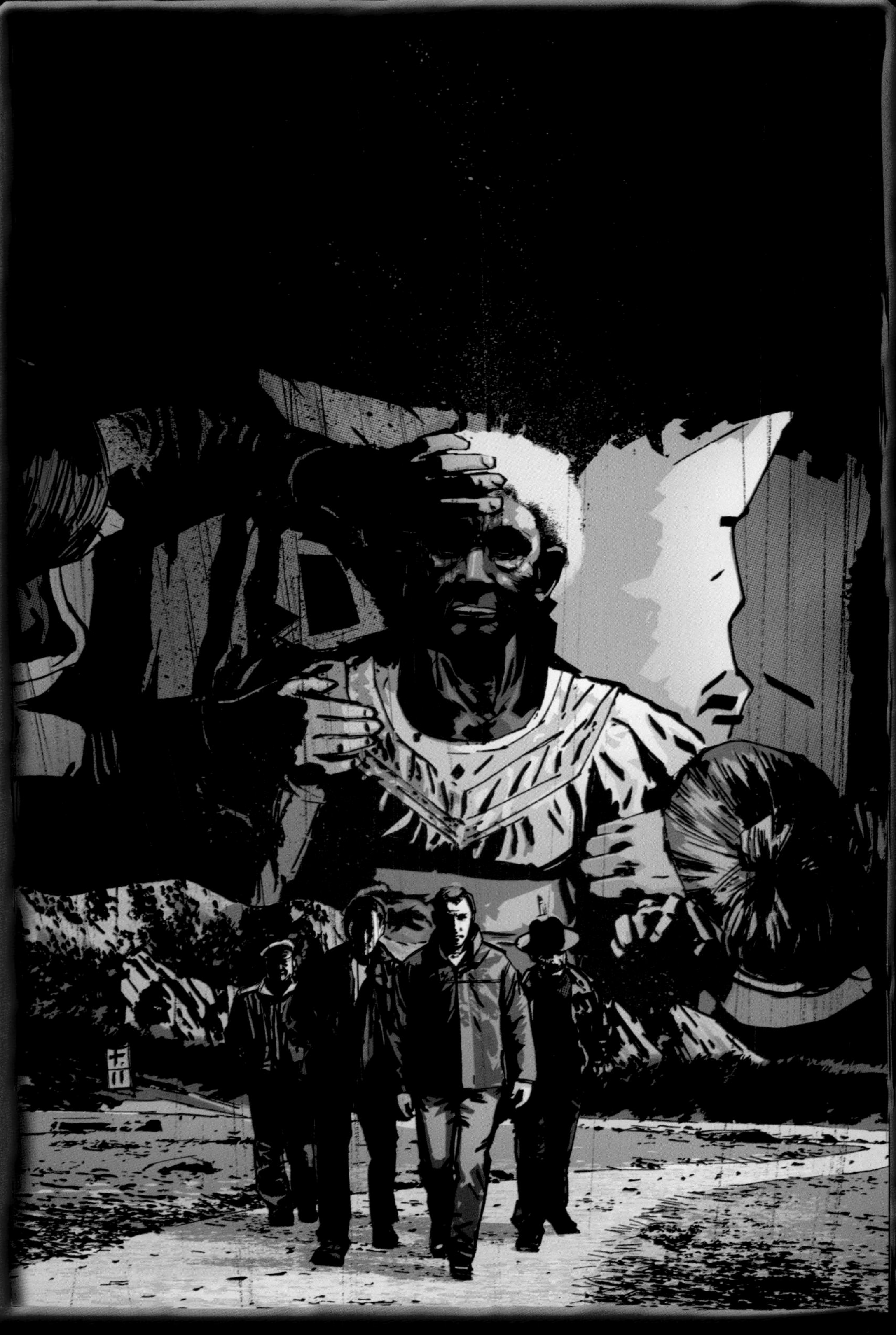

Artistic process from layouts to color by Mike Perkins and Laura Martin.

The Stand: No Man's Land # 4, page 14

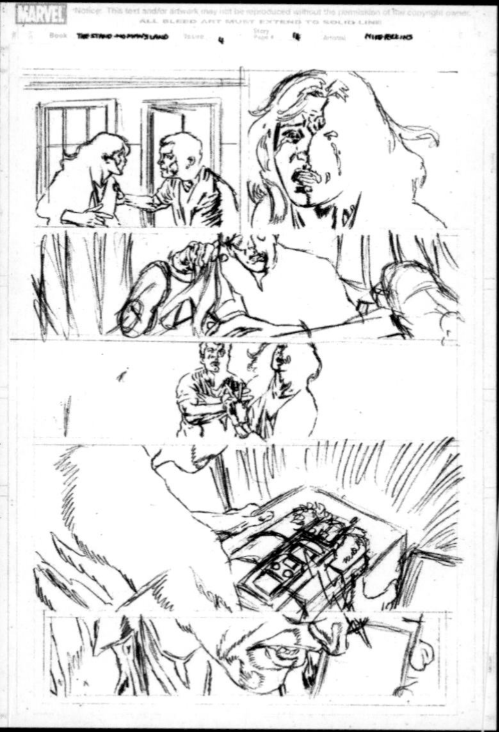
MARVEL
ALL BLEED ART MUST EXTEND TO SOLID LINE

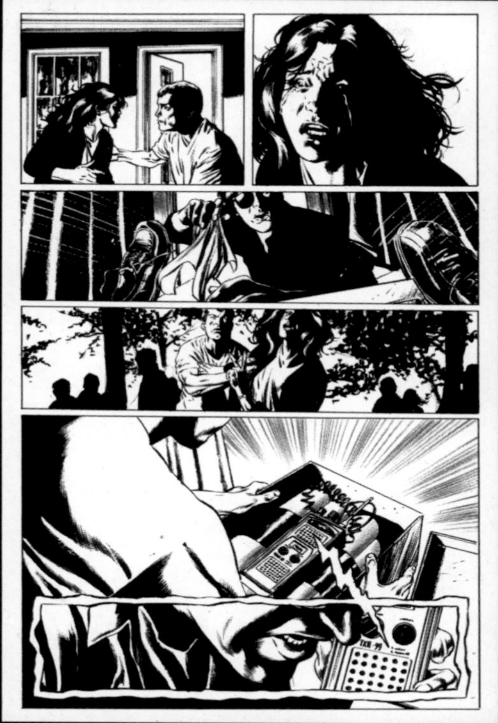
TXR-99

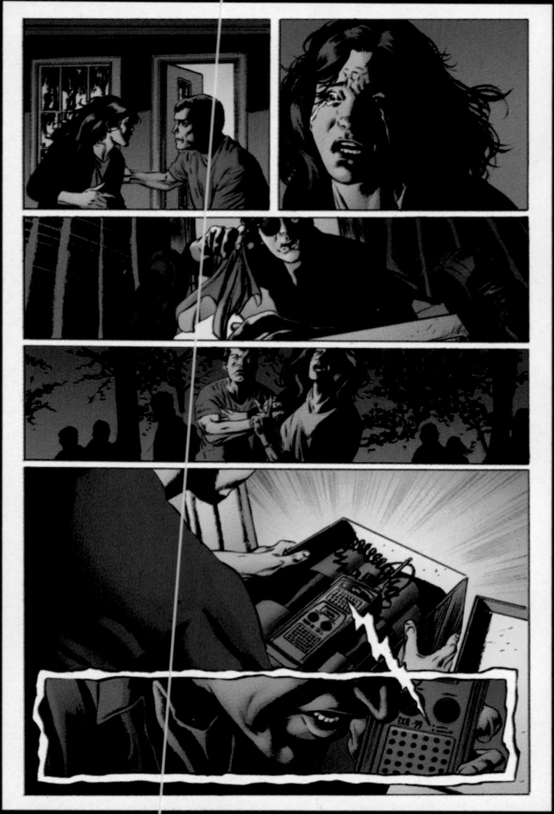
TXR-99

Artistic process from layouts to color by Mike Perkins and Laura Martin.

The Stand: No Man's Land # 4, page 15

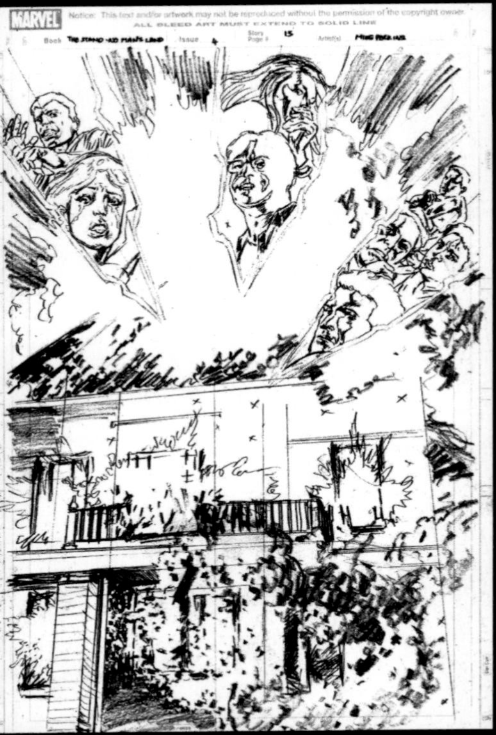
MARVEL
Notice: This text and/or artwork may not be reproduced without the permission of the copyright owner
ALL BLEED ART MUST EXTEND TO SOLID LINE
Book
Issue 4
Story Page # 15
Artist(s)

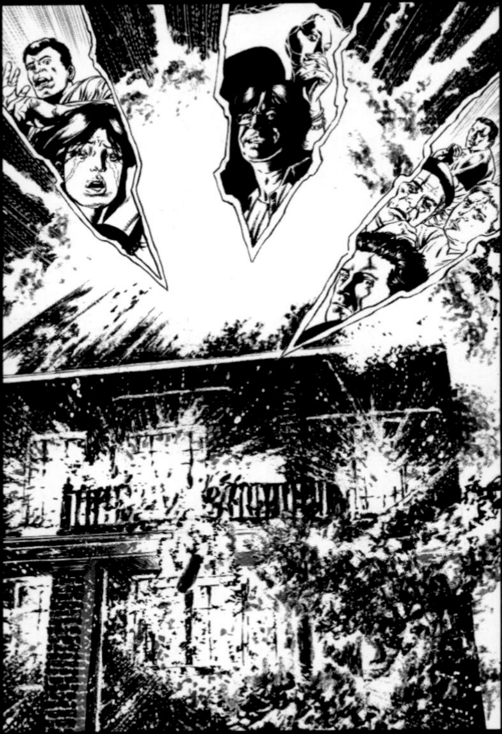

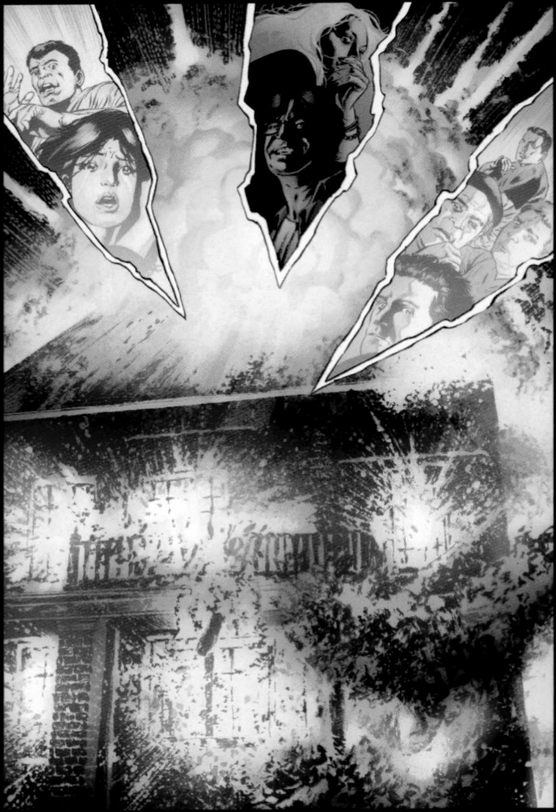

The Stand: No Man's Land # 4, page 18

THE BOULDE

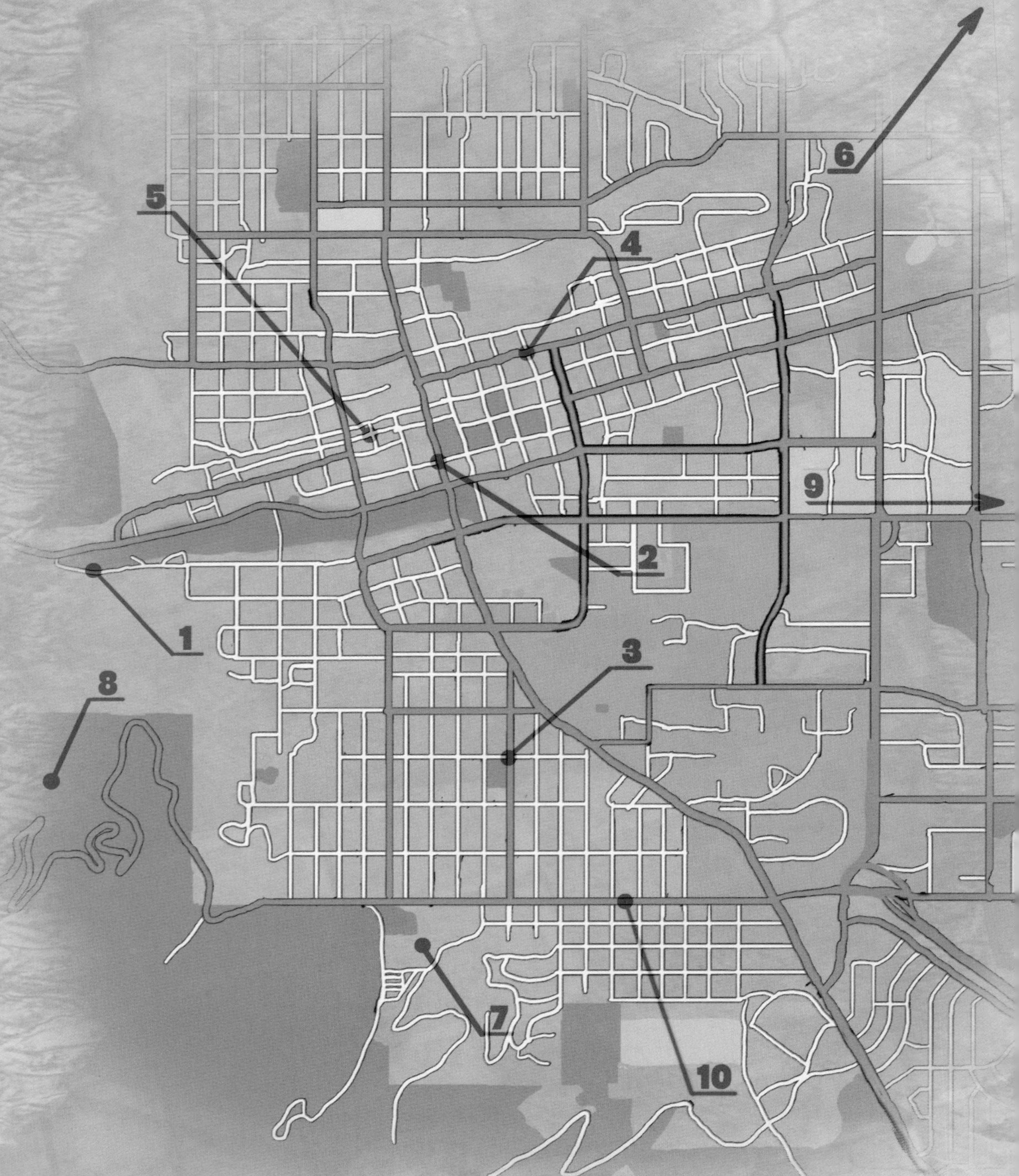

1
2
3
4
5
6
7
8
9
10

R FREE ZONE

1. Harold Lauder's house

2. Stu and Frannie's house

3. Judge Farris' house

4. Mother Abagail's house

5. Glen Bateman's house

6. To the Drive-In in Longmont, where Nadine was taken by the Dark Man

7. Chautauqua Auditoriom, location of the Free Zone Meeting

8. Sunrise Amphitheater, where Harold sets off the bomb

9. To the Boulder Power Station

10. Ralph Brentner and Nick Andros' house, and the site of the explosion.

The Stand: No Man's Land #2, page 2 inks by Mike Perkins.

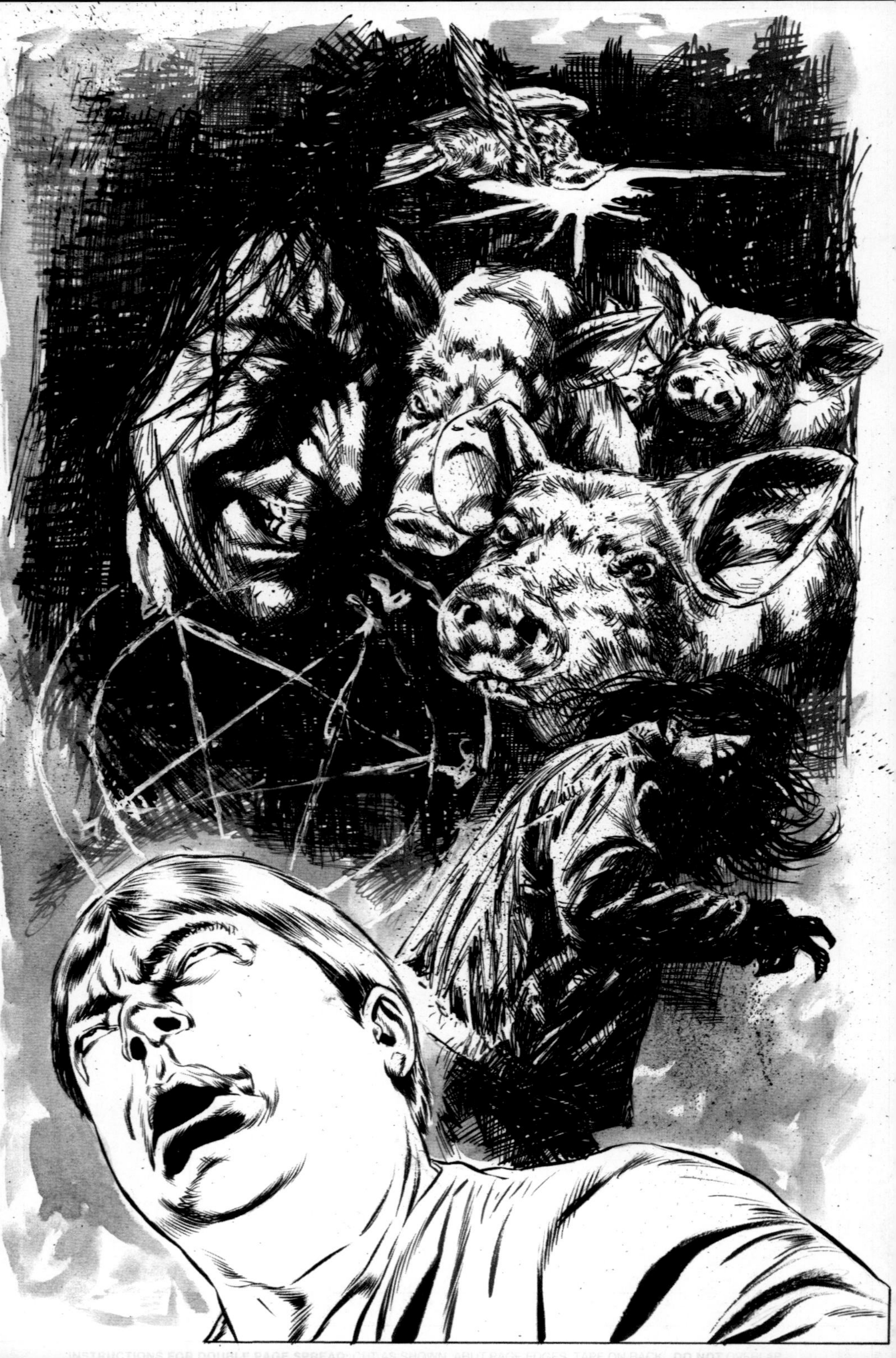
INSTRUCTIONS FOR DOUBLE PAGE SPREAD: CUT AS SHOWN. ABUT PAGE EDGES. TAPE ON BACK. DO NOT OVERLAP

The Stand: No Man's Land #3, page 15 inks by Mike Perkins

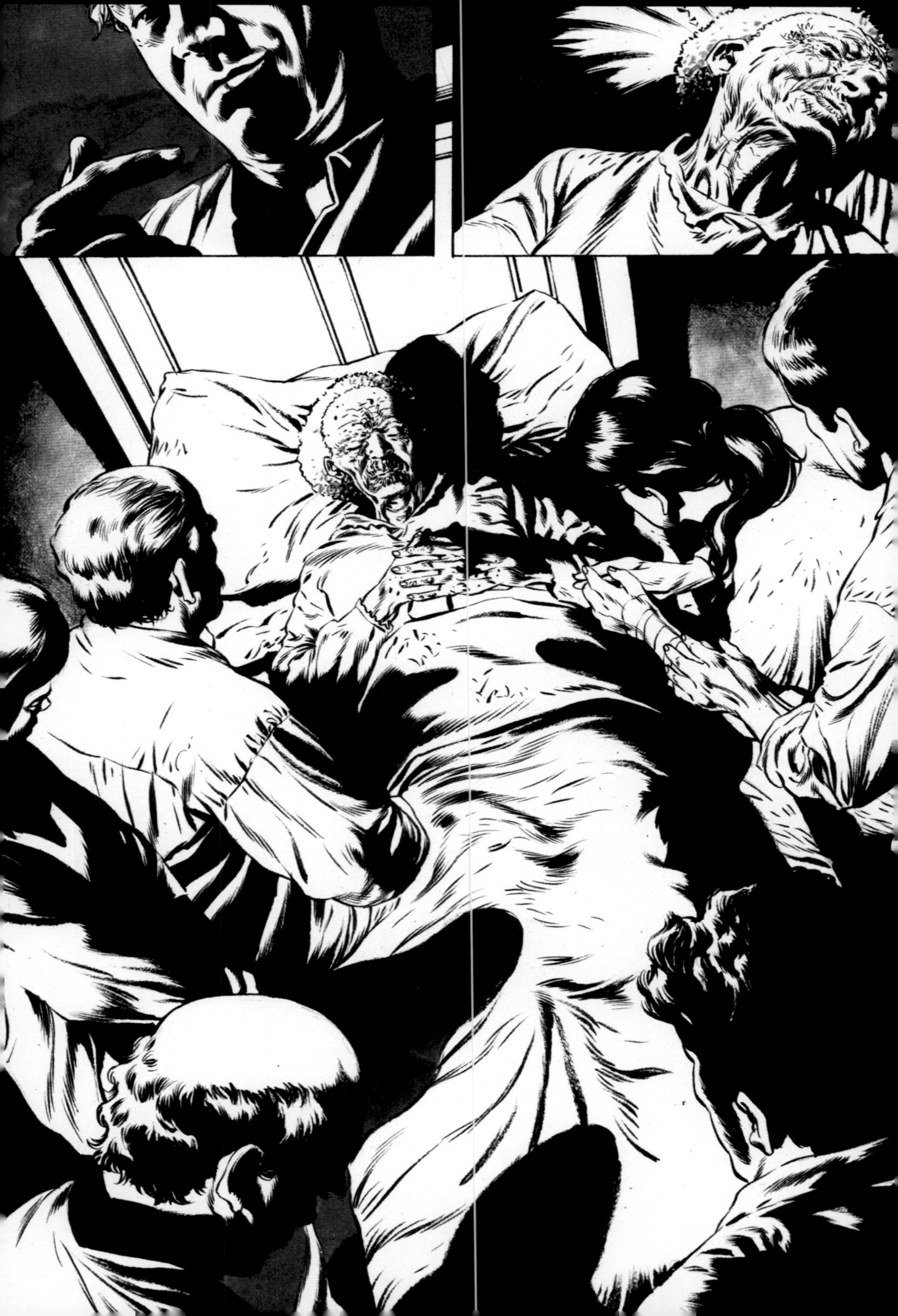

The Stand: No Man's Land #5, page 22 inks by Mike Perkins.

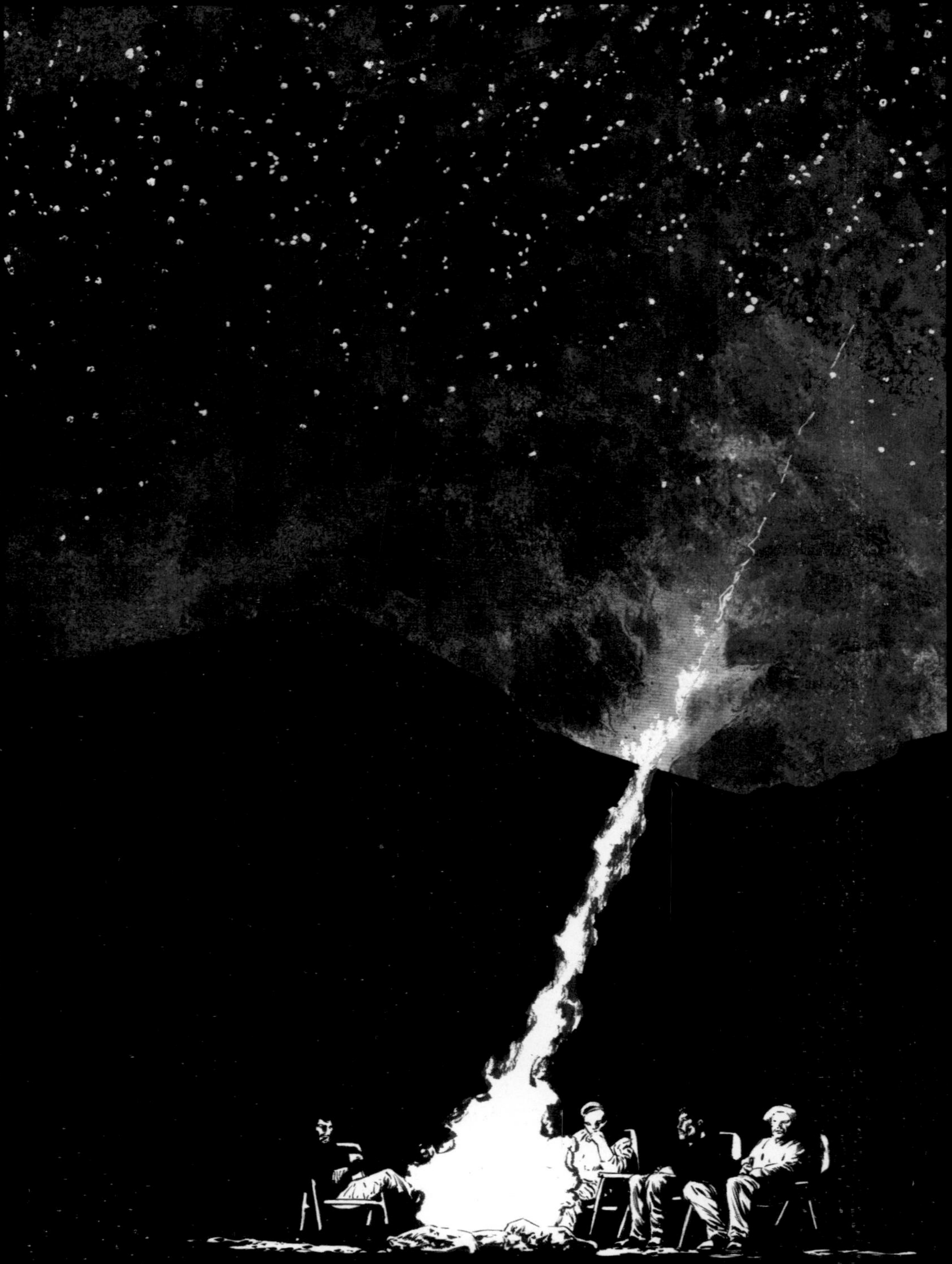